HOW MUSIC DIES

(OR LIVES)

FIELD RECORDING AND THE BATTLE FOR DEMOCRACY IN THE ARTS

IAN BRENNAN

PHOTOS BY MARILENA DELLI

FOREWORD BY CORIN TUCKER

ALLWORTH PRESS
NEW YORK

Allworth Press books may be purchased in bulk at special discounts for sales promotion, corporate gifts, fund-raising, or educational purposes. Special editions can also be created to specifications. For details, contact the Special Sales Department, Allworth Press, 307 West 36th Street, 11th Floor, New York, NY 10018 or info@skyhorsepublishing.com.

19 18 17 16   5 4 3 2

Published by Allworth Press, an imprint of Skyhorse Publishing, Inc.
307 West 36th Street, 11th Floor, New York, NY 10018.

Allworth Press® is a registered trademark of Skyhorse Publishing, Inc.®, a Delaware corporation.

www.allworth.com

Cover design by Mary Belibasakis
Cover photo credit Marilena Delli

Library of Congress Cataloging-in-Publication Data is available on file.

Print ISBN: 978-1-62153-487-7

Ebook ISBN: 978-1-62153-497-6

Printed in the United States of America.

Other Books by Ian Brennan

Fiction
Sister Maple Syrup Eyes

Nonfiction
Anger Antidotes: How Not to Lose Your S#&!
Hate-Less: Violence Prevention & How to Make Friends with a F&#!ed Up World

This book is not meant for academics.
Any words about music should at least
try to sing.

Table of Contents

SECTION VII:

Welcoming Magic: Heeding Wanderlust's Call   219

SECTION VIII:

How *Not* to Memorialize Music   249

SECTION IX:

Enlisting Limitations as Expressive Partners   261

SECTION X:

Racing Racism   273

SECTION XI:
The Battle for Democracy in the Arts   323

SECTION XII:
How Music Dies: $$ and Its Wake   347

SECTION XIII:

Odds and Endings: They Couldn't Keep Doing It Without All of the "Little People" 373

Acknowledgments

This book only exists because of the initiative and
encouragement of my wife, Marilena Delli.
It was all her idea.
Hopefully, the results are even *remotely* as good
as the wonderful person who inspired them.

S pecial thanks to Jason Moffat, Nels Cline, and Kevin Army for their time in reviewing the earliest drafts of this book and for having the courage to give me their candid and sometimes harsh feedback, not fearing to tell me things that I maybe "didn't want to hear."

Were it not for the kindness of every single person that has ever fed, sheltered, and/or driven us, none of this would've been possible. And of course, so many of the thoughts here are due to all that I've learned from every person I've ever had the good fortune of working with—both the musicians and the technicians.

Most of all, thanks goes to my mom and dad (. . . and two siblings) for tolerating an adolescence spent locked in my room and "rocking out" the entire household, morning to night.

Foreword

What has always interested me, as a music lover from a young age, and as a writer as well, are people's stories. And in particular, I like to hear from those voices that are not often heard from, those voices who are often rendered silent through lack of access to power or resources. The ability to bring someone inside your world experience, your viewpoint, and your story in a three-minute song is a special kind of magic. I think of a song like "Strange Fruit" by Billie Holiday, a woman who was without power in so many ways, and yet her vision of lynchings in the Southern United States helped open popular culture's eyes to the atrocities faced by the African American community.

Today, unfortunately, we still face many inequities in our country, and in the greater world. But by sharing stories and experience through song, we might be able to gain a greater understanding of someone else's viewpoint, of where they are coming from, and how they see things. The possibilities of opening up people's minds to a new way of thinking is very powerful.

However, creating art, of any kind, takes some resources. If the only money, or resources, for art, in our country, or the global community, is passed just from the rich and powerful corporations to their beneficiaries, we will lose the opportunity to hear those voices who are left marginalized. We will lose the deeper understanding of our entire community and how to make our society a more equitable one. As a culture, we need to reach out to those who may not have access to the equipment, the instruments, or the facilities to create art, in order to foster real democracy and a broader understanding between people from all walks of life.

—Corin Tucker
Sleater-Kinney
Portland, OR

Preface:
Proximity Bias and the
Irrationality of Fear

A s the ancient drum telegraphs of Africa and church bells of Europe attest, music is the original worldwide web, the invisible binding tissue bridging distances in a universe where all matter is made up of vibration, a galaxy that theoretically might've itself originated with sound.

A faceless Silicon Valley "leader" (deliberately left unnamed here so as not to add to his undeserved and exaggerated infamy) recently proclaimed that the most important issue of our time is that every child become connected to the Internet. What seemed to be lost on his privileged, provincial little mind was that being hooked up with clean water, health care, education, and electricity might first prove to be more pressing matters. Things humans truly "cannot live without."

Unless that 3-D printer is going to print them protein, it is all but useless.

And, rather than sharing "friends," the majority of people on earth remain in need of food to share.

Sound has the power to attract, ward off, give birth to emotion, and, on rare occasion, even kill (i.e., when subsonic sounds induce lung collapse).

Is this book intended to be authoritative or some sort of last word on the subject of music "for sale"?

Hell, no!

These are just reflections by one decidedly unfamous person who has spent decades in the cultural trenches. They are meant to raise questions, stimulate thought, and inspire debate, not to provide easy answers about the gradual, linguistic and cultural carnage crisis we are facing. And certainly by wading into the entire exercise of attempting to put into words something as disincarnate as music, the folly is not lost on me that one of music's main functions is to pick up where everyday verbalizations have fallen short, and express that which is otherwise inexpressable.

Though courting controversy is not the primary goal here, will some of this content probably piss off a few elitists and "experts"?

I sure hope so . . . (Lest we are just trudging along with the status quo.)

I owe almost all of my travel adventures to my wife, Marilena Delli. My passion for international music was piqued in the late 1980s when I began to tire of the carbon-copy turbine of rock music. But, in all likelihood, I never would have stepped foot into Africa except for her. Hell, I had not ever even been east of the Mississippi until I was twenty-four.

Marilena's mother is Rwandan, her father Italian. Our first trip was to accompany her mother home to Rwanda, when she was returning for the first time in over thirty years so that she could reunite with her best friend, a person that she had been misled, for over a decade, to believe had been lost in the third and biggest of Rwanda's genocides (1994).

In addition to visiting family, we hoped to record music while we were there and had the marvelous blessing of meeting a trio of "war" survivors who sang together like sandpaper angels.

Since then, we have returned to the continent almost a dozen times, as well as to other locations throughout the world (e.g., Asia, the Middle East). Marilena has been an invaluable photographic and film documentarian, and is charmed with powerful people skills, along with a command of five languages that can come in quite handy at times. This is particularly true when one is saddled with a monolingual, post-"voodoo" economics, public-schooled Americano.

Often people react in horror when we tell them of our upcoming journeys. The scenario plays out stereotypically, almost as if scripted. Usually the first response is "_____ *fill in name of developing country here*_____? *Really?!?*", which is then followed urgently, without fail, by "(But) *Why?!?*" And then, strained laughter . . . from their end.

Regardless of the high-profile and horrible tales of kidnapping and the like that circulate—and, in fact, sometimes even *occur*—the math bears out that the overwhelming majority of people on this planet live with peaceful intentions. In reality, no matter where one travels, the most likely cause of sudden death will be much more mundane—a car accident.

In the "developing" world (and what a horrible terminology that is as all places are developed, though maybe not industrialized fully), the most plentiful terrorists are nearly invisible: mosquitoes. Those tiny pests carry the potentially deadly disease of malaria and other afflictions, which kill an estimated one million-plus people annually. Admittedly, a commonplace insect bite is not nearly as dramatic and graphic as the mere thousand or so people who are held captive for ransom each year. Not that this number is to be scoffed at, but this ranks the odds of it happening to someone somewhere around .0000001. Statistically, the more routine calamities usually pose a *far* graver threat.

That said, the more highlighted risks can be horrendously real. In southeast Algeria, our camp was in the exact desert canyon where an Italian woman (my wife's own country) had been abducted a year earlier. And not long after we had departed, less than fifty miles away, the takeover of an oil refinery resulted in more than eighty deaths. Yet, our stay there in that area was about as idyllic as nature can offer.

Despite many loved one's well-intentioned protests and post-9/11 fed pleading, my resolve for making that particular trip to the Sahara was strengthened when, a few days prior to departing, two young men were shot thirty-eight times in broad daylight in front of dozens of witnesses a few blocks from where I was teaching "violence prevention" in Oakland, California. They died on a corner where I had passed shortly before on foot from the commuter train. In light of this and due to its having provided such a graphic contrast, from that point forward, my Western friends' cautions of how dangerous going to "emerging nations" can be have been thrown into almost comically sad relief.

On a personal level, my best friend growing up was raped and beaten nearly to death in her own bed by a "friend" on a posh cul-de-sac, and that certainly put an irreparable dent on my notions of what constitutes safety and peril.

Similarly, people caution of food contamination in foreign lands. But a moment's reflection on the soiled and soapless single sink bathrooms I've encountered all over the civilized world—from taquerias and diners to overly trendy gourmet places—puts that emphatically to rest as misplaced, superficial, and discriminatory. The fact remains that the worst food poisoning I ever contracted was in the Netherlands!

Truth be told, by all measures, I would be classified as a risk-averse person—I would never hop on a motorcycle except *maybe* as a last resort, I *always* wear a seat belt, detest extreme and contact sports, and am about as paranoid a pedestrian as ambulation allows. Instead of macho, to many people, I would likely be labelled as a "wimp." (But, considering that scooter-taxis are involved in almost *half* of the traffic fatalities in many major cities in Africa, skipping that one "experience" alone is a quite handy and simple way to slash your exposure in two.)

Not to make any sidelong commentary on just how cutthroat the entertainment business is, but I usually find myself more at ease in "Third World" countries than metro Los Angeles (which recently sported an intentional homicide rate that rivals Afghanistan, and that's *after* significant drops in LA crime).

The reality is, though, regardless of how far we roam or how "strange" any place may seem, wherever we end up is somewhere that many others feel *most* comfortable and call home. The center of the universe for almost everyone is *wherever they are standing* at that given moment, as much on the margins as cartographers may have consigned them.

There are no small countries, only small minds…waiting to be opened.

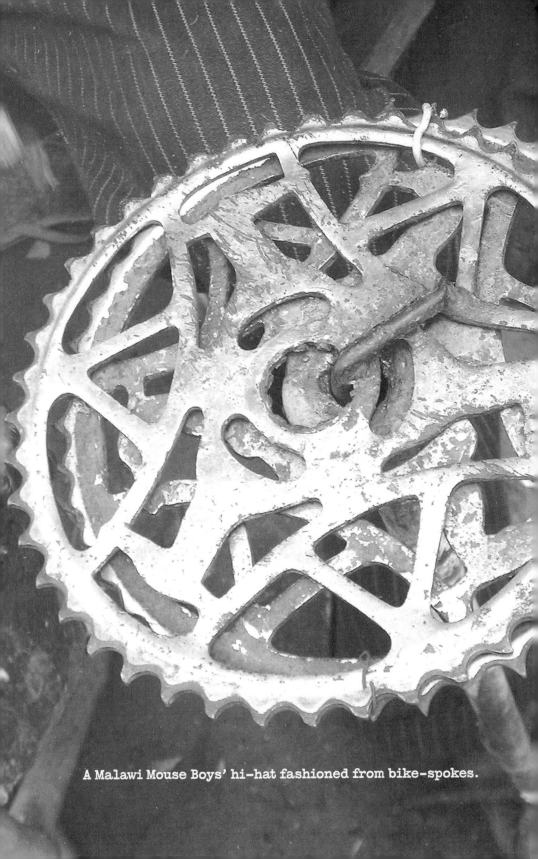

A Malawi Mouse Boys' hi-hat fashioned from bike-spokes.

Introduction: Learning Through Failure

Whatever little I might know about recording, I learned by making some of the more atrocious records imaginable. My own losses as an artist became others' gain, potentially. (Not to coddle any reverse-grandiosity, but one would be hard-pressed to put forth something more foibled than my debut LP at age twenty.) I failed to fulfill my own potential due in large part to a tendency to micromanage the creative process and, consequently, lose the forest for the trees. Much like the exemplary party-host, who makes sure every detail is in place but forgets to properly greet and engage the guests once the actual moment arrives, or the bride and groom who are too exhausted from stress to consummate on their wedding night.

My hard-earned and painful lessons in the guaranteed imperfection of perfectionism led to a liberation of sorts: the acceptance of my own shortcomings, if not the utter celebration of limits and "mistakes" as useful partners, however uninvited they might be.

In a nutshell, it boils down to, "If you can't beat 'em, join 'em." Keep it feral, is the theme.

First and foremost, a producer's job is to hopefully provide a *more* clear-eyed—though, undoubtedly, still highly subjective—point of view. It is the overall Big Picture arc of a work that needs tending to—to help find the heart of each song, the center, and clear away waste to bring clarity to the narrative.

An artist can no more fully understand what makes them special than a beautiful person can comprehend why others find them attractive. We are so poorly attuned to ourselves that one truism is how we almost always disown the very qualities that make us unique—despising the nose that makes our face interesting, refusing to play our best song(s).

Yet even the history of film and "glamour" themselves attest to some of the most arresting figures not only being blemished, but that feature as being the key ingredient to their appeal: Humphrey Bogart's lisp, Katharine Hepburn's tremor, Jimmy Stewart's stutter, supermodel Lauren Hutton's gap-tooth, Elizabeth Taylor's mole, and so on.

A fundamental task is to get the *ego* out of our ears.

Rather than trying to control outcomes, our energy is better utilized toward just "being *our*selves" and finding (*or creating*) a natural niche in the world. The challenge is not so dissimilar from the one facing those who are clinically depressed, a condition that is often largely based on people stubbornly insisting that circumstances "should" be a certain way, rather than better devoting attention to dealing with things as they are—to give up all hope, accept death as an inevitability, and engage with whatever *is*.

In my experience, almost without fail, artists will only play their standout songs last and highly reluctantly. This is because they do not, and ultimately *cannot*, know what their own most illustrative work is, any more than we can see our own face without a mirror. (And *even then*, can we ever really see ourselves in a manner undistorted from the noise of our own internal filters? Almost all information we receive arrives secondhand and preprocessed by our self-image. Despite even quite mighty efforts, most of us are bound to remain prisoners of our own subjectivity.)

This accounts for the shock most of us have experienced when seeing a stranger in a shop window, that after a split-second we realize is *us*. Or the rejection of our own voice that most of us express when we hear ourselves on a recording for the first time: "I don't sound like *that*." Beyond any of this is the fact that those engaged in that act of self-absorption literally change themselves—the very thing that they are looking at—as a result of that action.

And this is why every autobiography is, in fact, a work of fiction.

The better songs almost always have to be pried from the grip of an artist's vanity. The strongest performances and/or melodies usually occur during soundchecks, as gear is being broken down or on the way out the door, in the parking lot or hallways. Ironically, the bulk of magical moments happen in the candid breaks *between* the actual recording, and thus pass by, lost forever. For every great album, there is a shadow, unrecorded collection that would trounce that which exists. And the better of these two is irrecoverable.

One night I found the leader of Tinariwen crouching down between some trucks in the sheer blackness to "hide" from an overzealous engineer that the musician was dodging like an insolent student. With a long-lost friend, he was almost whispering an ancient lullaby that his mother used to sing to him and that he reported afterward he had not played in decades. It was fragile and transcendent, but he refused to share it officially outside that one mystical moment that kept the five people present breathless for those seconds' time that seemed to be temporarily suspended.

The strength of those "just one more" final tunes is the very freedom and ease with which they are delivered, liberated from the hindrance of formally sanctioned "performance." I've learned the hard way that equipment best never be unplugged until *after* the musicians are for certain long gone or finished, and the record button should almost always be on.

Often "the end" proves to actually be the beginning and everything else prior, just a warm-up. This is attested to by the wisdom of many ancient societies, where rehearsals attract the largest audiences and the shows themselves are secondary.

I continue to be motivated today by the same heady sensation that enchanted me to first pick up a guitar at age six, the identical rising feeling, high in the chest on those hallowed occasions that an undeniably exceptional creation is unexpectedly revealed. From day one of plucking out an instrument, my goal was not acclaim, but simply to be part of that process of sharing, hoping to catch a few of those unmistakable, lightning-in-a-bottle moments that lend an almost supernatural high. Over time, it dawned on me that my favorite tracks from most albums were often the more stripped down and raw ones—the B-sides—and also that I almost invariably preferred the "before" pictures in beauty-remedy ads.

In the end, what captivates me are those figures who could be categorized more as in supporting roles than in glamor roles.

My penny-pinching days of vinyl-record hunting in used bins and flipping through the mildewed, landfill-fated countless corporate cookie-cutter acts affirmed for me how much more value there was in an anonymous contribution to society's greater good than the napalm of fame. One sagacious maxim cast-off by a forgotten farmer, vagrant, or housewife (e.g., "A stitch in time, saves nine.") resonates constructively for generations, long after a thousand trendy death-metal, New Wave, or EDM albums have met their predestined end, only to *maybe,* at best, be revived as the butt of some danced and/or sung, ironic-nostalgia joke. That is, if they are remembered at all.

It is far better and more meaningful to be a Jo Jones (from Count Basie's band), who introduced the foot-pedal for the hi-hat cymbal or Gospel singer Julius "June" Cheeks who reputedly became the first performer to defy institutional gravity and walk into the audience while performing, collapsing boundaries with just a few short steps.

Acknowledged or not, we live as inheritors of the collective history and wisdom of the unknown, the "ghost writers" who shape most culture. The names may be forgotten, but the influences continue to long be felt.

By design, what follows here is neither scientific nor scholastic. It is just one person's opinions and observations from a life spent under the spell of recording's alchemy that makes it possible for the deceased to speak to the living.

The structure herein is composed of mini-chapters, designed to be opened to any page and read in random order, potentially. These words are humbly offered as stimulus for thought and reflection. "Riffs," as it were. I hope in some small way it proves helpful to your own expressive endeavors, whatever they may be.

In the end, I may not "know shit." But stealing another's voice—particularly when it may be the only material thing that they have left—not only speaks, but *screams* for itself. And if it is done with a smile on the face or a compliment on the tongue, that disingenuousness and denial only deepens the injury and divide. (It should not be forgotten that historically, among the first steps of enslaving a population is outlawing the enslaved's language to help insure their submission.)

SECTION I:

The Value of Democratizing Voices

1

We *Aren't* the World: All Music Is "Local Music"

W hat is World Music really anyway?

Isn't all music from somewhere in the world? We have yet to be exposed to martian countdowns.

There is no music that is not "local music." It comes from *some* place. But, distressingly, more and more sounds are disconnected from location, bearing no trace of their origins. Instead, they could literally be from anywhere. Thus, they ultimately come from *no*where.

All recordings are in the end "field recordings." They document life (. . . or lack thereof), arising from a specific time and place. If that place is artificial, then the results will often be as well. Ultimately, any recording technology exists only as a means to convey feeling, and has little to no value, otherwise, in and of itself.

At their best, recordings act as a form of eavesdropping, where it is as if the musician is speaking directly to only you, whispering in your ear in a privileged way that rises above ordinary experience and takes on a confessional air.

Good communicators mature from talking *at* someone (the affliction of egotistical individuals and performers) to speaking *to* them. But, in the most rarefied and illustrious instances, an artist seems to somehow be able to even converse *with* the audience—using his or her voice to conjure up a near three-dimensional experience, as if they were really "there" with the listener, serving as some spectral confidante. Certainly countless heartbroken people have cried themselves to sleep listening to their favorite singers, when no other or more fitting consolers were to be found.

In the final analysis of a recording, any musical endeavor is just the organizing of "noise" into sound. If the majority of sounds are increasingly banished culturally as nonmusic and the range of what is considered acceptable becomes constricted, this stands as evidence of a civilization in decline—asphyxiating on the fumes of its own heritage—and the more predictable and rubber-stamped becomes the output.

It is increasingly my belief that in our over-recorded, -duplicated, and -documented age, one of the last sonic frontiers is language. When we listen to someone sing in a foreign tongue, we are forced to pay attention not to what they are saying, but what they mean (. . . and *if* they really "*mean* it"). Instead, as is now frequently the case, anytime another language begins to sound like it *could* be English—even if just for a stray phrase—there is a shrinkage of musicality (e.g., vowel durations becoming unvaried). This is exemplified every time one hears some motor-mouthed, international DJ's downshift to half-speed, like they're going over a speed bump, for each borrowed English word (e.g., "SMS").

Mankind's end curse very well may *not* be Babel—many people speaking different tongues—but instead, a case where everyone is reduced to but one single language, and most differences and the possibility of random influence and couplings are lost.

This lack of diversity is reflected sonically by the ever-narrowing dynamic range, with the trend toward signals becoming more compressed electronically—squashing the quietest and loudest sounds closer together—so that the overall impression is the illusion that something is louder than it actually is.

2

The Fixation to Fixate

A pitfall of capturing music in any permanent, reproducible medium is that it can arrest the artistic growth and progress of that musical form. The archetypal field recordings that Alan Lomax did throughout America's South in the 1940s (or the forefather of all sonic "exotica" documentation, Jesse Fewkes in 1889), more than exemplifying exact musical genres like the blues, were in fact reflections of individual aesthetics at one exact moment in time. The assumption that bluegrass music always sounded like it did in the era in which it was first so faithfully documented is to disregard the fluidity of all musical creation. Not only would bluegrass have sounded different one hundred years earlier, it probably sounded markedly different even five years before (and would have more so five years *later,* had it not been for the permanence of the recordings themselves which led to more precise mimicry, turning music-making from a process, instead, into a "thing" that could literally be held and examined).

More than sacred scriptures, most folk music has been constantly retooled and adapted by each successive individual performer. The greatest pieces were cross-*generational* works in progress (e.g., *The Iliad*'s being seven hundred-plus years in the making).

The first recordings essentially caught improvisations that arbitrarily became benchmarks, snapshots stolen from an epic film, that was then disrupted violently, damming up its stream, midnarrative. And, those pictures will inevitably be, in the first place, blurry ones, for they are capturing something elusive and in motion, much like the ambiguous images offered as evidence of UFOs or Loch Ness monster sightings.

Art is designed to reveal, not to show us what we already see and know. Yet, the gigantic copying machine that is the music industry, by necessity, thrives on repetition. And when a system ceases changing, it has become a cadaver.

A psychological appeal of fixing something vaporous into a physical state is that it appeases people's fear of their own impermanence. But one hundred years from now—if we have even survived as a species—no one but the most erudite will know or care *who* sang "Sexual Healing" or "Every Breath You Take" or the like. But the sturdiest songs—the most unshakable melodies, a lyrical bit that hooks listeners' psyches—will have lived on in some altered and evolving form, liberated from celebrity.

3

Message Monopolization

"We would not have conquered Germany . . . without the loudspeaker."
—Adolf Hitler, 1938

How can it be that for decades, hundreds of thousands of "artists" from cities like Los Angeles, New York, and London have been given deafening megaphones, while entire countries are left unrepresented globally? This computational absurdity of superiority only reflects society's greater inequities.

Is it not in order to ensure fairness that the US Senate has a compensatory composition—one that provides the exact same number of representatives for *every* state regardless of the size of its population?

Perspectives must be democratized. In order to thrive as a species, it is imperative that we learn to listen to one another more attentively.

Equitable representation in music and other popular arts is critical to the health of our society and the world, and the ever-reeping corporatization of sound enacts a form of sonic and cultural genocide. Rotation of power is vital to democracy.

Relatedly, African Americans make up 12.5 percent of the US population, but 40 percent of those incarcerated in the United States. Unjustified, inequity in this and all forms is best exposed and confronted.

A dozen people can be murdered on one street in a single weekend in a city like Chicago and go mostly unreported and unnoticed nationally, but a non-story about a celebrity's bedhead or latest online tiff in some other higher-rent district such as Beverly Hills is worldwide news for days on end—a VIP hangnail goes viral. These are manufactured controversies to keep us distracted from the more pressing issues at hand.

Eight hundred immigrants go down off the coast of Libya, capsized and drowned without a sound, and we barely hear a peep about it. Around that same period, I witnessed the immediate aftermath of a car chase and shooting in West Oakland—a teenager dangling, twisted and supine out his driver's side door—but was never able to find even a single mention of it in "the news."

Akin to the ancient political concept that "those who desire to lead, should be prohibited from doing so, and those who are reluctant, must be forced to," those who most want to be noticed, should be quieted and, in their place, the humble nudged to the forefront.

Too often, less wealthy nations are treated paternalistically: like "good" children, who should be seen, but not heard.

I honor my country. I love my language. But too few people with too much power equals injustice. Ethical sliding almost always occurs in the smaller places first, where we aren't looking or have disregarded—such as with "kid's" music. Physical danger itself most often presents from whatever we've underestimated and allowed the upper-hand (e.g., being mugged in broad daylight while brunching in a "safe" area). And, it is the "little," last-straw things that usually prove most catastrophic to relationships.

This is not about protectionism. In the end, art should always be a case of letting the best song/voice/story prevail regardless of the politics. But if only a select spattering are even allowed to speak, it is de facto censorship. And the lessons of history are weakened when only partial accounts are heard, by way of this sneaky and indirect tyranny.

For democracy to thrive, contrary voices must not be muffled and ignored, but *amplified*. Even on the rare occasions when "smaller" countries are heard from (and, is it not an absurdity that we can even ever dare to regard any country with millions of citizens as "small"?), it is almost always only from members of the ruling sect, who not only do *not* customarily voice the concerns of the masses, but frequently oppose them.

The concept that music "centers" itself is diseased at its core. Music is universal. It exists everywhere and is a necessity for survival, spiritually. The hope is to help tip the scales, even in the most minuscule way, back to fairer representation. The majority of countries in the world have been rendered so invisible that most "educated" people on the planet would have a hard time even locating them on a map.

There is a lot of discussion of physical mobility and universal access for the physically disabled, but almost no comment about regional immobility. Most citizens of impoverished countries are seen as suspects for defection just by virtue of their origins. Consequently, freedom of movement beyond their own borders is an almost unattainable dream—freedom to wander, to discover and explore, to literally become airborne. This is something that those of us with power passports, like the United States or Japan, can barely imagine, since we instead are welcomed with open arms almost anywhere we show up—even if traveling on a whim. Contrastingly, every band that I have worked with has been rejected for travel visas on their first application and a legal plea must be made for them just to be granted reluctant days-long entry.

A hallmark of totalitarianism is that it favors the one over the many.

The rich get richer, indeed. Endowment by entitlement, where opportunity is not just expected and/or demanded, but *taken*.

Yet, nepotism and academia are both antithetical to major pop-culture uprisings. Innovation in pop culture has almost, without fail, routinely risen culturally from the bottom to the top, not from the aristocracy that now rules much of the misnomered "indie" rock world. Folk artistry is rarely a trickle-down affair. Be it James Brown, Elvis Presley, Bob Marley, Sister Rosetta Tharpe, Louis Armstrong, Grandmaster Flash, Johnny Rotten, the Carter Family, Miriam Makeba, Woody Guthrie, Kurt Cobain, Blind Lemon Jefferson, Edith Piaf, or Eminem—to name just a few—many of the most prescient artists historically have originated from less than auspicious circumstances.

It is not sheer coincidence that so many innovations incubate in garages, vacant lots, and abandoned warehouses. Yet, try to name even one great penthouse or villa-estate band. It is in the former "empty" spaces that there is a liberty to the process, an absence of fear and expectations that squarely puts the priority on results.

Cultural piracy is most often a case of downward mobility, with the well-heeled rummaging through the basement thrift shop of the underclass to try to toughen and spice up their facade. Such is the common case of boarding-school-bred boys adopting Cockney accents or suburban soccer-league kids fronting as if they are "ghetto" (which is a word borrowed from late Middle Ages' Italian, by the way).

And the call for greater diversity is not just to right regional deficits. Any music must shine on its own, but if all other factors are more or less equal, shouldn't whoever *represents the underrepresented* be the one given an opportunity to be heard—be they of the nonmajority and/or nondominant sexual orientation, gender, physical ability, or age group? Would there not be some benefit if a fully clothed female was given the nod over a thong-clad, crotch-thrusting peer?

And all of this is not nearly so much for any given artist's gain as for *ours*. To feast on as wide a range of information and perspectives as possible is enriching. It nourishes, strengthens, and even heals the listener. Is it really healthy and balanced for a "just" society to still have an estimated 86 percent of the voice-of-God emcees be male?

When was the last time you heard a lesbian, Filipino Canadian group or a double-amputee singing in Oriya (hardly a fringe language, with over thirty-three million speakers)? Ever? Didn't think so. Yet, how many whining, upper-middle-class Caucasian boys playing standardly tuned guitars have been shoved down our collective throats for decades, through every possible distribution outlet, traded as if they are the gold standard?

Variety benefits us in diet. It also benefits us mentally. To challenge ourselves cerebrally helps build new neural pathways, which literally helps keep us alive since ongoing curiosity is the strongest predictor of longevity. This is likely why so many scientists live long lives.

And often when "alternative" voices are heard, they serve more as phallic or racial substitutes, guests in someone else's world, slotted into an otherwise unaltered aesthetic framework.

Instead, we are offered unity through shopping, with calculatedly integrated fashion campaigns chock-full of ecstatic cross-cultural chums, rainbow-hues that rarely appear in real life. Worse, do we ever see an actual Benetton or Esprit store in the 'hood or the barrio? They visit these corners only via the wish-fulfillment land of propaganda.

This is much the same as bastions of "freedom" like the United States, United Kingdom, and Germany celebrating "world peace" and the abolishment of slavery. Yet what has changed in actuality is applicable only to the richer regions of the globe, since the same sufferings have been displaced or continue elsewhere, without ever breaking stride.

Overemphasis of any one individual or region can only beat a path to facism. Just as a body must have a circulatory system and a method for dealing with waste, so should culture.

Is not the very basis of any *just* justice system that every last person is entitled to a "fair hearing"?

Alfred from the Malawi Mouse Boys' vocal take is crashed by some uninvited groupies.

FIELD RECORDING CHRONICLE
MALAWIAN MIRACLE:
THE MEEK SHALL INHERIT THE GROOVE

It was just around the corner from the "Pack-and-Go" coffin shop that any trace of music was found in Malawi, on a skinny stretch of road that marks the only place where the tradition of selling barbecued mice-on-a-stick as snacks for passing travelers continues.

Literally working around the clock, whistling and waving their wares at oncoming traffic, the Malawi Mouse Boys spend the downtime of their days (and nights) beside the highway, strumming rudimentary guitars tailored from recycled scrap-metal parts.

Using stones for kick-drum mallets, they are a literal "rock" band. And, their hand carved and sheet-metal guitars give true thrust to the term DIY (do-it-yourself). One of the member's mother gave him a birth name that translates to "I hate you," expressing the not-so-subtle hostility of the environment that they were born into.

Having crisscrossed almost two thousand miles along the bumpy dirt roads and undivided two-lane, main highway of this tiny, agricultural, and narrow land, until then—in over two weeks—not a single instrument of any kind at all had been sighted.

At one roadside bar-stall that served banana-beer by the half gallon, "Play that Funky Music, White Boy" came blasting on the cracked speaker teetering on the counter, upping the irony quota to *post* post-modern dimensions. Whether the song had been put on intentionally as mockery or was just a case of someone simply liking the tune with or without knowledge as to its literal meaning seemed beside the point.

Along the journey, the person driving had made a wrong turn, dead-ending into an outdoor market. There was a standoff as he and one of the shopkeepers argued back and forth. The vehicle was soon surrounded by dozens of onlookers and other proprietors. The fact that the person with us was white seemed to only worsen matters. Finally, after many minutes of suspense, the crowd erupted into uproarious laughter, due at least in part to their befuddlement that a "British" person (who actually was Italian) could speak Chichewa so well *and* was willing to stand his ground so fearlessly. It turns out it had all been for amusement. To be allowed passage, we had paid a toll in theater.

Rural Malawi is a place where wealth is demarcated by whether there is a thatch or tin roof over one's hut. This alternating pattern dots the countryside in bursts, like some sort of patchwork binary code.

Subsisting in one of the poorest countries (e.g., the mean income is less than forty cents a day and life expectancy narrowly surpasses forty years of age) with nearly the highest rates of AIDS, the populace seems poised, just one gram of protein a day away from revolution. The group of young villagers that founded the Malawi Mouse Boys live in one of the most impoverished districts of an already ravaged land and have been writing songs of faith and love together since they were young children. The earnestness and passion of their voices hark back to an earlier and more trusting, pre-"modern" time.

After spotting one of the members beside the road, strumming a guitar, we made a hasty U-turn and introduced ourselves. Following some negotiation through a translator, a recording session was organized for later that week.

What had started out as a plan to record one single singer-songwriter snowballed into a full collective of eight musicians that piled in along the way, overfilling the truck-bed for a chance to play their handmade and repurposed instruments (e.g., the hi-hat was made from two rusted bicycle gears) for prosperity's sake.

People talk of one-stoplight towns. Malawi could be called a one-stoplight *nation*. A place where shoes remain a luxury item. There literally is no road into the Mouse Boys' small village since cars never go there, so the band had to improvise a way through the bush.

It is an area where people define themselves not by what they have, but what they can *do*. The only real obstacle to catching something magic musically with these men was the tiny, manic spiders that kept racing into the slots of the hard drive.

Yes, dogs, chickens, and children are audible in the background of the recordings. But the great thing about animals and kids is that they always bark, chirp, and/or whine in time to the music. Intuitively, they blend.

4

The Real King(s) of Rock 'n' Roll

A bit before the turn of the twentieth century, while the European superpowers were busy dividing up the African continent as their "Wild West" in order to expand kingdoms, the United States—having run out of physical space—had started the process of colonizing the minds of the world through media.

America's physical and cultural isolation are exemplified by the fact that in the one-hundred-plus-year history of recorded music—a medium that we invented, nonetheless—there has sadly only ever been three (!) indisputable hit songs in the United States in any language other than English: "Volare" in *partial*-Italian in 1958, Los Lobos's reworking of "La Bamba" in 1987, and the recent "Gangnam Style" YouTube craze.

This linguistic separatism is a breeding ground for wrong-headed notions of what is "foreign." If we cannot even coexist on the radio and/or on our own playlists, then the potential to do so in the flesh is made even more dismal. Few things are more silently nefarious though than a pseudo-familiarity with other cultures (e.g., third-generation American kids claiming that they are "French"), and the poorly constructed stereotypes that result.

If every casual music aficionado would force themselves to listen to even one song a day in an unfamiliar language, the world would become a slightly more nuanced and connected place. Multilingualism, even in its most piecemeal form, acts as a bridge between people, literally helping connect the dots.

One of the most disheartening moments I've experienced as to the possibility of America opening its heart and ears more to global music was having a supposedly hip New York City music professional recently ask me if I "spoke *African*"—without even the faintest hint of awareness as to the downright wrongheadedness of his question and how it negated the over three thousand languages found on that continent (not even counting the innumerable dialects!). And, this came from a forty-something, masters degree–educated, Manhattan-raised, bilingual man, from a "minority" group, whom one might expect to know better.

Similarly shocking was hearing a liberal, gay Berkeley blogger activist declare that "the whole world speaks English" and also that "they all want to live here (in the USA)." My time residing in kissing-cousin countries like Italy and France has violently dissuaded me of such notions. Even these quasi-similar lands remain places where it is extremely rare to find someone outside the tourist districts that can communicate in English beyond "hello" . . . if that. As a rule, figuratively and literally, it seems that Americans need to "get out a bit more."

As a first step, no real progress can be made around these issues until Africa stops being referred to as a country, but instead is identified as the grand, intricate continent that it is with a massive geography and cultural diversity to be celebrated (e.g., the Sahara desert alone is bigger than *all* of the contiguous United States).

Almost every person who has emigrated that I've ever asked, says they plan to return to their homeland—that they "love" it there. But few ever can or do. And still today most people live their lives within fifty miles of where they were born.

The dividends of this geographic spoon-feeding continue today with English still being the official business language globally (though, Bollywood and the like, as well as ascending economic powers like China and Brazil, are causing some overdue threat to that supremacy). A telling observation is how readily many Americans will claim to "speak" another language if they know even a few words, which is a mortifying contrast to most other sectors of the world where people tend to protest that they "*don't* know" a language—even when they very well do—unless they have completely mastered it.

Anytime a piece of media is imported, it pirates with it not just the language, but the affect of that culture—facial expressions, hand movements, pace, and posture. Creepily, via dubbed films and programs, many people in foreign lands have spent tens of thousands of hours (or more) of their life subliminally reading lips in English, almost like some sort of bizarre cult-induction.

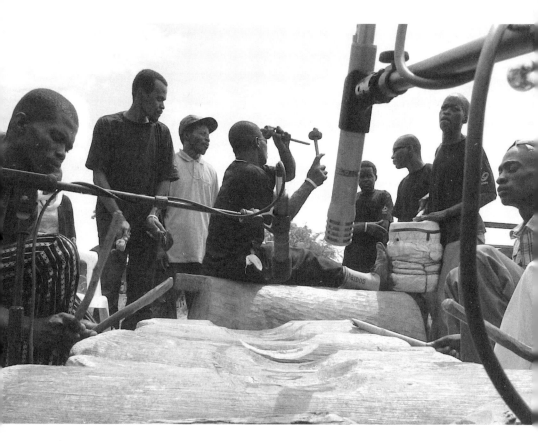

The Zande tribe's ten-foot-long, five-person zylophone sits
at the center of the village and acts as its "heart."

FIELD RECORDING CHRONICLE
OPEN ERROR:
IF YOU HAVE TO ASK, YOU'LL NEVER KNOW

Maybe you are not a true field-recordist until you've been detained by a tribal chief—backed up by over one hundred people—and then been extorted for four times as much money as originally agreed to. Or been taken to "the Somalians" for a trial-viewing as a possible sale, but who thankfully decided that we weren't apparently up to snuff on the terror-network marketplace. (Sometimes a backlog of existing inventory can work in one's favor. This was one casting for which I was happy to have not made the cut . . . loads better than all of the times that I was the last one picked for games of hoop on the schoolyard.)

Earlier, it probably should have come as some sort of omen when, as Marilena took some photos of one of the elder band members, a young, drunk Westernized male got up in my face, taunting, "How's about we take your picture? Want us to come and take *your* picture," his LA Dodgers hat hanging lopsidedly and oh-so precariously balanced on the side of his curls. Obviously, the Chief's blessing that any recording and photos were "okay" had not been passed onto this young upstart.

Taking into consideration that some countries will imprison you for even snapping pictures of certain buildings and that it is quite common for people to accost photographers and confiscate their cameras and/or demand money if a viewfinder has as much as been pointed in their general direction, the sort of comment made by the young resident was not to be dismissed too lightly.

Hillary Clinton might've said it "takes a village to raise a child." Instead, with the Zande tribe, an entire village is needed to raise the roof (figuratively) off the place.

The "heart" of the village is a xylophone that is over ten feet long and requires five people to play it simultaneously. With sacred wood carried from three countries away in Africa, the "kpaningbo" is built in the center of the village, and is so immense that it cannot be moved henceforth. (Never again will complaints from weekend-warriors about having to shlep around Marshall half-stacks or Hammond organs ring quite true!)

When we arrived, there was a raucous midday crowd awaiting us. Since the party seemed to already be in full swing, with dozens of dancers circling the players, and vocalists trading off in a seemingly spontaneous, ragtag fashion, there was little choice but to throw up a coverage of mics as quickly as possible. As a default, I loosely followed "Sound Engineering 101" principles and placed the microphones:

1. as close to the source as feasible, but

2. as far away from each other as allowable.

In such instances it usually helps to bear in mind that in post-production it is easier to take away frequencies than add. It is not usually viable to enhance sonics that aren't there at all to begin with. And microphone placement best starts with simply getting down on the ground and listening with the naked ear, and letting the sound—not user manuals—dictate where things should go.

Our taxi driver, who had agreed to be on standby and help translate and mediate, vanished into the crowd, and there were few options but to live the experience and hope for the best.

Close-by, a straw-and-plywood bar blasted dub music that might send a schooled engineer to the edge of a psychotic break. The villagers said it would be impolite to ask him to turn it down. But, to my great pleasure, I was amazed later how completely absent this intrusive sound was on the actual recording. It stood as further affirmation that you can record just about anywhere, with the outdoors providing about as close to a neutral sonic sphere as is possible, since there is minimal reflection compared to that which usually occurs from surfaces like windows and walls.

Music should bleed and breathe, and not be vacuum-sealed. If silence is the goal, then we are doomed to failure, since silence does not exist. Sound is always found. Silence is merely noise that has stabilized or been masked or ignored. That is why filmmakers almost never utilize actual silence for effect, but instead when indicating it, emphasize the meeker details that normally wouldn't be evident at all (e.g., a fly's buzzing) if things were louder. And "noise" is nothing more than whatever is classified as homeless and unwelcome sound.

Of any equipment that is needed to record outdoors, one of the most valuable is actually the cheapest. Above all items, duct tape is king. Plumbers tape can affix a microphone to almost anything, making de facto mic-stands out of tree limbs or anything else perpendicular.

Yes, and that very tape is the one thing that authorities have most often tried to confiscate from me. This is similar to the great suspicion that ferrying such contraband cargo as a backpack full of books routinely arouses. More so than the microphones and cameras that could easily mark me a spy, ideas seem to be an even more threatening import.

The core of the group's instrument—thirteen keyed bars of varying lengths—are stacked just a matter of inches off the ground. The recording equipment and mics had to be situated there in the dirt. By the end of the session, the gear and myself were covered in thick coats of claylike dust, temporarily turning my hair a fluorescent orange.

One technical reality of recording outdoors is that often pieces of machinery have to be ceded to the cause, fallen—sometimes, *quite literally*, with microphones—in the line of duty. Certainly, in the field is no place for fastidiousness. Shure SM57's microphones have a well-deserved reputation for their versatility and durable nature, but, as I experienced in this case, we all have our limits.

Since wind was gusting intermittently, I improvised pop-screens for the mics from the sweaty socks off my own feet, since almost any cloth barrier will do.

Similar to encounters I'd observed elsewhere, an ingenious recycling here was the use of Igloo coolers as tom-drums (. . .
news which may or may not be music to the ears of certain
refrigeration-industry executives). Since the musicians held
these between their thighs as they shuffled about, a more-or-
less centrally aimed shotgun microphone had the only prayer of
capturing the (*mostly*) quarter-note pulse.

The bass drum itself is fashioned from half of a hollowed-out
tree trunk. It is so large that the player must sit atop its con-
cave shell and use their entire leg to alter the tone by opening
and closing the sound hole via the bending and raising of their
entire limb at the knee. The activity is so tiring that over
the almost two hours of playing, a crew of musicians rotated to
trade off the role mid-song, without ever once losing the beat.

Later in Hollywood, with great excitement, I tried to concisely
relate this experience to the president of one of the last
remaining major-label companies. To my ears—I guess, somewhat
bugged-out ones—this was some of the best trance dance music
that I'd ever heard, capable of making Skrillex and Deadmau5
blush with envy.

As I had been expecting to receive back the same enthusiasm that
many musician-artistic types had expressed when they heard of
this experience, the chill that came over the room seconds into
the story was jolting in its instantaneousness and palpability.
As if on cue, a phone call from a Euro-techno artist that the
executive "had to take" ended our meeting abruptly on the spot,
and I was summarily escorted out by an assistant, with about as
much urgency and contempt as if I were a shirtless, drunk pedo-
phile being bounced from a toddler's pizza party. Apparently I
was never to return, and now bore the African-xylophone story as
the equivalent of a sort of show-biz scarlet letter.

5

*Un*labelling Labels

A Belgian international music "expert" once authoritatively proclaimed to me that "there is no good music in Rwanda. They are not a musical people."

I took this as a bit of a personal challenge. There no more is an "amusical" culture than there is an asexual one or any group lacking in any other basic survival instincts. For, if this were true, then the said people would have ceased to exist, *long ago*. In fact, it can be argued that music, in and of itself, *is* a necessity for human survival. (And, for that matter, there is no amusical place, either. In fact, "instruments" surround us on every surface. The world is a drum-kit, awaiting greater animation. There are only two types of sound: struck and unstruck. It is merely our task to free sounds that are trapped. They are our partners in this.)

Furthermore, with a population of over twelve million people, what could "Rwandan music" possibly mean? Would anyone be so naive as to ask what American music is? Would that be jazz, blues, country, rap, rock, or any of their hyphenated prodigy? What, pray tell, is the California or, even more pinpointedly, the West London sound? To make even the most ham-handed attempt, we would have to embark on such an iffy process by at least first demanding more specifics—what era, what neighborhood(s), what gender and class, etc.? So therefore, why would it be that, at a minimum, every country would not likely display a similar—*or even greater*—diversity? Particularly since the drive for individuation is universal.

Anyone who dares to claim to have comprehensive knowledge of a country's potential is instead unwittingly revealing their own ignorance and small-mindedness. There simply is no generic, representative Armenian or Hebrew person, any more than all one billion Chinese or Hindus are the same. All lands are lands of contrast.

One band from Myanmar does not equal all of Myanmar nor its people, any more than Justin Bieber could be construed as the sole or exemplary representative of Canada (. . . God forbid).

Bloodcurdlingly, a festival exhibitor once refused outright—without even a courtesy listening first—an artist I worked with by declaring, "We've already *done* Uganda," as if the aim were to collect countries like nesting dolls, not to mention the notion that millions upon millions of individuals could be summed up in one fell swoop. (That the double-entrendre seemed lost on her of having "done" a country with such a history of exploitation, only added to the sting.)

Next time anyone claims to be a World Music expert, try asking them to explain some of the ways that Celtic music was born from English folk. (Hint: It *wasn't*. Celtic culture predates the arrival of Anglo-Saxons by *at least* one thousand years.) Or comment on how much you admire pre-Christian music from Cape Verde and wait for their response. (There is no such thing as this form of music in Cape Verde. The island was not settled by man until much later, *after* the fifteenth century.)

You get the idea.

Anyone doubting that we are still living in the shell of imperial rule of a sneakier sort was clearly not present at the international music panel I sat on for one of the most prestigious and influential music organizations on the planet. That there was not one citizen of an African, Asian, South American, or mainland European country present was cause for embarrassment. But that no one present seemed to even blink an eye at the fact that there wasn't even a single person in attendance of African or East Asian descent at all, nor a soul under the age of forty, was appalling and made me start to question whether we were even convening in the twenty-first century. It was as if a time-warp had been passed through and the others seated around me could easily be wearing powdered-wigs and corsets (. . . and, come to think of it, I guess maybe some of them very well could have been doing the latter). I feared that maybe I should more properly be addressing some of them with averted eyes and as "his/her excellency," that is, if daring to speak in their presence at all.

Distressingly, "World Music" is usually unofficially reduced to a few populous countries: India, Mali, South Africa, Cuba, the Congo, and Brazil, as if they were aesthetically superior rather than simply numerically advantaged *and* also wealthier historically due to their participation in trading routes.

The trend is that, more than a regional or racial issue, being heard has become one of class. Every country has a division between the rural and urban inhabitants (and, when applicable, the suburban, too). Usually it is only the elite-stratosphere—clustered in capital cities—that are granted a forum, regardless of whatever culture is in question. Just like in the West, elsewhere the well-heeled are the most likely to make *and* have connections, along with the ability to more easily maintain them.

The result is a broadcasting of the bourgeois.

Further, the bulk of "international" artists given a leg up are usually actually citizens of Western countries. Ones that sing in English or French, but have exotic surnames. Not that there is anything at all wrong with the voices of first-generation immigrants being heard, but certainly someone born and raised in America is not interchangeable with an artist from an entirely different country who has never ventured outside its borders, or maybe even the surroundings of their own tiny village.

The strange practice of referring to people by distant, rather than direct, biographical origins would be equivalent to someone claiming that they had heard this great "Mexican singer," when speaking of Jerry Garcia from the Grateful Dead. Or a wonderful British artist who goes by the name of Garth Brooks.

Rather than dismissing the significance or deeper impact of this sort of invasion and dominance—when one culture acts like an occupying force to another—it would be best to attempt envisioning for even a moment what the feeling might be like if for decades the major radio and television stations in your hometown broadcast almost nothing but, say, Pakistani singers and films for decades, and almost exclusively what was held up as beauty ideals were images of people whose facial color, hair type, and predominant features differed noticeably from yourself as well as the majority of your fellow citizens and peers. Or what must be the sensation to see men of a different skin color continually coming to your birthplace and taking away children and young women, as if their own. The transit-connection areas of many African and Asian airports often appear to be abduction sites, with multitudes of crying and confused toddlers, having just been wrested away from their families or longtime caretakers by strangers. Or try pondering the jolt of having foreigners come up to you on the street daily, attempting to speak to you in a language other than your own, and then having the audacity to become irritated when you don't immediately respond or completely comprehend what they've just said. Such is already the experience of many citizens around the globe.

Stani from The Good Ones (Rwanda) makes it more than clear
that he's seen a few things in his lifetime.

FIELD RECORDING CHRONICLE
RWANDA:
LOVE SONGS FROM THE ASHES OF A GENOCIDE

They were standing in the dark, their eyes downcast and furtive, and holding only one guitar between them. From one hundred feet away, I knew instantly that there was something special about them, a feeling one is lucky to experience even once in a lifetime. By that point, for over two weeks we'd already visited literally every recording studio in the capital (Kigali) and surrounding areas, and listened to hundreds of artists, all to no avail.

We even attended a Kigali music festival where every performer seemed to be nothing more than a cookie-cutter version of a corresponding Western celebrity—same dress, affect, gestures, intonation, and hyperkinetic, but empty moves—with the only alteration being that the local language was grafted on top. (In the darkness that night, groups of pre-adolescents kept strutting up to us in mass, busting moves, "calling us out" to a dance-off, for which we were clearly out of our league and probably quite wisely declined.)

The meeting with the band, the Good Ones, had been set up through a mutual friend—someone who was quite talented himself, but was adamant that they were far better. The instant the band opened their mouths to sing, it was as if the universe reached down to tap me on the shoulder and say, "What these guys do is precious and rare. Don't f*&! it up."

It felt like being carried away on a wave, but with no fear of drowning.

Earlier on the trip I experienced a cross-cultural, mini-epiphany when, Akim, who had driven us to all four corners of Rwanda in search of music, angrily ejected from his car stereo the

8-track tape that I had found of 1970s Rwandan singer Kagambage Alexandre. Akim immediately replaced it with the only collection he owned. It was of Mandarin pop, the strain that is played in cheesy Chinese-American restaurants.

Alexandre's music featured vintage synths and elegantly analog saturation that would make a Brooklyn hipster weak in the knees. But, to our local friend, the recording just sounded like "God" music and the saccharine tripe from Asia was "*much* cooler," which he made *ultra*-clear by way of his endlessly looping it at all hours throughout the multitudinous miles, making our way south-west by following the lines of satellite dishes like sextants.

Since the multitrack was "lost" in transit by the airline, the entire Good Ones' album had to be recorded on a video cam-era. Fortunately, the old-school camcorder had two XLR-inputs, allowing for the connection of higher-grade microphones. I was provided little choice but to set up two ribbon condenser-mi-crophones that I'd had for decades, and position each one in the gap between the three seated singers (two of whom also played guitar), in a quasi-stereo. I used a chair for one mic-stand, and a potted plant for the other—duct-taping the mics to each of them. I then rolled the dice: having set the band up, seated, on a covered porch with their backs to a wall that provided some natural reverb, as well as helping shield away much of the exter-nal sounds, from at least that one side.

The session was proffered under the disapproving eyes of many of the locals who declared the band members "filthy street bums" and ridiculed their "old-fashioned" music. One elder declared, "I've never even met such trashy people before." Often, I would look up and catch glimpses of faces peering out, sardonically, at them. That after the success of the record overseas, many of these same individuals became the group's most enthusiastic supporters, thereby modifying their personal memories as to their own initial opinion, proved once again the universality of human nature: that hypocrisy is not exclusive to Hollywood, everyone loves a winner, and things that are too alike or "too close to home," tend to be the most threatening (thus, the love-hate dynamic of most families).

From where I am sitting, unadorned but thoughtful lyrics of theirs, like the following, stand toe-to-toe with some of the best romantic poetry from any canon.

"I remember the day when we first met and I left right away, and that is the day when, Belthilde, made herself known to me. When I met her, I remained there for a little while, chatting. I knew her deeply, I kept her in my heart."

Their simple, direct, and plaintive love songs are sung in the street dialect of the outskirts of the nation's capital, and speak more to the healing power of peace than a thousand academic treatises or preachy goodwill ambassadors ever could—literally four of the songs on their debut record are titled with the names of the amores whom they are written for. And their follow-up album continued this trend.

They are as punk rock as they come: barefoot, bandaged, and jaundiced, armed with broken, mismatched-stringed, and borrowed guitars, but singing angelically from amid a landlocked country that the world abandoned . . . literally.

Some sad lessons from Rwanda are how radio played such a sizable role to incite hatred and violence, with one tribe seizing the lone major broadcast signal in the country, and then using it around the clock to convince others to attack. Due to an ensuing onslaught of disinformation, the masses were mislead to believe the exact opposite of what was occurring—that the aggressors were actually the victims and that, therefore, the aggressors needed to kill the victimized tribe first, as self-defense. This is a portent reminder that the mass-media issues grappled with here in this book are far from merely philosophical in nature. And this knowledge makes it particularly chilling today to hear a European media giant's catchphrase proudly proclaim, "One nation, one station."

Like so much strife in this world, fear was at the core.

It is astounding to think that Rwanda's most recent genocide was so severe—claiming the lives of at least one-eighth of the citizens, by even the most conservative estimates—that it can almost erase the fact that two *other* massacres (in 1959 and 1973) preceded this biggest one. Those unthinkable, earlier injuries have become all but forgotten internationally. For the survivors, though, the effects linger. Yet, throughout the populace, suffering similar to their own is so widespread and commonplace that few wallow in having had family members killed. Strikingly, the majority opt for the more subdued verb "died" instead or "murdered," in such sharp contrast to the glorified culture of victimization that sometimes plagues America.

What we didn't learn until later is that the band actually serves as a spontaneous realization of the unification of Rwanda's three tribes, with the original trio's members each having Tutsi, Hutu, or Twa (Pygmy) origins, respectively.

Later, while overseas I witnessed the attempted rapport, but insensitivity, of people attempting to speak French to the band. French was the tongue of the colonial rulers who had spurned the country and its people after the massacre broke out. So it hardly is a welcome sound. Not to mention that three out of four members were from the rural areas where formal schooling ends at an early age and they had never learned French, beyond basic greetings, even though in their formative years it was the nation's official language.

And it is languages that usually continue to occupy long after the formal rule has ended. As an example of this, in Portugal, after almost two hundred years since their empire's fall, there are 2,000 percent more people who speak Portugese living *outside*, than within, the borders of that modestly sized country.

In the words of one elder Rwandan, "Yes, I know French fluently. But, no, I do not *speak* French. And I never will again."

Years later, the lead singer, Adrien, explained to me that, "I can't sing low anymore. I sing differently now. My voice has aged." Counter to the general assumption that vocal tone drops as we mature, he felt that his had become *higher* with time and experience, so that he could sing more spiritually and "closer to heaven."

6

Regressive Superlatives: The "G"-Word . . . and Other Demons

A triumph of mass media is that their messages have become the communications that people receive more often than any other. Rather than speaking *with* one another, we are spoken to. Even if one attempts to escape television and radio, there is the papering of municipalities and printed word, due to billboards and other campaigns.

Being talked at bleeds over onto face-to-face communication. And that canned content then gets regurgitated, with people often speaking in quotes.

It is no wonder that so many people are confused. They witness a supermodel crying on television that she is a "strong" woman because she can withstand people calling her "fat" (which is in turn, something that she is *not* by any measure), but then that same person somersaults over to another program and cruelly berates a meek teenage contestant for having put on a *single* pound. Later that same afternoon, we are confronted by the breaking story that a famous rapper has started a brawl at a charity sporting event promoting nonviolence. Later, an exalted one-name superstar changes her costume four times (!) at an internationally televised benefit concert to combat world poverty, and no one raises a cry at the contradiction. These are the subtextual discombobulations that we're bombarded with and by.

To work the magic sales-scam of provoking unrest while simultaneously promising to have the solution for it, propagandists traffic in the untruthful confidence of extreme language (i.e., depicting reality in oversimplified, all-or-nothing terms: best/worst, always/never, hate/love, etc.). The excessive use *of excess* leads to oversimplified expectations of reality. And demands for the "best" in "everything" are unlikely to end well.

At this stage of population explosion, the concept of genius, particularly, begs for retirement. It is primarily only corporate battalions that benefit from maintaining the farce of there being a chosen one(s), whose skills are trumpeted because of their rumored superiority, rather than being revealed as to only having superiorness due to the dandy firepower of their pulpit.

The division of art from life and performer from audience creates a bogus supply-and-demand, where talent comes to be seen as something that has to be purchased materially outside oneself, and by making it seem much rarer than it actually is, its value, thereby, inflates for the brokers.

This entire approach treats music as if it *belongs* to someone and can be contained, rather than its being a gift to be shared by all. And by this, the majority are transformed from producers to consumers, as happens with nations when they modernize from agricultural economies to service-based ones.

The reality is that the most eloquent songs almost never make it fully realized outside the writer's head, that whatever was heard interiorly was more sublime than anything which can be brought forth externally into the world. And, the majority of the great works that still do now arise are buried amid the sheer volume of competition and/or walled off in their localized languages, never to be recognized by any but a choice few . . . if at all.

Tragically, most of the greatest songs ever written are doomed to never be heard.

It can be conjectured that in actuality, composition is more a matter of discovery than invention: that every possible melody already exists and merely awaits being unveiled.

And science shows us that no sound ever dies entirely, it simply dissipates.

The recording studio at Zomba Federal Prison.

FIELD RECORDING CHRONICLE
ZOMBA:
FREEING MUSIC FROM BEHIND BARS

Q. How do you record in the maximum-security prison of the world's 1 poorest country?

A. Very carefully.

Though it may sound like the setup to some long-lost, Borscht-belt comedy routine, the fact is that this answer is sincere.

My wife and I traveled a three-day journey, specifically to record with inmates in southern Malawi, a lanky territory with a topography whose height is approximately seven times its width. Since the prisoners outnumber the guards by a ratio of about eighteen to one, once you are within the walls of the penitentiary, it is the inmates that keep control, having established and maintaining their own, sometimes violent and exploitative, order.

Never before agreeing to record have I been quizzed as stringently by a group of musicians, than by the convicts at Zomba Maximum Prison. Amid an arid and decaying brick fortress built in the nineteenth century, their utmost concern was that they wanted to be sure that the process would involve multitrack recording and be "professional."

Many of them became sour-faced after I informed them that "no Reggae!" was a (tongue-in-cheek) rule, and that we were only interested in local music. That every single person was to contribute at least one song was another stipulation.

The star of the group, who had been a professional performer before prison—and had actually murdered someone in the process of trying to rob them of their gear—was none too pleased when he was asked to step aside and let other members take their turns. (In the end, from over six hours of music, none of his songs made the album.) The best tune of the bunch came as an afterthought, when one man who had hid around the corner to strum a ukulele that I had brought, returned and pronounced, "I think I might have one more." He proceeded to perform "Please Don't Kill my Child," as ethereal a ballad as I have ever heard in my existence. The room became still, as if wedded in a collective prayer that nothing would interfere with those few sacred moments. And as tends to be the truest divining-rod for a performance, tears began to stream my face (an experience I had also had previously with Bob Forrest *and* Jovanotti, an Italian superstar rapper who insisted he couldn't play guitar at all, but ended up outshining most full-time folkies).

Only one of the men held out, refusing to put forth a number of his own. I made a pact with him that I would return two days later expressly to record whatever song he could write in the meantime. When we returned as promised on the appointed day, he stayed seated and his eyes never left the piece of paper he'd scribbled the lyrics on. With just he, a bass player, and one falsetto harmony vocalist in the background, they freestyled in one take and laid down a sing-speak groove funkier than a thousand "boogie" bands could ever hope to.

In Malawi, children often pay too for their mother's misdeeds.

They are born into it, literally. Serving the same sentence as their parent, from birth they are locked up, with people wall-to-wall in a ten-by-ten cell from midafternoon until dawn every day, without light or access to a toilet, but populated plentifully by rats. It's like some nightmarish embodiment of Original Sin.

But, it gets even worse: one boy's mother died when he was two. Now, the child remains imprisoned with the grandmother who is also a resident. But children can only stay until age five, at which point they then are kicked out.

That is how three generations of the same family—grandmother, mother, son—ended up serving time together. A "family affair" of a whole other sort.

Last year, another imprisoned woman's three-year-old daughter died within the prison, due to dehydration. (And then, as it was, that mother died suddenly the following year.) Mothers can only have one child with them, so those with more than one offspring are forced to choose. For the additional children left behind, the sentence can be even more severe. Yet, even more sobering is that it is not uncommon for women to be held due to charges arising from accusations of their having used "withcraft.", with no compelling evidence that they have committed a crime other than that they were an easily available scapegoat.

There are over 2,000 inmates in the 340-person capacity maximum-security prison. Every inch of floor space is covered as they sleep, alternately head-to-toe.

The space is so limited indoors that at night the men literally have to lie atop one another in a zigzag formation, one's toes to the other's head, then the next's head to the other's toes. And together they stave off those many rodents that invade at night. Often these and seasonal swarms of locusts provide the only protein to be found.

One of the saddest details that was repeated to me more than once is "If you don't have AIDS before entering the prison, you will when you leave." In that way, every sentence at the prison is a de facto death sentence.

Built near the turn of the 20th century, it is staffed with just 153 officers. Not exactly fighting-odds for the guards.

Many of the staff live on the grounds with the prisoners, in conditions only slightly better than their charges'. Uniforms aside, the boundaries between the guards and inmates can be fuzzy, and the music-making is often an integrated and communal affair.

The officers are unarmed, except for some of them carrying a thin wooden stick not unlike a riding crop of a bygone, imperial era. Only those on the perimeter have guns, with orders to "shoot to kill" anyone foolish enough to try to escape.

Not so different than their countrymen outside, the most inhospitable periods are surviving the rainy season without proper shelter, and the food shortages in the gaps between crop harvests, during which time captives sometimes resort to eating bugs for sustenance.

Miscarriages of justice are nearly inevitable due to the judicial hearings being in the former colonial language of English, while the less privileged often speak only the local tongue of Chichewa and, therefore, may have little awareness of what is being said or decided during their own legal proceedings. Appeals are made all the more difficult due to the courts often located many hours drive from the prison itself and the prison not having available transport for the defendants.

As one of the poorest countries in the world with a correspondingly high murder rate, the sad reality is that as dismal as their jail environment is, for many of those held, the conditions are no worse than what they faced at home. And in some cases—particularly with the aged—prison provides even greater luxury and comfort than they had prior, and some come to dread returning back to communities that have now shunned or "forgotten" them.

During the making of the album, the female prisoners steadfastly swore that none of them wrote songs. But then after much encouragement, miraculously, one woman stepped forward. This bold opening was immediately followed by an hours-long line rushing of the mic—with many cueing up a a second or third time—to sing some of the most heartfelt, self-composed odes of our entire ten-day stay.

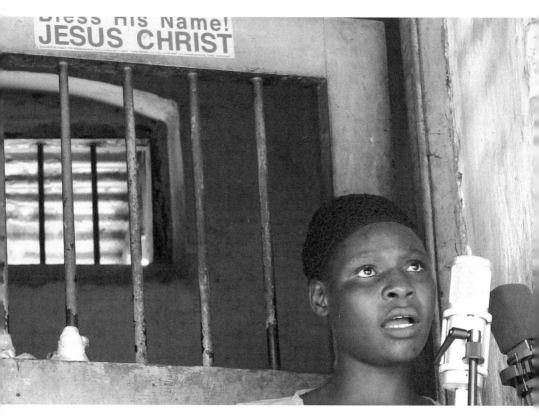

An imprisoned singer just steps from her cell.

7

Winning Hearts, Not Breaking Backs: All We Are Saying Is Give *Art* a Chance

When a terrorist soldier on night watch laughs at a dubbed American comedy streaming on his laptop or a skinhead, alone in his car at dawn, accidentally raps along with a song by a black artist, then some sort of victory has been won.

Rather than unloading bombs on people, we should shell them with books, for the arts permeate. They penetrate and erode people's defense mechanisms, rather than provoking head-on the way violence does, and then inspire ever greater fortresses to be erected. The arts position us with—rather than against—one another, linking instead of dividing. Any person who is beguiled to voluntarily enlist with a fiction, no longer needs to be conquered.

If people laugh, dance, sing, or make love together, then the opposite of war has occurred. Peace has been embodied and common ground found.

Yes, there will always be subjectivity and debate as to the relative quality of different aesthetic works. But if educational systems already have various apparatus in place specifically to ensure that identified written "classics" are read and preserved, while film schools work to educate students as to why certain films are important, then how is it that popular music is discounted to such a degree that recordings are simply set loose in the wild and fed to the wolves? It can only be that we as a society continue to have a highly ambivalent and disrespectful view toward popular music's social value, even though it is arguably the single greatest art form of the past century. Plus, even more importantly, it is the most powerful one to ever arise from the people. For the first time, what had always previously been looked down on as "peasant" and "beggar" music has displaced formally sanctioned art, and noises and sound effects that had previously been banished to only the circus, cartoons, and burlesque have been pushed from the margins and background to the forefront.

None of this is to posit that any issues related to creativity in and of themselves are life and death, but when increasing arrays of people claim that music hardly matters at all—as demonstrated by the expectation that it should be given for free—or that it has no real lasting impact, it is a negligent debasement that saps our own collective potential. Surely, any song that somehow cosmically gets people to move their bodies and/or alters their mood, possesses—much like with romantic love and attraction—the ability to break down barriers and unite people more than even the mightiest intellectual arguments or governmental interventions almost ever can.

SECTION II:

A Call for a Return to Naturalism: The Need for Randomness

8

Building an Arc

With a pop song, you have approximately three and a half minutes to try to change someone's life. Within the boundaries of its duration, we enter a holding environment that affords escape to where rules of ordinary time do not necessarily apply and instead, multiple, overlapping rhythms can be found. And through this it even becomes possible to travel into the past, figuratively.

The greatest records tend to provide just such an immersive experience. They reclaim "recording" from the category of a noun and return the music into action.

It is oft quoted that "architecture is frozen music." Therefore, is not music then something constructed that can be lived inside, providing temporary shelter?

And, through the options of a mixing console, that world can literally be mapped out in seconds, without the need for physical materials or additional laborers or city building permits.

All but the moment of a tune's inception are facsimiles. My goal, if possible, is to capture the genesis of a song—its moment of birth, that most unalloyed form. The instance of composition.

Rather than retreading the same worn-out patterns, music should raise questions, ones that the answers to cannot automatically nor easily be predicted. Just as poets stretch the frontiers of language in a search for new grammar, music can chart new syntax. Instead, just as a bigotry in favor of privileged regions has become entrenched, certain sonic frequencies are favored and overemphasized, while their counterparts are largely ignored and under-heard.

But in fact, any single sound is many sounds, blended.

A truism of sonics is that, paradoxically, isolated sounds rarely sound like *themselves*. The reason is that they have been taken out of context. In order to simulate the sensation that, say, rainfall produces, it must be rejoined with the layers of other secondary and tertiary elements (rustling branches, birds singing, etc.) that populate and complement it. Otherwise, if strictly sequestered, the sound becomes unrecognizable and, ironically, not "credible" in its purest form. For example, in actuality, we can never record the sound of wind, only its effects on something else, like leaves or shutters.

Every note is a world to itself, with the web of overtones varying depending on how an instrument is touched or struck, and melodies chart the distance between notes. (Free jazz pioneer Cecil Taylor demonstrated to me how he sits and plays the same key on the piano for hours, acting as a detective to its potential. This is very reminiscent of twentieth-century Italian composer Scelsi, who wrote entire symphonies comprised of only one note, exploring it intimately through microtones.) The journey is to find the rhythm in the spacing between any two notes or bodies, and be "carried away" by what that sound carries.

Music, at its most potent, can take us beyond ourselves, in the hope of finding a truer state of being.

9

Everything, *Including* the Kitchen Sink

We need not so much to invent new instruments, but to find new voices within each existing instrument, beyond their stereotyped usages. Anywhere we go we have access to the original bass drum—our stomping feet—and the snare drum of clapped hands, and can play our own body to unlock the score written within each of us. All instruments are at birth, first and foremost, speech surrogates.

Every object and material is literally peppered with stored harmonic energy that can literally be rubbed out of it, releasing its inner life. (And, this is not some touchy-feely hippie stuff, which tends to be too aggressively blissed out for the nitty-gritty truth that is necessitated for heightened communication.)

It is theorized that the genesis of toolmaking might not have been for hunting, but for music-making. In the least, it is clear that most hunting weapons definitely served a secondary purpose to create sound (e.g., the bow). And the genesis of so many instruments are repurposed household items like pots and pans, saws, washboards: using whatever is at hand.

Modern musical systems try to restrict music to prescribed objects only, ones that require purchase and that increasingly divorce music from daily life.

Music is as vital to the lifeblood of any culture as food and sex, with similar binding, procreative, and spiritually nurturing capacities. It has an indispensable facility to heighten emotion and thereby help with the education of children, aid in the courting process, embolden soldiers toward war, ease labor's efforts, and repair interpersonal wounds. Songs synchronize groups.

Even in stillness and sleep, we are a particularly vibration-generating species.

Acting as proto-musical force, our planetary system is said to emit a diatonic scale (i.e., the blues), with the Earth and Mars serving as the tonics. And there certainly must be something to be made of the fact that oxygen atoms contain twelve steps, with five of them being empty, exactly as is found in the Western musical scale.

When someone pompously posits, "I am a musician," a good rejoinder is, "As opposed to *what*?"

For who is not a musician, no matter how unintentionally so?

10

The Primordial "Social Work": Why Music Heals

Music and other forms of art are by far the most effective kinds of social work that exist. A single, nameless one-hit wonder brings more comfort to the world than almost any single psychologist can hope to in a lifetime.

There is no religion worldwide that does not use music as a ritual cornerstone to try to reach for the majestic sublime. This is fundamental, since all humans live in air and causing it to vibrate is a primal act. It can be asserted that music was the first specialization, since being able to make people dance is such an occultist action, not to mention that music acts to intensify or purge existing emotional states.

For example, regardless of what someone's opinion might be of Adele's music, with one wistful lullaby ("Someone Like You"), she did more to assist diverse individuals through heartache than the entire history of psychiatry could hope to. And, by all appearances, that one song will go on to do so far into the future.

Similarly, Michael Jackson's first nationally televised moonwalk dance did more in an instant to reverse racial roles culturally than a cavernous library packed with social-science books.

If I had a dollar for every time that someone told me that a certain recording or artist had "saved" their life, I would be a much wealthier person, indeed.

Obviously, a pop-ditty or a stanza of poetry will not protect you from a bullet wound or Ebola (though the ancient Pugliese did believe you could dance away the poison of a tarantula bite), but countless blood pressures have been lowered, adrenaline released, courage fortified, suppressed tears thawed, and sexual unions consummated with the benefit of music *and* without the need for pharmaceuticals or other unwholesome supplements.

How many songs have ridden shotgun, escorting lonely drivers home (or helped beget towers of speeding tickets just as the refrain was reached)?

There exists healing properties in any record that cause the majority of people who hear it to almost involuntarily reach out and turn it up. It is not surely by chance alone that two of the bedrocks of Western medicine are [1] percussion (striking the body to hear the reactions) and [2] listening to the voice itself as an aural x-ray of the speaker's interior. It would be challenging to name any single, collective element other than music that has done as much good for humanity.

Art processes pain. We can become almost drunk with it as a shortcut to a different state of being. Music alters and can even help install an updated nervous system, bolder and more rhythmical.

Songs act as emotional sonar—assisting us to figure out what we feel or to enhance existing sentiments. Music helps us map our way through the world, to reveal who we want to be, and even possibly how to get there.

Without these aural companions, how many of us might have been left adrift somewhere along the way?

Nguyễn Thị Lân sings out for the first time
since the Vietnam War.

FIELD RECORDING CHRONICLE
WAR IS A WOUND,
PEACE IS A SCAR

They call it the "American War." For a country who fought off consecutive and sometimes overlapping invaders from Japan, France, China, and the United States, our Vietnam War doesn't necessarily carry the same weight as it does in the states, due to its being the first war the American military ever "lost." Like so many other misguided interventions, there had been a fatal failure to appreciate in advance the potential challenges of engaging in combat with a populace that had proven to be so successful in the past at resisting other much more heavily armed forces.

We had gone to Hanoi to record veterans from *their* side. Some were music "masters," one of whom had joined the army at age thirteen and whose job it was to sing to the troops to boost morale and provide solace . . . while in the trenches!

Another was a former AK-47-issued village leader who had not sung in over five decades. And she proved to be the most dead-on vocally. She did not hide or adorn, but quietly exposed muted emotions that a microphone—much like an internist's stethoscope—can, on occasion, detect more easily than face-to-face interaction. Then, immediately afterward, she withdrew back into her stoic shell and fell mute.

The streets of Hanoi are an almost direct inversion of western cities, with scooters displacing and outnumbering cars. The chaotic ballet of riders, sometimes four or five to a motorcycle, is offset by the stoicism of the drivers. Many are masked to ward off pollution, and only once did I see any reaction whatsoever to the incessant horns and traffic violations of others.

Those who dismiss Asian music as without a pulse have maybe missed the intricacy. With a whammy-bar technology that dates back to the ninth century, it is fair to say that their tradition's had

a bit of a headstart over the headbangers of the 1980s. (In much
the same way that it appears many musicians in Africa have long
valued the distortion and sound modification of instruments,
which they achieve without electricity through the addition of
beads and rattles to instruments. In fact, in less central-cen-
tric cultures, the tuning of the overtones of an instrument can
be as important, if not *more* so, than the dominant note.)

For years I had been interested in doing a project with Vietnam
veterans from the other side of the war. The emotional trauma that
slews of American veterans suffered was so profound, and yet the
pain of the other country's soldiers—those from Vietnam—I had
never heard mentioned once in the United States, yet it seemed
clear that there must be a similar depth of experience there.
Growing up in the San Francisco Bay area, I directly witnessed the
refugees arriving in overloaded fishing boats after the war, as
well as saw the American soldiers, many of whom ended up homeless
on the streets. The sad irony was that these two populations found
themselves once again in direct contact, with dire circumstances
anew, now on another continent.

Musician Van Anh-Vo has commented how upon first arriving in
California, she expected a warm welcome from her fellow expatri-
ates. But instead she was met with the shock that most of her
fellow immigrants had also smuggled their prejudices over the
new borders, and vented open resentment for her since she hailed
from the north of their shared country.

At dinner one night in Hanoi, we witnessed a cross-cultural
collision as a raucous family of Chinese tourists took over
a Vietnamese restaurant. A Japanese family looked on disgust-
edly, as the other family's children raced around the room and
ducked under tables, and a German couple commented on "*those*
Vietnamese." Meanwhile, at that moment, not one Vietnamese person was present in our upstairs dining area. Thus is the whirl-
wind of essentializing others.

By far the most enlightening find musically was the K'ni, a bowed
instrument that is clasped between the teeth and a local dialec-
tic language is spoken *through* the single string. Again, "futur-
ist" innovators like Theremin maybe arrived a little later to the

party than popularly thought. On this instrument, what sounds like extraterrestrial, nonvocal atmospherics to the uninitiated, actually carries coded, poetic lyrics.

This musician was a shy man, and each time I moved the microphones closer to him, he inched back and it became as if I were unintentionally shoving him around the room until he was finally cornered. Seeing this, I realized it was time to fall back on my default theory—meet people where they are at, don't force them to come to you. Bring the studio to where the music is happening. If that is the parking lot or while they are lying on the ground, and the mics are farther away than is optimal, so be it.

This is an outgrowth of a practice that I learned decades before, working in the psychiatric emergency rooms, which was to use nonlinear interviewing. If someone did not want to answer a question, I would simply move on. Almost invariably, when the earlier question was circled back to, the resistor's charge was neutralized and they then supplied the requested information . . . and then some, usually! Similarly, if a person does not want to do a song, they usually end up being willing to later. That is, if they have not previously been pushed.

To create a nonthreatening environment, I often duct-tape equipment to deglamorize it. The theme is "We are just warming up. Practicing. 'Trying' things. No pressure." This taping method has the additional advantages of making the merchandise look less appealing to would-be thieves, as well as garnering less censure from authorities, who might otherwise harbor concerns that a person with a camera is a "journalist."

There in the thick of July, the humidity misted the camera lens so repletely that photographs had to be taken in that slim interlude before the images became completely unreadable.

Let it suffice to say that all of the master's music was a far cry from the lip-synching karaoke show that we saw on the local cable television, with groups of teenagers cavorting onstage and mouthing the words—*air*-karaoke, if you will—that managed to make something pre-fab, even less real.

The elders carry a haunting but dampened melancholy with them that seems only fully revealed through the music that they valiantly keep alive in the face of the industrialization and "progress" overtaking their homeland.

One master, Pham Mong Hai, trafficked in a two-stringed blues. His son arrived late and grabbed the instrument from his father mid-song, sat down cross-legged on the floor without saying hello, and with that, we were off and recording, literally within thirty seconds of his arrival. This was yet another experience of how seamless life and music can be, when undue preciousness is checked at the door. It was as if he were simply tapping into an existing stream—from riding on his moped to rockin' out—in seconds. Rather than needing to warm up and ritualize, instead life and art were not so harshly segregated.

Hanoi master musician Xuân Hoạch
at home with his foot-pedals.

11

Consumerism Masquerading as Creativity

M usic is not a physical object. It cannot be held. It can only be enacted. And with each action, it changes. Even the effects of recorded music itself alters in the echo-chamber of personal and/or collective history. Who has not had the experience of a formerly maligned or disregarded artist unexpectedly hitting you for the first time and "getting" it (usually at a time when we are already in a vulnerable emotional state, such as post-breakup)? Or, contrastingly, revisiting an all-time favorite and finding that the thrill is now gone, from what was at one time so uplifting and aerial?

Recording's permanency arrests the aural and oral, and freezes an event as one unchangeable etching. Thereby, music becomes something no longer to be shared in real-time, but hoarded. And, paradoxically, rather than increasing the art's worth, this stockpiling contains within it the potential for the music to be discarded when it loses its currency to provide reflected power and splendor for the owner.

By divorcing music from labor, it becomes something which can be bought and traded at will, without the need for further direct involvement of any artist.

Music before recording was ephemeral and without visible form, existing and dissolving in air. But now it has been captured and enslaved.

The appeal of replicable sound is its portability and intimacy—that anyone can mount their own private experience almost any time, anywhere. But this also contains its downside. These properties not only provoke fracture, but do so straight at the heart of rituals that have historically been what helped bind communities together. For most of history, you could only experience non-solo music in the presence of others—in the very least there were the other participating group members, and, almost always also, an audience gathered for that rarified happening.

Whereas participatory music's subtext is to reinforce existing cultural traditions as a way of unification and belonging, recorded music often results in listeners attempting to distinguish themselves as apart, by way of what they select or reject. It becomes a social filter. Ironically, the manner of division that recordings possess eliminates one's ability to interactively influence the musical event itself in the manner that intrinsically occurs when a collective, mutual face-to-face musical exchange takes place.

In the "First World," rather than a reciprocal relationship with live music-making, audiences generally are expected—and sometimes even *commanded*—to stay seated and express their appreciation only in explosive bursts of applause at the predetermined, "appropriate" time. It is sadly common occurrence for audience members to shush others, tell them to sit down, and/or *not* to sing along (and even for people to be thrown out against their will for being too demonstrative), concepts that were nearly unthinkable before music's transformation from activity to "thing."

FIELD RECORDING CHRONICLE
PALESTINE:
ANOTHER BRICK IN THE WALL

Tamer Nafar almost single-handedly started the hip-hop revolution in the Middle East, being the first person to rap publicly in Arabic. He was originally inspired by the vignettes he saw in urban rap videos from the United States and noticed how closely they resembled his own war-torn environment.

We flew to Israel to record with him and his group DAM (Da Arabian MC's) in the West Bank. Our visit was just weeks before all hell broke loose there again in the Gaza Strip, which made my wife and I both feel fortunate, as well as a little spooked that we seemed to be harbingers of bad luck to places we'd just visited, as had also been the case in Algeria, Kenya, and South Sudan, each of which coincidentally went berserk with violence within days of our departure.

There could be few more graphic embodiments of the hurdles for peace in the region than the twenty-six-foot-high wall topped with tilted barbwire that encircles many of the Palestinian residents into open-air prisons. There is an additional cheerless irony in seeing many of the Jewish "settler" compounds closing *themselves* voluntarily within razor-top fences for protection, fortifications that all-too-eerily resemble concentration camp imagery.

When an eighteen-year-old solider with an assault weapon sits for forty + hours a week, looking into a city that he has never once stepped foot in and has only seen up-close through a sniper-lens, or a PhD in "peace studies" nonchalantly relates that the only Arabs he knows are "housekeepers or gardeners," then even deeper divisions become apparent.

The band changed the initial meeting location three times at the last minute, then had us stand at the corner of a busy intersection so they could eye us first from a distance to make sure that we weren't informants. Once at the café, they arrived separately, staggered one-by-one, and then left in the same manner at the end, as a precaution. This same basic routine was then repeated the next day, when they gave us different addresses, each successively nearer to their actual home, before finally ambushing us on foot near one of the locations, and then walking us back up the block to the correct house, on the opposite side of the street than they had indicated.

The site of the recording was the shell of a once palatial Palestinian hotel that had been bombed out and never rebuilt. As the afternoon wore on, kids ranging from toddlers to late teens gathered. Many of them ultimately joined in the choral singing, while others also engaged in the region's infamous rock-throwing, taking out an aged five-hundred-dollar condenser microphone in the process.

The cops quite fortunately showed up *after* a rousing rendition of "Fuck the Police" (a different song than the NWA tune) had already happened. With the rampant drug and gang problems in the area, the lawmen—to their credit—assessed that an impromptu afternoon concert in the mud was the least of their worries and continued on their rounds without citing us.

A local tagger had previously sprayed neighboring storefronts with the broken English phrase "Fuck police," probably not realizing that this seemingly slight change of words actually inaugurated a whole new area of law enforcement specialization. Or in the very least, had coined a novel name for the Vice Squad.

Later, there was an eye-opening instant when the only association the grade-school kids told us that they had of America was that it was "that place with the 'exotic' animals," an almost direct inversion of our own African savannah, wildlife channel cliches. Similarly, often when people from less industrialized nations use the term "savages," I've come to realize later that they were referring to Europeans and/or Americans.

DAM's song "Who's the Terrorist?" was downloaded over one million times, clearly striking a chord with many young people in the diaspora. With lyrics like "she said her dream was to be a pilot, my dream is to not be searched every time I fly," it is not all that hard to see the appeal.

"Born Here"
A destroyed house
and in the garden
eight railway tracks.
During the day
at least 200 trains pass,
and behind those ruins,
a separation wall.

Despite my passport photo looking more or less like me, the border patrol at the airport, after examining my face via a stare-down contest in excess of a minute, insisted that I show her a secondary identification, something that I'd never been asked to do *anywhere* in the world before. Then, after vetting with a boss man, I was finally motioned through.

12

Parallel Rituals: The Insularity of Technological "Advances"

As multitrack recording developed in the 1960s, people began to record in seclusion from one another—playing in separate rooms or even at different times became standard. Today, musicians often even shuttle files back and forth across oceans, collaborating without ever having even once met face-to-face. (This is not to dispute in any way that remote recording can be a miraculous and great thing, *when* it works.)

Almost simultaneously with multitracking's advances, in order to fully appreciate this newly available higher-fidelity, partakers were obligated themselves to also listen in greater seclusion and to remain stationary. A proper stereo experience requires being seated dead-center between two speakers, at equal distance from them as they are from each other and with the speakers hung at ear-level, not too near to or ever touching any walls. (99.99 percent of the time these inconvenient requirements led users to wrongly setting up their top-dollar systems, thereby deriving almost none of the benefits they'd splurged for.) Later with car stereos, almost no mix engineers were savvy enough to factor into the making of panning choices, just how heavily biased to the left side drivers sit.

With headphones, others were shut out entirely. Music was no longer shared. The experience became fragmented, stymieing communalism. It was a divisive act that furthered television's positioning audiences as passive, being trained for hours in their own helplessness and inability to change the outcomes that they witnessed—to not intervene toward simulated murders or react to danger when their bodies were compelling them to—thus setting their brainwaves to a less-active state than when sleeping (!), since sleep is a time during which our minds are busied with the act of creation and reorganization (e.g., filing data) through dreaming.

Some sobering parallels are that for victims of assault, isolation is most often a factor. While with psychological and interpersonal dysfunction of all stripes, secrecy rather than transparency is usually found. There could be fewer concrete proofs of the endangerment of voluntarily plugging-up one's ears than the deaths of countless pedestrians listening to music *instead* of their environment, who are struck by trains or automobiles as a result. Or there is almost nowhere a more petrifying piece of footage than that of a young man repeatedly waving a pistol around a crowded municipal train, yet no one noticing due to their being absorbed in the minutiae of their cell phones. This gunman went on minutes later to execute a student he didn't know, point-blank in the back of the skull as the two randomly crossed paths. Similarly, it is staggering to hear the number of people who are shot after failing to respond to the police command "halt," when the reality was that they were not being disobedient, but simply weren't able to hear.

Whenever music amplification gets louder, people become more divided in dance. Since they can then hear rather than feel the beat, there is no longer the need to hold each other (e.g., waltz) to maintain a mutual connection to the pulse.

In a matter of generations, we have gone from symphonies to big bands to quartets to one-man turntablists locked away in their rooms. From playing together to "falling apart". . . alone. It seems only logical on a certain level that systems founded on a binary interface would contribute to some degree to a larger polarization socially.

When asked to sing, seeing people first put a hand to their mouth to mime a microphone before they make a sound is eloquent evidence that they feel they do not have a voice without something external and technological, that they need to be plugged in.

That almost every "live" concert album made is underlain with the soundtrack of the same ecstatic, unrelated audience floated in and grafted on to beef up the excitement, is all the more dismaying when one realizes that the majority of that applause is from a massive crowd comprised of people that are now dead and have long since passed on from this world.

The Malawi Mouse Boys' head security honcho
guards their gear at home.

13

Sound Before Volume

Equipment is almost the least important thing in recording, and instruments can often be secondary to music-making. Without a pervasive aesthetic and a burning desire to communicate, these paraphernalia are merely meaningless objects. Owning a good camera does not instantly make you a photographer. Having unusual powers of perception and an eye for details, meaning, and context do. (With a crap circa 1998 flip-phone, Dorothea Lange would've been able to take a better photo than I *ever* could, even with a Zeiss Olympia Sonar lens.)

Gear is the weather, not the climate, so to speak. Music-making, fundamentally, doesn't change. All technology sold is based on planned obsolescence, to perpetuate renewed cycles of consumption. Rest assured, the "latest thing" will not be good enough, *soon enough*. And, ironically, as technology has exploded, a period of stagnation in musical forms has coincided commensurately (compared to the unprecedented surge of creativity in the first two-thirds of the twentieth century that immediately preceded the home computer, cell phone, and Internet revolution).

Despite the lofty claims of the most devout, technology does not change human nature. It not only does not usurp the reptilian stem of our brain. It customarily indulges it.

Behavioral issues are almost never a problem of information. They are nearly always primarily of emotion. That's why you can't talk an alcoholic or abuser out of their behavior. They *know* what they are doing is wrong, but intellectualization is not the key. The "information age" cannot solve matters and the inundation of data can even make things more confusing.

Tools do not increase the powers of imagination, they merely facilitate it. Did the typewriter or word processing lead to the works of Shakespeare or Joyce becoming immediately irrelevant and their observations obsolete, beneath the surge of never-before-witnessed and unparalleled writing? Has a single, entirely new musical form emerged since computerized recording's landing? Where is the deluge of records that come close to diminishing the powers of Cab Calloway or Alvin Lucier's "I Am Sitting in a Room"?

Spiritual health is balanced when what we can imagine continues to outstrip and far outpace what we "know."

Those that build war-rooms of gizmos often do so as an unconscious defense mechanism to avoid confronting their own vulnerability and mortality, the acts of courage that are necessary for transcendence from everyday life, efforts that no amount of money can buy or play substitute to. The former approach wallows in the masterbation of temporary, soon-to-be-outmoded expert status.

Instead, those without easy access to instruments distill music in memory. Not having instruments means being forced to write music in your mind as a practice, so that when that person does finally place his or her hands on an instrument, they are hungry and ready. It also means that the best songs are usually the ones that survive due to *their* memorability, so there is a pre-process of involuntary selection through attrition.

Literally, three of the most gifted songwriters I have ever known were illiterate. One of them signed a contract with an *X*. But this technical ability had little bearing on (or maybe was even an unintended boost to) their uncanny way with words.

The added and unforeseen bonus of having broken or low-quality instruments is that those limitations can in the end spur someone to try to make up for them by singing and/or writing better. And also, often such instruments accidentally provide a unique sound, with no tweaking or nod-twiddling necessary.

Musicians have paid up to forty-five million dollars for a Stradivarius violin, but in blind-tastes, less than two-thirds of the musicians tested preferred the storied brand.

It is almost sickening to contrast the scarcity of instruments that are found in most impoverished regions, with the arsenals of unused acoustic guitars that stay shuttered within the closets, cellars, and storage sheds of almost every would-be bohemian in the western world. (And it need be noted that this bounty itself was a quick escalation in the West. As the culture tried to collectively catch its breath during that odd and often overlooked latency and fermentation period between the first shock of Elvis's debut and the interstellar, one-two wallop of President JFK's assassination and the Beatles' USA debut, Grateful Dead leader Jerry Garcia recounted that he could not find a single person at that time in the entire city of San Francisco—that liberal bastion, of all places—that could give him electric-guitar lessons. And so he had to drive a half hour south to the suburbs to find any suitable candidate. To say times have changed is much more than an understatement.)

Not dissimilarly, those with "disabilities" often prove to be the most expressive dancers, since you don't really dance with your legs, but your soul. Despite the common misconception, scientifically, "muscle memory" is a myth. *All* memory is stored in the nervous system, not "the body" itself.

Those who grow up in geographically small areas—never leaving the village where they are born—usually possess a wisdom-bank of fine detail as to that one area, their own tiny corner of the world: the various residents, the weather, the history and cadence, that others are oblivious to. Vast data can be held in those microcosms. Maybe someone has not traveled far physically, but that does not mean that they have failed to learn from where they are—understanding extensively and deeply a few, select tiny things, rather than fleeting bits about *(too)* many.

Information alone does not ensure knowledge. Knowledge is not what we've been taught, but whatever we've actually learned. A double PhD in psychology does not prevent insanity (and, in fact, can even *induce* it). Nor does chronological age grant gumption, if an individual stubbornly remains emotionally immature and arrested.

Being "old" far from automatically makes one wise.

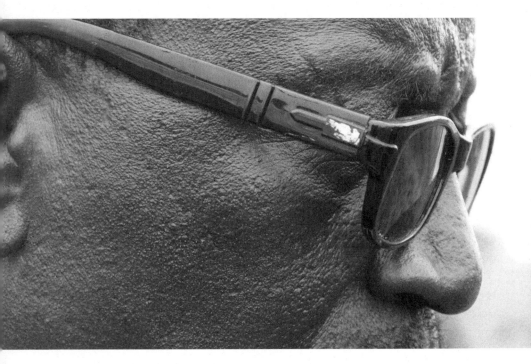

General Paolino, a blind singer from the youngest nation in the world, South Sudan.

FIELD RECORDING CHRONICLE
SOUTH SUDAN:
SONGS FROM A DIFFERENT CIVIL WAR

Just after arriving at Juba airport, we saw three dead bodies on the ground (an experience similar to that which also greeted us during our first visit to Malawi, only there the individual had been stepped over and ignored), all fallen from the same motorbike and now draped with sheets. A vigilante group of over one hundred people had gathered in search of the driver who had fled, obviously knowing full well that the practice there is reportedly to murder the driver, regardless of fault.

There were no driving schools in South Sudan. People instead just pay those fortunate few who own cars one dollar per lap around empty lots, and then go to take their licensing test whenever they feel they're well-enough prepared, thereafter hitting the road with next to nil experience. This in part accounts for the astronomical number of accidents and the common sight of seeing more oncoming cars headed in the wrong direction than the right one.

Upon arrival earlier we had been refused entry across their border. Fortunately for us, we were on the last flight of the day and it was closing time at the airport, so after quite a bit of haggling and hubbub, they were left little choice but to just allow us in.

General Paolino is a blind musical legend in South Sudan, whom many locals speak of in the hushed, reverent tones reserved for the chosen few. He has written a wealth of standards for his countrymen, utilizing five different languages from the region. Throughout his nation's fifty-year civil war against their northern Arabic rulers, black African southerners have found solace in Paolino's chronicling of their struggles via anthems such as "No Segregation" that have earned him the title of "the blind Bob Marley."

The night we first met, the General played with a bar-band in a suffocating eight-by-ten back room crammed with equipment and musicians. The ancient Peavey-amps were stacked perilously high and cranked up to eleven while two young, scantily clad female backup singers were left without microphones, inaudible amid the din. They were there more for appearances than sonics, it seemed.

Halting abruptly in the middle of only the second song, Paolino angrily fired the preteen drummer on the spot and decided in that drunken moment that he wanted to make this record solo, instead.

And so we did, the next day in an unfinished building at a construction site on the outskirts of town. Using a guitar-pick, hand-cut out of necessity on demand from a plastic bottle we scrounged, he played the battered, acoustic nylon-string he calls, "My only friend. My wife. My husband."

It is hard to imagine what sound-engineering course could prepare one for the mine-shaft din of an unfurnished apartment, built of cinder block, wood flooring, and glass. The bulldozers and dump trucks circling and backing up just outside the side door, along with the chatter and laughter of dozens of laborers and gatherers, did little to help matters.

I defaulted to a little-known and counterintuitive principle, that to *open* windows is the best remedy for reducing reverberation. An open window absorbs—by releasing energy to the exterior—forty times *more* than an equal wall surface can absorb. In such a cavernous case, whatever you're letting out can be far more important than anything that might sneak in.

Mostly due to his visual limitations, but seemingly intensified by his hangover and overall fidgety nature, Paolino regularly walloped the delicate, ribbon-microphones in such way that could send a traditional audiophile into conniptions. The spaciousness of his voice, though—with its crusty vulnerability—could transcend most any limitations of the equipment, not to mention the technologically impaired capabilities of this operator (i.e., me).

When we were through with the hours of recording that were dominated more by his verbal rambling and rants than actual playing, Paolino spit in my hand and closed it firmly in his, as a dubious "blessing."

14

Recording as a Leap of Faith

Paradoxically, the act of recording is one of investing in the future while simultaneously giving emphasis to the past (i.e., the faith that someone later will choose to revisit that which has already occurred, rather than create anew in their own living instant).

This undertaking very easily can detach the performer from the life at hand, in favor of some abstract future and audience. When the process of recording (i.e., the technical aspect) takes precedence over that which is actually being recorded, then the origin of the entire endeavor has been subsumed and the vitality of the music suffers.

But no matter how bleak the material, recording is ultimately a gesture of hope. If someone truly didn't "give a fuck," then they wouldn't be recording whatever it is they are doing to begin with.

Erecting these temples for tomorrow is done with the twain belief that there will, in fact, be a future *and* that future matters enough to invest the present toward it. It is a scream into the hereafter and if even one person retrieves that audio message in a bottle—these SOS calls—and if through that listening, their life is enriched by it, then, all commercial considerations aside, the entire effort has been a success.

Almost every record ever purchased, now rotting away somewhere in an attic or bin, represents one person's desire for a better life, the hope that the music contained within would answer some of their questions or needs. The music itself merely acts as a go-between to experience, the quest to find pleasure, reduce pain, and grow inside—that place where singing and/or listening become regained as acts of self-preservation and help us access another world, transcending even the music itself, bringing us back to our birth, leading us home, and reminding us that we are *still* alive.

SECTION III:

How To Get "There": Some Possible Roads Home

15

Surrendering to Sound

My intention as a "producer" is to tread lightly. It is my belief that the best production is invisible, adding to and helping shape or even act as a catalyst for the process, but drawing no undue attention to itself. Often this entails an exercise in subtraction, more than addition, to remove clutter in order to make room for the life to find fuller expression and not be masked by extraneousness. As with visuals, the "empty," negative space can be as or more meaningful than the drawn and busy areas.

Acting more like a midwife, the end result should not be of the producer's DNA. Many of the best producers go unnoticed—blamed if something goes wrong and having credit stolen from them when things do succeed. A driven, young band leader with control issues recently commented to me how amazed he was and how much he'd learned from my being able to "disappear" during takes, even though I was still physically there in the room with them. For me, this was the highest of compliments (though I am not sure that is entirely how he intended it). I should be forgotten (and it is almost a surety that I will be). All that should remain are the sounds. What must stand alone are the songs.

It is not about trying to make somebody something that they are not. But more of what they really *are*. How many times when you ask someone what they are playing, they reply befuddled with, "This!? I don't know. Just something I was making up." But it is almost always difficult to get them to continue exploring the vein they have found. They want to get back to what they've prepared because the candid moments look *too much* like them. Instead, personal will should be abdicated in favor of chance.

Often, the primary role is managing people's egos. To get artists out of their own way and keep them from being their own worst enemies due to overthinking something, when instead what is needed is the wisdom of the heart and unconscious. They must be moved beyond their heads, to free their bodies and intuition.

Largely, the task is one of problem-solving and setting realistic expectations. Jobs tend expand to whatever the time is allotted them. Something that could be done quite quickly often drags on. But, in the time it takes to debate whether to take an action or not, usually you could've already recorded the song(s) in question.

The most mature engineers are willing to do *nothing*, if nothing is needed. To leave a work untouched. In almost every medium, restraint is rare and invaluable, the willingness to step aside and *not* contribute, if it is not necessary, as well as having a recognition of when the time has come to check compulsive tendencies and stop short of things becoming overcooked. Attention is often the most precious tribute we can offer someone. Most people are starved for it, far too many entire groups have been neglected, and people are willing to pay exorbitantly and sometimes even kill to receive it.

Immature artists need to feel and make known that they have "done something," rather than acknowledging that some things simply happen. And the inability to explain them entirely is the very mystery that in part grants the creation its power.

My personal goal has always been *not* to try to give people a voice—they already have one!—but a microphone. A platform internationally to be more widely exposed. Relatedly, it is *not* possible to "discover" someone. They preexist. Our witnessing them does not demarcate any greater validity to their being. It just *might* give them wider—though not necessarily "better"—opportunities.

How can one discover a culture that is thousands of years older than your own?

Sadly, so many today globally can recognize Beyonce's vocals or Homer Simpson's face, but have turned away from their own regional heritages.

They say you are "never a hero in your hometown." This maxim is made all the more true, now that far too many downtowns globally begin to look hauntingly the same.

Zondiwe Kachingwe digs deep inside himself for the source of true "soul" music.

16

Voices Within the Voice

Being a singer is an incredibly arduous task.

Simplicity is often the most complex endeavor since it requires suppressing and forfeiting all other options in the sole pursuit of just being.

Listeners may not be able to articulate the particular reasons why, but they commonly have emotional experiences that are alike when a vocalist "speaks" to them.

Having a strong, genetically granted voice in no way guarantees that one can sing convincingly, no more than having a pair of Nike "Air Jordans" makes it possible to sail through the air as advertised. In fact, physical prowess can even act as a crutch hindering further development. In the end, the thorax is just another piece of gear. What matters is how it is used. And the lungs are nothing if not the original "wind instrument."

Even the most reserved among us speak daily, but often we practice and/or are encouraged to *not* express our true feelings—to keep a stiff upper lip or put a smile on our face—especially in business environments. And this is tragic.

All language speakers must act as composers and poetry is the bridge from words to song.

Emotions and meaning are carried on our breath, literally on what sustains our life. And almost all musical phrases fall within and are limited by the parameters of the lungs' capacity (i.e., ranging from two to twenty-plus seconds in most cases). Words represent only the surface of the voice, which comes from somewhere deeper and gives rise to greater dimension than mere text in black-and-white.

Air travels around the room at about the same velocity as bullets do (approximately 720 mph). And sound travels even more quickly through solids (i.e., *us*) than air. You cannot outrun a drum.

Though we are made of matter—and so are our brains—our soul and mind exist only through process, in action. They literally cannot be contained physically.

With the introduction of the Industrial Era technologies, people for the first time began to be exposed to voices that were uncoupled from time and place. Previously, one could only ever witness a small bank of voices and never ones that were not somewhere within our immediate presence, within "shouting distance," as it were. Somewhat paradoxically, the voices during that time often were more greatly varied versus the creeping homogenization we find today. And the extent of one's vocal reach was limited almost entirely by the powers of the human voice, contained in real time.

But today, we can choose our own ghosts, and with music we rarely hear original sounds emanating directly from their source, dislodged instead by things that are replayed.

It is an increasing rarity that someone is able to speak with their own voice, outside the echoing maze of their influences. More and more people have lost their acoustic identity. Human speech—which was once signatory and as individualized as fingerprints—liquifies into a generalized male/female mush (and, even that gets muddier with the popularization of androgyny).

In fact, many everyday interactions now play out as scripted conversational exchanges, very much like replays of television reruns. Far too many seem as if they are providing a voice-over to their own life, as if they aren't even actually there.

Over-singing is a plight known almost exclusively to cultures where performance is artificially divided from audience, a schism which is enforced for economic reasons. This power structure puts the majority in the passive position where they cannot possess magic intrinsically, but only rent it vicariously and temporarily from another more active and societally identified superior being.

Structured performance leads to competition: the drive to be "good," correct, or better than. An artificially rigid system provides contest as the primary path to gaining those precious few coveted slots, the rare places where one literally has a voice and is heard. This competitiveness then leads to cementing in place things that were initially arbitrary measurements, as is exemplified by adolescent-male music culture, where being heaviest, faster, and loudest are key. (And, showing weakness of any kind is the ultimate offense.)

Ethical behavior has been defined by virtually every philosopher throughout time as doing the same thing regardless of whether or not there is an audience, no matter what the punishments or rewards. To not be wavered by environmental factors, but instead, remain consistent. Art, at its most realized, should do the same.

Great singers rather than "making" a sound, liberate it and *then* play with it. The sound comes from within, not outside them.

They allow the tone to occur, rather than endeavoring to manipulate it. This is very much akin to the sculptor whose goal is to free a preexisting image by removing only what shouldn't have been there in the first place amid the form—the excess, surrounding and obscuring it—so all that remains is the finished piece that was previously trapped inside each particular block of stone.

Rather than trying to "sound natural," stellar vocalists *are* natural.

Instead of trying to *be* something, it is better to simply be. This is why untrained but gifted actors (often children or animals) sometimes give more believable performances on film, outshining their multimillion-dollar costars.

Subjectivity is found in the suppression of emotion, not its true expression, which is instead universal—a genuine smile or tears are understood unequivocally. But caution is required, since revelation is a world apart from the needy exhibitionism it is often confused with.

Revealing is about having the courage to drop our facade(s).

Vocal basics are to relax your body, open your throat (more necessarily than your mouth) so that there is a clear channel from the lungs upward, and then *breathe*. Consequently, it is mystifying and ironic how a paradigm that restricts and interrupts expression and stimulates bodily tension has become dominant. The most powerful singers aspire for their entire skeleton to act as a resonator, and to feel themselves not just grounded, but drawing energy *from* the ground (or even far *beneath* the ground, by being rooted to the earth). Instead, the dead giveaway of immature singing is when people force their voice into the nose, up high, in an effort to fake tone by using their sinuses like a distortion-pedal. Not coincidentally, studies have shown that less authentic tones of laughter are more nasal—whereas our involuntary belly-laughs never come through the nose, at all.

Paradoxically, often artists are at their most true when they speak with their *other* voice. A singer who doesn't consider himself a "good" guitar player or the drummer who is not a singer, may actually find greater expression on those instruments due to the deliverance from their own ego and practiced patterns, whereby the new instrument acts as some sort of prosthesis. Similarly, when people sing phonetically in a language that they aren't fluent in, they often give their most spot-on interpretations. Intuitively, by becoming freed from logic.

I once saw 83 year old jazz legend, Roy Haynes, appearing with an overly reverent, undercooked band. After more than an hour of languidness, he suddenly let loose a solo, using only the parts of the drum-kit that you are *not* supposed to play. And it was as if a wrongly accused man had come uncuffed. Similarly, one of the most tortuous vocals imaginable was sung by Eddie Harris *through* his saxophone on "I Don't Want Nobody."

Often we are better at what we disown and are most *dis*interested in. We maybe "can't help it" and sometimes simply *are* good at something—instead of *wanting to be* (i.e., literally "wannabes")—and are unable to stop not being able. The rash of famous and skilled actors who try to hustle their own subpar bands—the projects that they claim are their true passion—exemplify a form of this.

Technique often insulates us from the heart and takes over from the soul, when instead "remembering to forget" is what is more often needed.

17

Using the Microphone as a Telescope

Recording is an inexplicable alchemy. It is a dynamic process, with each variable, embellishing, displacing or altering another. Some of the best recordings I have participated in have been with the lamest equipment or under the most inadvisable circumstances, and vice versa. What is critical is working *with* whatever you're given, regardless of how little it resembles any preconceived notions or prescriptions. Preparation has a place, but only *as preparation* for anything and all that may come.

Ultimately, methods should matter little. Great art has been born from virtually every possible route. And that elusiveness is part of its ethereality. I love some audiophile masterpieces years in the making, as well as spontaneous cell phone a cappella recordings. In the end, any works that feed you have unweighable value and attempts at comparisons otherwise are mostly silly. How one gets there is not the issue, but the fact that on occasion, some actually *do* miraculously arrive, is what is at stake.

There is a constant interaction between elements. Things change meaning within contexts. For instance, a loud note is perceived as longer than a soft one, a higher frequency more loud than a low one, and the same volume, through repetition appears to weaken over time, *even while* remaining stable. Generally, distance equals depth. Most times, rather than crowding, if you move a microphone further back from the source, its sound grows bigger.

Almost inevitably, whichever songs were expected to be the best by those involved in the process arrive stillborn, and other orphans emerge, bearing fruit. When it comes to albums, many times a perfectly good tune needs to be martyred for the health of the whole, set aside as reserve—like starter-dough for the future. A mark of a great work is one that has the luxury of an excess of sturdy material, and even grade A can be treated as B class. These are lucky "problems" to have.

Overconceptualization can be bad, as it can keep people trapped in their head and interfere with their objectivity. For growth to occur during any creative process, the result *has* to be different than originally envisioned. Otherwise, what is the point of even having put forth all of the effort and stress of actualizing ideas? And if everyone involved is happy, then something is terribly amiss: compromise has been placed ahead of point of view. It has become everything *and* nothing at the same time, something that is compromised to a degree that everybody likes, but no one *loves*.

We must let the record tell us what it wants to be, to inform, in the same way that healthy parenting encourages a child to journey, stray, and become more fully themselves, rather than fulfilling any preformed expectations.

The goal is reducing attachment, which is the opposite of materialism. To instead, seek substance over concepts or labels—to accept mortality and advance voluntarily into the void.

Technology often acts mostly as an enabler to procrastination, feeding the fear of commitment. Thereby, what we end up with is enameled audio.

Far too many prefer to masquerade as someone else, rather than accepting themselves, as is. And, the compulsive drive to perform—to always be "on," as if every moment were a quiz—is fed by a culture that often gives attention to the young only when they "do" something and not for the sake of simply being.

Artists don't need a gimmick. Instead, they just need to simply not disown whatever makes them novel. And to celebrate it, instead.

If people don't feel judged, they have a greater sense of freedom to *"play"* music, a goal that tends to go missing when potential loss is made part of the equation and the threat of failure thwarts pleasure.

To cope with the overwhelming onslaught of stimulus, many people now *pre*-interpret music (e.g., "I don't like ballads."), invalidating entire spectrums wholesale. This is the antithesis of receptivity, burrowing bunkers to hide within, and in the process denying vast realms of experience.

The audiences that I most often played to were empty barstools and dance-*less* dance floors in dingy clubs. Worse than the shame of no applause was the delayed, sarcastic, lone clap from the solitary, smug drinker in the back who seemed to be serving as some sort of undergird for the building, perennially at their post.

It took me three decades of being a vocalist in bands before I really even *started* to learn to sing. My breakthrough was in a downtown laundromat where I staged a free show every Monday night for half a decade.

There were two primary things that I learned there.

First, that you had to use the "noises" in the room as accompaniment. It paid not only to harmonize *with* the espresso-maker, but to listen closely to the entire room and *anticipate* sounds. To play in-time to and in-tune with the room. And both these elements were constantly unfolding (e.g., a drunk schizo-affective passing with a shopping cart that's back wheels are rattling in a different time-signature entirely than the front).

Second, in doing field recordings of sundry local bands, a pattern emerged where the most dynamic live renditions often fell flat on playback, and many disastrous performances had veiled a phantom force that was revealed only through the mysterious spiritual shadow discovered by way of a pair of headphones. It can be much like the negative photographic process, where what you ultimately end up with is the reverse of the actual impression that has been captured. And some moments just turn out to be inexplicably "phonogenic."

FIELD RECORDING CHRONICLE
"CAPTURING LIFE" IN ARTIFICIAL ENVIRONMENTS

Is it possible to record during a thunder and lightning storm, in a roomful of croaking toads and crickets?

In the case of the Juba Orphanage, the answer is yes.

The concern for "noise" interference is largely overemphasized. Generally the only sounds that intrude are the sudden, "transient" ones. Constants, by nature, drone and generally can be adapted to.

Bass sounds travel the farthest and through walls. But it is the high frequencies of the voice that we hear when someone leans in close to whisper. With proximity, the low-end drops away, as does the reflected sound. That is why vocals drenched in reverb—as is the norm with "professional" recordings (e.g., think of the echo we experience when someone shouts into a cave)—actually distance listeners from the source. For a voice to truly be foregrounded, present, and intimate, it needs to be as dry as possible. No additional insulation should come between the artist and the listener, but instead the two should be brought closer to each other.

When high frequencies are cut, sound is usually unrecognizable, but not so, when the bottom disappears from a signal. Ninety-five percent of the volume of the voice comes from bass resonance, but in an exact reversal, 95 percent of the voiced information that is actually used for comprehension comes from treble, the sibilance. Most sounds are distinguished by the upper-partials alone and we subliminally fill in the lows. This is how telephone transmission works, by conveying only the uppermost frequencies and leaving us to imagine most of the rest.

With the the advent of multitrack recording in the 1960s, the gold standard of audio-engineering for decades has become the quest for completely antiseptic and air-brushed sound. Pro Tools and the ilk have made recording an even more "we'll fi-it-in-the-mix" affair. Performance has become secondary and the cart *is* before the horse, with sonic "perfection" taking precedence and engineers often fascistically interfering with the slithering current of life and music. This is not unlike major film productions where the actors are made to wait endlessly until the lighting is just perfect, and then directors complain if the actors aren't "in the moment" at 3:43 a.m. They probably were, but they aren't *now*.

Often, perspective is lost. Of all the massive expenses and elaborate equipment put forth for projects, the most invaluable of all elements often gets overlooked: human energy and attention. Not to say that lush cinematography or spacious sound don't have their places, but without a central spark (or better yet, frisson), all will fall flat.

The history of all-time classic records (think "Louie, Louie" or Dylan's "Like a Rolling Stone") is how many of them are plagued with mistakes that end up having been serendipitous—a botched EQ or tattered equipment that creates an oddly pleasing sound. Or a band speeding up naturally due to their own excitement, as a singer's voice cracks in a certain way that imbues it with a depth of forthright, unconscious emotion that could never be produced "on cue," and, if attempted to be re-created later, turns out sounding like a caricature, as Michael Jackson became, post-Thriller.

In the same way that there is alarm socially regarding deformation of body image due to the omnipresence of Barbie-like images, shouldn't overconsumption of unrealistic and inorganic sound be of some concern? In Juba, our goal was to make a children's record with the elementary school choir, but the kids proved more intent on chattering than singing.

Instead, we ended up being subjected to a string of aspiring performers of radically varying degrees of talent who had gathered, uninvited, to audition for the "American" producer.

A sad development of rap globally is how few people play instruments anymore. And, with the advent of television singing-battles (and, what a despicable jock-like model they are, to begin with), almost every narcissist below the age of thirty whose grandmother and/or coworker has ever told them they have a "nice" voice, now thinks that they can have a career or be a star. Consequently, a mumbled melody and a single lyric for the chorus now is often passed off as making somebody a "songwriter." The manufactured accomplishment of these artificial competitions rewards glamour singers for their preening in the fulfillment of some predetermined concepts of beauty, like sonic Miss America pageants.

In Africa, frequently westerners are duped into believing that if someone has a primitive instrument, then they are automatically authentic. There is also the inverted discrimination, that "*all*" Africans are musical. That's an awful burdensome crown for over one billion people to carry, on a continent that—despite white cartographers' historical shrinking of its size—is actually larger than the United States, China, India, and almost all of Europe *conjoined*! Though, many African countries are inherently musical in the rhythms of their daily life, language, and culture, *no populace* is without tremendous diversity, both the good *and* bad. And the plethora of truly awful players that I have encountered over the years, and then had to try to politely refuse, serve as painfully disappointing reminders of this reality.

Throughout time, the exceptional family member was the one who didn't play music. Now today instead, you are exceptional if you *do.*

It is not that the inhabitants of rural regions in less pampered places are superior. They just haven't usually been indoctrinated as to how *not* to be creative. That trust has not yet been broken. Instead, they remain awash in it, with expressive action being as seamless, close to the surface, and natural as walking, talking, or laughing, instead of having art severed from life, barely reachable or discernible, and stashed away as if only located in a museum in some distant, restricted place.

18

Acoustic Illumination

At their optimum, microphones can help us learn to hear the world *better*, to listen more carefully.

Rather than dressing up sounds (e.g., voices drenched in delay), what is often needed is to revel in their nakedness and focus attention on what is already present, though ignored. To shine a light *into* the shadows.

A formerly deaf acquaintance related that after she had implant surgery to make hearing possible, she lost her previous ability to imagine sound and that also for the first time, she became aware of silence, something that she was unable to distinguish before.

In our hoarding society, founded on amassing material objects, productions are generally built on addition: a "the more, the better" mind-set. With that, sparseness becomes devalued.

Subtraction, instead, often can restore, rather than distort, the truth. Allowing elements to relish in their own *self*-ness, without the compulsion to change them into something "more" and/or what they are not. Restraint can reveal greater candor and complexity, by letting sounds to speak for themselves and not be manipulated by preconceptions of what is best or better. The literal truth can't be revised (with alternative alibis). It is complete, in and of itself.

Rather than monopolizing every possibility, the absence of notes, the rests, leave space for the listener, and it is there that they can potentially act as partner to fill in the blanks. Silence is sound's ghost.

By nature, we listen most attentively in the absence of volume. We become more alert, preparing to hear what follows. Like with slasher films, the scariest moments are often when nothing happens, in the same way that a partially revealed body can be far more alluring than a full-frontal view.

Often if a musical section or song is repeatedly problematic or error-ridden, that is an informant—like sickness being a wake-up call that our body needs rest. Maybe that "problem" part needs to be left alone or cut, rather than overworked, and we best cease hitting our head against the same wall over and over via some misguided masochism.

Referencing physics, the basic test is if an element can be removed and the structure does not falter, then it has been proven superfluous and not essential. That piece is the equivalent of a non-weight-bearing wall, and can just as well be torn down.

19

What's "Left"?

Art is a web neurologically, but predominantly acts as a right-brain activity. The more a performer concerns themselves with left-brain details like budget and scheduling issues, the more they are likely to *not* get lost in the moment, and, instead, perform in prescribed ways that lack the freedom that allows for true growth.

That is part of the function that drugs and alcohol have often played: helping people get out of their intellect . . . and into their souls, so to speak. The complication is finding the balance where liberation does not lead to overkill and mayhem, and become counterproductive in the long run.

When recording, I discourage listening back to performances. This switching to and fro, from creator to critic, can wreak havoc on the acquiescence and full commitment that are necessary for profound expressive actions to occur. The duties of performing and reviewing are not only separate roles, but can act at cross-purposes to one another and result in deadlock or worse, backsliding.

More often than not, "first thought, best thought," rules. And a person's "worst note" is often their most disarming.

The hardest part usually is simply getting started and generating some kind of momentum. That is why so many successful writers give themselves set office hours daily or work on a laptop *without* Internet capability. Once people are on a roll, an interruption of their focus is an enemy and traitor to the process.

It is preferable instead to almost never make musicians stop. Flow is the goal, not fragmentation and atomization of experience. Yet, so much recording becomes a fraught-ridden enterprise, with discontinuity being the rule.

In actuality, people *can't* sing out of tune relative to themselves, only to one another. Music is not calculus, as is commonly touted. If someone believes his guitar is in tune, no matter how anomalous, I usually only correct him *if* he becomes progressively *more* out of tune and does not reset it to his own established and self-determined baseline.

20

Element(s) of Surprise

An almost surefire music-making ploy is to try to add something new—no matter how minor—at least every eight-bars as a song develops and build the song rather than it simply being off or on, started/ended.

If nothing in a work of art surprises you, then it has failed. It has literally not progressed and has little (or contrary-value) since our cognitive system is designed to work economically, by design only paying close attention to things that are novel and adapting to and ignoring whatever is stable.

One of the most daunting challenges of recorded music is that it must be able to stand up to repeated listenings, levels of scrutiny that are not possible in a live performance. It is exactly there where the layers come in. Sound without the pull of at least some undertow is usually lacking.

Masterful singers can do almost this same thing single-handedly, through just their phrasing alone—slurring a word, holding a note a hair longer—ongoingly revealing the unexpected and keeping listeners on the edge of their seat, willing to follow the artist throughout their trek. A musician's expressiveness is usually not so much in the notes they play—particularly in pop music—but in *how* they travel from one note to another (e.g., a downward bent D-string). It lies in what they don't play—their breath and own particular way of counting.

FIELD RECORDING CHRONICLE
TARANTA:
I ♥ ITALIA?

Many Americans have visited Italy and/or have descended from there. But there is a danger in pseudo-familiarity. It can create unintended prejudice that may actually impede closer examination of that which is largely unknown or misapprehended.

The Italian nation was formed not due to the will of the people, but as an ideological exercise of the aristocracy to unify the motley regions. The persistence in the use of local dialects, versus textbook Italian, are remnants of this fact.

In Puglia, the southern heel of the country, the dialect spoken in the south section is indecipherable to those who reside just a little over an hour to the north. This is where the Adriatic Sea narrows, almost touching Albania and Greece, and thusly bears those influences. Like so many places, the core population seems to have sprung out of the region like trees, just as rootedly. Antique faces that hang in the atmosphere as if they always have been there, a part of the nucleus of the land.

Taranta dance was developed as a communal antidote to depression for women from the "peasant" class. The belief was that it was possible to twirl themselves out of an emotional state. Similarly, lullabies often served a dual purpose of not just soothing the infant, but providing an outlet for mothers to vent their dissatisfactions, fears, and disappointments. A standard tune from the period features the refrain "sleep well . . . and please don't ever become as stupid as your father."

Taranta is believed to potentially be related to or even the source of the Irish jig, having migrated and mutated westward over time. For eons, traveling minstrels acted as newscasters, disseminating information and ideas in much the same way that griots do to this day in many parts of Africa.

The barbershops served as music schools, as well as offering the only medical and dental services in villages. With much downtime, barbers practiced musical forms that were often believed to possess their own medicinal properties.

The musical idioms were not just regional, but often familial. Clans routinely developed their own distinct styles, largely formulated by the midweek music sessions that were practiced as a way of reinforcing relational bonds. When someone married into another family, this could entail having to learn a whole new set of practices musically, as if a new idiom.

But since this music was associated with poverty, it was disowned as the population moved from agricultural to urban life following WWII. It skipped a generation, with the grandchildren going back to their elders to try to retrace and pick up the threads that had been lost.

By candlelight, we recorded the album totally live with the six musicians—plus an additional guest player for a few songs and an audience on the final night—in the basement of a centuries-old masseria (vineyard), built from massive stones.

Canzoniere Grecanico Salentino has been in existence over forty years. It was established as a counterweight to globalization, celebrating a local dialect (Grecanico) that had been brought across the sea by ancient Greeks to one village, and that is now a dying tongue, with only a handful of practitioners left. The founders passed the music and group on to their children who continue to mine the tradition, while also expanding upon it and confronting the harsh economic realities of modern-day Italy, ones that are overlooked by the busloads of tourists chauffeured daily around the countryside.

21

Cooked by Culture: Ever Beware the "Experts"

Ethnomusicologists are the cultural equivalents of crime-scene investigators. They are usually a few steps behind the curve, showing up too late, and after the fact. Academics attempt to catalog what is constantly in flux, as if their recognition and documentation sets it permanently in place, a benediction whereby the music seemingly gains significance due to their blessed presence, music which then from that point onward, becomes *theirs*. An unintentional irony is the degree of straight-up puritanicalism that so many bring to cross-cultural affairs.

A primary danger is when "developed" countries position themselves along a timeline and regard themselves as ahead and other nonindustrialized nations as behind. In reality, the past *is* the future. There are no cultures better suited to deal with global warming than the ancient ones—Venetians, Sahara dwellers, and any that use their feet or other nonmotorized transport as well as those who have to haul their own water. Little adjustment is needed for them to cope with lessening access to mechanized energy sources, as these populations continue to do things much as they always have. They don't need to learn to cut back on what they never had. If a bomb wiped out Paris or Tokyo, their lives would change little.

Ethnomusicologists like to try to box things up in trim packages. But it is never that simple. Bob Marley does not represent all Jamaicans, nor Fela all Nigerians. And Bob Dylan is far from a humdrum Minnesotan. They transcended their origins, and thereby helped lead all mankind forward.

Habitually, the studious mistakenly attempt to define individual expression as tradition. I instead have little interest in the heritage (or not) of what someone is doing. My concern is the present—the most textured voices, the most sinewy songs. Not where the music has been. Nor even where it's going, but, instead, where it *is*. By the time musicality can be diagrammed and analyzed, the life and breath have moved elsewhere, seeking fresher expression.

Ingenuity is a vagrant. Veritable flair, a rover.

My concern is not cultural authenticity, but emotional truth and uncloying performances. Purity, without baggage. And, every song should be viewed with the same tough-mindedness and standards as "the best," regardless of its origin.

One of the follies of most anthropological research is failing to factor that those most willing to provide information about their own "native" culture . . .

1. Might not be the brightest and most insightful of the bunch.
2. Could be downright mentally unstable (hence, their willingness to speak so freely to outsiders).
3. Possibly are pulling the leg of the researcher by providing deliberately false, fantastical, and/or arcane information.
4. Just because someone is there where they are currently does not mean they are "natives." We are a wandering species, and anywhere you go there are a good percentage of people present who are also foreigners, even if they are the "right" color. They, too, might just be visitors, minorities, and/or immigrants. Often, what ends up happening is a bit like asking a tourist from the bayou for directions in lower Manhattan. Every "foreign country" has foreigners living in their midst.
5. Much accuracy might be lost and/or disfigured in the translation from one language to another. Not to mention that in many such cases, the translation itself might require being passed through a third or fourth intermediary language, usually one that neither the sender nor receiver are particularly fluent in.
   a) Plus, all translators also work as editors. The protracted and heated exchanges that I've sat through, that then get comically reduced down to a curt "yes/no" answer, have always reminded me of this prevalent fact. It is made bluntly clear that what I am receiving back is a summary, at best.
6. They may feel compelled to make up an answer rather than admit that they do not know whatever information has been requested.

The fallacy of authority by proximity is very real. Just because someone is from somewhere, that in no way means that they know everything or much of anything about the topic at hand or, furthermore, that they even possess semi-decent judgment.

You can try this test in your own country: Ask any three random acquaintances to refer you to the "best" music and/or food. Odds are you will be amazed by the ineptitude or ignorance of most responses from your guides.

The thing is, locals anywhere cannot really be expected to be a refined resource culturally. The majority of people in the United States would direct you to pap like Michael Bublé and the latest Adam Sandler kiddie-pic sequel, not Elliott Smith or P. T. Anderson.

How many, "I like everything . . . except country and/or opera," and, "Whatever is on the radio," answers can you receive without it becoming clear that for most people music is not life-and-death, but convenient wallpaper.

To even have a prayer of being shepherded in the right direction, we have to be ultraspecific. What is the "best" food is far too open to interpretation. Inquiring if someone knows of a "good, independently owned, pescatarian Pakistani place with some ambience, but reasonably friendly staff," you just *might* be sent somewhere that even vaguely resembles what you are searching for. Otherwise, a vegan is going to end up sent to a *churracscaria* (Brazilian meat grill).

Even with "professionals," bias plays a huge role. My epiphany back in my teens was once having the nerve to ask yet another callously indifferent or openly hostile college-station music director what kind of music she liked to listen to. When I came to realize that it was a Goth metal teenager who was rejecting my acoustic folk, and not someone who loved or even knew who Townes Van Zant was, the personal sting of it all somewhat softened. It is too easy to assume that others share our same sensibilities.

Another mistake of anthropologists is not accounting for the liberal bias of most artists. Just because a local songwriter drinks a certain herb or sports a bonkers haircut or sartorial ensemble, that in no way means that the majority in the same society do, *would* do so, or even approve. In my limited experience, wherever you travel in the world, most musicians and artists are as much outsiders to their own culture, as in the west. (And, many of those who might at first glance appear Zen are simply stoned.)

I am far from a preservationist. Blends and drift are not only necessary for health, they are inevitable. Those who attempt to catalog culture are largely chasing their own tail.

For, no time or place is simply of one era, but instead is dotted with layers of nostalgia. And, yes, even faux-vintage things actually do age and turn old *eventually*, potentially gaining a certain luster (as Los Angeles did in a matter of a generation, due to its relative youth as a city). When nearly everything is new, almost anything older will seem dignified. Scads of sightseers refer to elements as either "old" or modern, but in fact cities like Prague and Paris have differing ages juxtaposed millennially, and are not all of one single category.

Care should be given to how things might age. Creative integrity demands that the concern is not foremost with how someone feels before or even during an event, but *after* it has concluded, once the initial intoxication of its own novelty has lapsed.

Most folkloric performing outfits more or less portray staid cartoons of the past for the comfort of tourists. It ventures toward a politically correct freak show or human zoo. The real vernacular pulse of any region is to be found in what clothing the performers are wearing *beneath* their traditional garb; it is revealed by the sounds they make offstage and/or listen to on their mobile phones in the taxi home.

In misguided attempts to be accommodating, people will often make assumptions about what it is that you really want, and then play the things that they think that you want to hear. Some of the worst miscommunications occur when the person responding *over*-interprets and adjusts their answer in the belief that the speaker has made an error in the question, rather than the receiver just accepting it at face value.

I decided years ago to ask staff at far east Asian restaurants if I could try any tea that *they* drink in the back, if it is different than what they serve. Almost always they've seemed shocked that could truly be what I desired, usually cautioning me that I "wouldn't like it" because "it's too strong," but then later becoming bemused by the fact that it was tolerable at all, and even more so that I actually enjoyed it.

From this revelation, I routinely ask artists to play their "unfinished" and "stupid" songs. And my motto is to request that people help us find, "the *worst* music you have. Not the professionals, but the amateurs. Not the people with 'good' voices, but interesting and strange." Those with character, but without caricature.

The best direction to give any performer is: "Play *badly*. (And have fun.)"

22

What Can't Be Owned?

Did Elvis steal "black" music? Is Tejano based on German waltzes brought to Texas from Europe by immigrants? Was Reggae's one-drop rhythm born simply out of fledgling Jamaican musicians' misapprehension of American R&B as they were trying to decipher the truncated, static-y signals coming off the coast of south Florida, ones that they could only tenuously pick up, at best, on their transistor radios?

Well, yes, to all three.

Kind of.

But, also, no. It's never quite as simple, cut-and-dried, and orderly as that. Art and influence are a messy saga.

Like the reflexive question, "How long did it take you to write that?"

The most accurate answer would almost always be, "My *whole* life," for art draws on every impression, though mostly unconsciously. And very few things on this earth are monocausal . . . *except* for the homage-dependent music of recent eras, where people import an entire aesthetic—lock, stock, and barrel.

Similarly, to the query, "How did you do that (creation)?", the most truthful reply would usually be, "I really don't know. It just sort of happened."

To paraphrase ancient Arabic thinkers, we never really can say which person wrote what or where it came from. We only know for certain who it is *attributed* to.

At its most grounded, music is not used as a mirror to seek glorification, but as a microscope to better understand one's own existence or as a floodlight to shed light where we otherwise cannot reach.

Prior to microphone technology, "quiet singing" was not ever perceptible beyond a *very* immediate audience. Others would have to strain to hear such insular sounds. The magic of mix-board faders enables the possibility of championing the softest sound as the loudest, and muting the loud, entirely. It can be a tool for democracy.

A friend recounted to me, how as a child in communist Hungary, a visitor smuggled in a portable tape-player for her. There was only one song on the tape, which she played endlessly until it snapped. This exposure was like a flying-saucer crash landing from the clouds. But the thing that "changed her world" more than the music was that the machine had an "equalizer" on it, where sounds could be altered and not just passively accepted, as dictated. That opened galaxies of possibility to her, in contrast to such an otherwise oppressive and regimented environment.

Art, at its best, finds an opening and lends some way out for the exiled.

SECTION IV:

Products of Our Environment

23

Making Sense of the *First* Sense

Hearing is the first sense to emerge (being fully formed in utero), and usually the last one to leave us. Illustrating the importance of listening, we have three times as many neurological pathways connecting our ears and brain, than to our eyes.

In infancy, we can hear before we can see. Before we're born, we are already listening. In fact, for the baby in the womb, the volume level is the equivalent of a rock concert or a construction site—which seems fitting since the mother's belly *is*, in fact, a construction site of sorts.

Though sight might dominate our consciousness, it is not necessarily the most *influential*. For instance, our sense of smell functions beneath our awareness usually, but is the only sense with a direct link to our emotions—bypassing the intellect and tapping the limbic system straight away.

And hearing is the only continuous sense. We hear even when we are asleep. Closing our ears is not an option. At least, not without the aide of accoutrements. Our ears remain on call at all times.

Being our first link with the world, sound is deeply fused with our primal emotions. Also, we hear 360 degrees of our surroundings, while our eyes take in, at maximum, less than half of what's actually present. We have to turn our heads to see, but not to listen. We are all partially blind at best and while in states of fear, our peripheral vision narrows farther. We cannot see in the dark, but we *can* hear in the dark. Arguably, even better under those circumstances.

Due to the absorption of vibrations, our whole body acts as hearing device, a receptor. (Relatedly, some hearing-impaired individuals report that they experience music best by holding a balloon between their hands in order to emphasize the pulsations. Just because someone's ears don't work well does not mean that they can't still "hear.")

In overcoming their own inertia, every sound, as well as our own ears, introduces distortion to what is heard. There is always some degree of subjectivity, and that is even beyond the fact that all sound has its own resident-noise.

The structure of being equipped with two ears and only one mouth is a fairly clear indication of which sense is more crucial to our survival. Hearing's foremost job is to keep us alive by alerting us to imminent danger. And, every person's receptive vocabulary is stronger than their expressive one. That means, upon first being exposed to a word, we can potentially ascertain the gist of what we've never heard before, and are especially astute at deducing meaning when there is a clear context present. We invariably can comprehend far more than we can articulate, otherwise, we never could've learned to speak.

Clinically, the social solitude experienced by the "deaf" is generally more severe than any by the visually impaired. Those with vision can see what they are missing or at least see *that* they are missing something. The "blind," more often, are able to act as full participants to the verbal content, and therefore tend to feel less shut out.

Aurality itself is intimate since for sound to register, it must *enter* another's body. A human voice itself is a most carnal sound due to its arising from within someone in the first place—a direct connection from one interior to another. It enables us to be tactile from afar, to reach others at a distance. And that is what most listeners ideally seek: music that lifts one out of themselves and anchors them to something deeper and infinite.

In much the same way that faces tend to be particularly riveting, voices tend to be the hardest sound to ignore, and therefore, often are the most provocative and/or irritating as well.

Playing mechanical instruments is once removed from this source. The impulse is interior, but the sound arises only exteriorly. And, with computer-based technologies, there is a further removal, with the majority of sounds being triggered through one identical mechanism (a typewriter keyboard) and motion (tapping a finger, or "hardly lifting a finger" to be more accurate). This continuum is akin to the difference between striking someone with your own fist, stabbing them with a sword or air-bombing them from miles above, and the greater distance and desensitization that each bears.

A tried-and-true method for musicians to connect better is for them to play in the dark and be forced to feel the instrument and become more at one with it.

Listening actually requires *more* action than speaking, for optimally, the listener acquires new or deepened insight. It is an act of growth, which demands effort and concentration.

Unfortunately, though music at its best can help deepen our sensitivities and act as a lubricant emotionally, it now contributes increasingly to many people's mounting desensitization via the staggering surplus of sensory overload that we are besieged with daily.

As an antidote, we can try to let your ears "go for a walk" daily. Not passively, but actively. To close our eyes and let sound lead instead. Quite literally, those who are blind often learn to "see with their ears," navigating space using the echo's reflection.

If we snap our fingers, a room replies. In regards to this sort of accompaniment, we are never truly alone since even when outdoors, the ground acts as a reflective surface, parroting and *Amen*-ing whatever has just transpired.

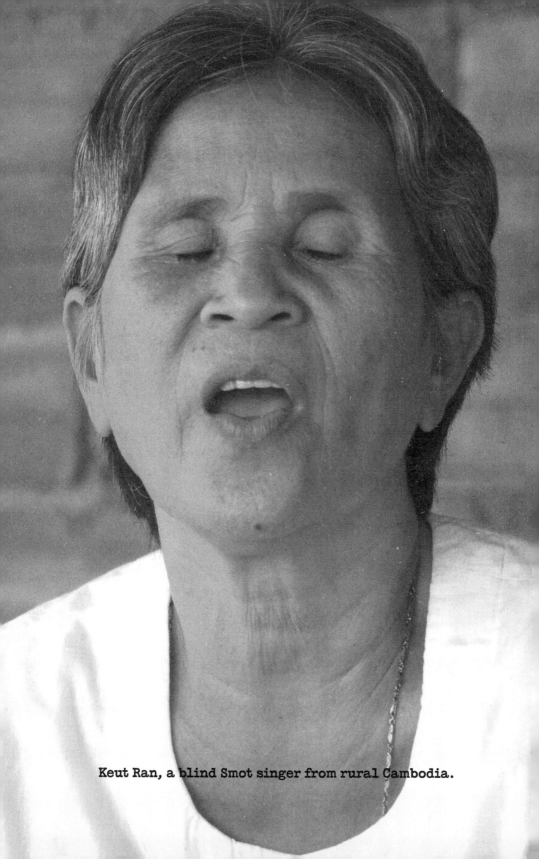

Keut Ran, a blind Smot singer from rural Cambodia.

24

S-urr-ounded: The Inescapable Symphonies of Our Everyday Life

In post-industrial society, rather than strengthening our own listening skills, what we more often practice is selective inattention to the world around us. Akin to the loss of peripheral vision that has resulted due to the dual assault of television viewing *and* interacting with computer screens more than people, the dawning of automated noise has led to a particular form of deafness.

If we truly open our ears—or at least don't try to plug them—we discover a multilayered soundscape around us: a clicking clock's eighth-notes, underscored by a pile-driver in the distance, a random dog's plaintive complaint, and the drone of the passing cars on the expressway. None of which are visible, but all of which are still *very* present.

To our heart's ever rising-and-falling tempo of *almost* triplets, mini-suites are played out in our movements, voice, and thoughts.

Historically, noise ordinances only came into existence after the introduction of massive mechanization. Prior to that, personal soundmaking (e.g., being "loud") was as natural a right as breathing or movement. Instead today, machine's shrieks-and-cries are tolerated in ways we individually never would be.

With the Sony Walkman's introduction in 1980, deliberate deafness as we moved through our immediate surroundings was pioneered. In stark contrast to the aggressive sharing of a boom box being carried down a city block or a car stereo's subs thudding (or Venetian teens cruising slowly in motorboats, using entire waterways as their resonator to get true "subs" out of their sound), headphones allow someone to divorce themselves from their environment by way of an exclusive and customized experience that can have an entirely arbitrary relationship to that specific location.

This was a harbinger for a revolution of disregard for the random and a suspicion of the unexpected, supplanted by a compulsive need to schedule every last moment—"schedule," by the way, being a word that did not exist as a verb until quite recently. As that use of that word has risen, spontaneity has largely been brushed aside.

Consciousness is comprised of two processes. First is filtering out the majority of information we are subjected to, since the immense details in our surrounding are far too vast to be dealt with piece by piece. Second is organizing *and* binding of these impressions. This creates our subjective experience, with no two people taking away the very same recollections of the "same" experience.

Nowadays, much stimulus is *pre*-filtered, with a bias toward repetition of attentions that are market sanctioned, and a rejection of the stray sights and noises of everyday life, the half-missed moments that are merely awaiting us to assign them meaning (e.g., some of the most beautiful clouds I've ever witnessed, I nearly missed by not simply looking up or turning around).

Paradoxically, self-knowledge is self-limited because our consciousness is actually largely made up of our *unconscious*, which is never *directly* accessible to us. The unconscious is a gnarled fantasy world that operates as a much-contorted arbiter between thought and reality.

What is often lost when people speak of intuition is that even it comes heavily weighted. Intuition, at its best, is *not* blind. It is better based on a trust in whatever resources we have deliberately developed in a given area, but that are far too vast to be processed by the conscious mind alone—a form of "learning the rules, so that we can forget them." As we advance in any activity, what was once conscious becomes automatic, freeing up more of our energy to circle back for even more intricate refinements: the progression from novice to intermediate to expert, with the learning-curve spiking at initiation—the vast void from zero to *some* initial knowledge—but then flattening ever more, the deeper we advance into a subject.

Far from undisciplined or merely whimsy, the wisdom of our experience guides us almost exclusively in areas where we are already quite well-prepared.

Though not as known as the legendary Kong Nai, Mr. Soun San is another master of the *chapey dong veng* (long-neck "guitar").

FIELD RECORDING CHRONICLE
KHMER ROUGE SURVIVORS (CAMBODIA):
"THEY WILL KILL YOU, IF YOU CRY"

It would be disturbing anywhere to see a mob gathered around a street pole as an electrocuted utility worker's lifeless body was lowered down by rope as if lynched, but especially in a land with so many ghosts. Amid skin-whitening overdoses and marijuana-pizza for the sex tourists, the stench of colonialism does more than just linger in Phnom Penh.

"We hate the Vietnamese," said the taxi driver as a stark naked child ran into the street to urinate, "but our people are tired of war. We are tired of fighting."

A reported three million tons of carpet bombs were dropped on Cambodia by the United States in the 1970s, more than were unleashed on Germany during all of WWII. And still today, Cambodia is laced with more land mines than anywhere else in the world, which results in two or three deaths on average daily, mostly to "peasants" in the field.

Following the bombings, dictator Pol Pot seized the moment, emptying the cities into shells, then pitting rural residents against the urbanites and launching a genocide that claimed somewhere around two million lives (i.e., nearly one-fourth of the population). This particular holocaust was especially catastrophic culturally as it specifically targeted the artists and "intellectuals," of whom it is estimated that less than 10 percent survived. During this period, daring to wear eyeglasses—which had become a stereotyped symbol between classes—guaranteed almost certain death.

Singer Thorn Seyma had discovered by chance just days before our arrival that her father, Thom Mouy, had apparently been quite a famous singer in the sixties before perishing himself in the killing fields.

As in many post-genocidal countries, communal living is common, with people assembling ad hoc, surrogate families. With a large group of such survivors, we visited a crowded shopping mall full of things that no one buys, just display after display of what people can't have. And there singer Chea Sean (age forty-five)—who has spent her life nearby as a rice farmer—rode an escalator for the first time, which was a main attraction for having brought us there.

With the majority of the population under age twenty-five, the populace has been shaken by a secondary, post-traumatic wave: that of the majority having little memory of the relatively recent tragic events that ravaged the country. That so many of the elite who were involved with engineering those massacres have remained unbrokenly in power ever since, and are now conducting mass evictions and selling off nearly half the landmass of the nation to private foreign investors, is chilling.

The roads are dotted with glamour-shot posters of aging military men in makeup. And along the lone stretch of oceanfront area, vacationing Russian gangsters openly assassinate one another in the streets and set luxury cars afire at beachside resorts. A recurring theme of resignation among residents is "if you have money here, you can do whatever you want."

We had the good fortune of recording with sixty-year-old Han Nai, from the mountainous far north, near the border of Thailand. He is reportedly one of two people left in the world who play the *Kann* (a bamboo horn). In a country where the pop-charts revealed that nineteen out of twenty hit songs were in English, concerns about cultural extinction in this region are far from hyperbole.

Fifty-year-old poet and guitarist Thuch Savanj bears the scars of war on his face, having been deformed by the same shrapnel that claimed his mother's life.

Musical director, flautist, and percussion player Arn Chorn Pond managed to survive, first by playing music to entertain the Khemer Rouge troops, and later by himself becoming a child soldier against the Vietnamese, in a kill or be killed scenario. His weight had dropped down to thirty pounds due to lack of rations, before he was rescued by an American adoptive father.

"If you're a soldier, they will kill you if you cry. Now I cry and feel better. The turning point for me was learning to cry and listen to my own words, rather than just preaching peace and forgiveness to others."

On the road to visit the legendary Kong Nai ("the Ray Charles of Cambodia") we passed aging bomb craters the size of ponds that had filled with stagnant rain water. Parents commonly warn their children, "If you try to play like Kong Nai, you too will go blind," as a way to scare youngsters away from music, so that they will hopefully instead follow some other, more respectable career pursuit.

But as amazing a musician as Kong Nai is, he was rivaled by another virtually unknown *chapey dong veng* (long-neck "guitar") master, Soun San. San was left with a crooked leg and walks with a crutch, but all struggle seems to vanish from his being when he enters trance-like blues states, where he literally tears the shirt from his own chest and beats the floor and walls to emphasize vocal phrases. Being that he lives in the capital's flight path, that is a jet airliner that is audible, almost clipping his building and dovetailing exactly at the end of one song.

Another blind singer, sixty-year-old Keut Ran, keeps the *Smot* vocal style alive, one that bears an uncanny resemblance to the hollerin' style of America's backwoods in the Deep South.

When a young hipster from the city talked of knowing elders that played "country music," it was intriguing. But upon further examination, it was discovered that what she meant was not cowboy hats and fiddles, but the murdered music of Cambodia's own roots tradition.

There is an inherent disconnection of logic among Westerners who claim a culture like Cambodia—who speak a tone-language, where the meaning of many otherwise identical words is dependent on the pitch with which they are spoken—is not musical by nature. And, prejudice's self-destructiveness is nowhere more apparent than in the common write-off of an entire racial group as "passive," particularly one with such a history of upheaval, perseverance, and resistance.

25

Disposable Music

A s labor is divided, almost every endeavor becomes commercialized—
until we reach a strangling cyclical algebra, where people must pay to
have someone care for their children so that they themselves can go to
work *to pay* for the childcare. Similarly, when modern cities are built not to human
scale, but instead are designed for cars, then even the simplest task requires money
to be achieved, since *nothing* is easy walking distance, the way that historically
almost everything has been in towns, cities, and villages. (The telltale sign that you
are in one of these such car-communities is that almost the only people you will
ever see walking are ones whose cars have just broken down.)

A by-product of this is that musicality is moved out of the domain of everyday life—how one talks and moves, communicating animatedly with the entire
body—and compartmentalized to specially restricted areas, such as nightclubs,
football stadiums, and select churches, and even then, only for precisely designated intervals and extents.

To see as unmusical a group of folks as you can find anywhere, look no further
than your average corporate entertainment company, where speech patterns have
more in common with the "always on 11," compressed, tension-ridden vocalizations of car salesmen than anyone with even a rudimentary, bohemian sense.

This is an epoch of corporate-centric sound destruction. The earth's aural
ecology has been disrupted—first by machinery's domination beginning in the
Industrial Age, and now by way of the global clear-cutting culturally to make
room for *du jour* paint-by-numbers, gimmick-driven pap the synergy-sniffing
overlords are selling.

Historically and tragically, the western world as a group tends to speak rather than listen. As inventors of one-way communicational gadgets like radio and television, that proximity also allows the developers to put forth their own tribe as the stand-in for all humanity (e.g., in much the same way that Christ and his apostles ended up resembling ruffians from Michelangelo's local penitentiary—whom he often used as models—rather than the northeast Africans that Jesus's peers actually were).

The West is the equivalent of the indulged and entitled child, one born born of geographic isolation and military might.

Look no further for global homogenization than the standard-issue wedding-reception soundtrack that almost demands that the Village People, Bee Gees, and Louis Armstrong's "What a Wonderful World," have an airing, lest their absence be almost as conspicuous as the cake-cutting or bouquet toss being left out.

And now prepackaged sounds have become almost inescapable—blasting overhead at *al fresco* malls, cluttering cafes, and sticking it to you even while you try to pump your gas. Formally heartfelt words and melodies are increasingly being used not just to sell themselves, but completely unrelated, other shit as well.

Yes, unexpected juxtapositions of music can sometimes be a positive thing. Ideally, that is a song popping up on random play that matches one's mood synchronistically at just that precise moment. The negatives are the escalating and blasphemous, excessive incorporations of art, that through their exploitation weaken the core impact of a piece. Overhearing Kurt Cobain sing his last breath "All Apologies" exorcism while you're standing in line at a McDonald's? What the fuck!

The trend that records are now sold in places with drive-throughs like Starbucks sort of speaks for itself, as to music's disposability factor for many. This stands far, far from the not so long ago days of people camping out and queuing up to be among the first to buy a new album when it was released at midnight (and stores opening at that late hour especially just for such occasions). For many, music is now just a low-res file you download or stream for free and then trash, or an impulsive add-on value to your burger and fries. People now line up days in advance for the latest device model *itself*, having transferred their excitement from the content to the piece of plastic and poisonous elements that can channel the content.

Long gone is the just pre-Napster era of mail-away music clubs, where members would pour over the sparsest of details in a printed catalog to try to decipher how to make the best crapshoot of the dozen albums that they were granted. Basing the choices on just the name, hearsay, a cover image, good old-fashioned word of mouth, and/or a hunch—the order-form prayer was that it would provide delayed-gratification deliverance many weeks later when a package finally appeared in the post-box, to then be unwrapped and spun, using the turntable like a roulette wheel.

The paradox is that the more sound there is present, the less we are able to hear. Detail and nuances of our environment disappear, and every experience hits like a hatchet, bludgeoning us into believing that all of this is perfectly natural. (With all of the calls to reduce carbon footprints, why is there nary a word about the dams of electricity wasted on unwatched and ignored loops of sound and images that idle 24/7 on just about every restaurant's and shopping center's flat-screens throughout the "developed" world?)

In an information-overdosed environment, attention becomes the rarest commodity. And no one need worry what might be your mind, if your thoughts are constantly occupied with those procured by others. Impotent imaginations leave a void just waiting to be stuffed.

We suffer from an overpopulation of sound, but a dearth of diversity.

And this volume makes it even harder to speak *with* one another.

26

Inter-Specific Artistry: "I Am *Not* an Animal!"

The discovery that whales actually have "hit songs" seasonally, that travel the ocean if catchy enough, sort of speaks for itself. That these enormous creatures—who are close cousins to us intellectually—actually rotate their forty-six-foot-long frames vertically to assume the proper singing posture, only adds to the meaningfulness.

That various bird species have been found to have raised their pitch over recent decades in order to be better heard above the din of urbanization, leads one to ponder who really is the more sympathetic accompanist. When studied, sing-ing-species brains are almost double in size to their more silent counterparts. And many life-paired couples soldier on, performing *both* halves of a duet long after their partner has passed on from this earth.

Then there is the discovery that orphaned birds sing the dialect of their adop-tive parents, *not* of their own bloodline, clearly a case of nurture eclipsing nature. Or that scores of birds have chosen to return to the badlands of Chernobyl—one of the only large, open swaths of uninhabited land to be found—begs the question of what they find more toxic: nuclear waste or the intrusion of humans on their environment?

That crickets fashion instruments from leaves and dirt—cylindrical horns that amplify—debunks the misconception that we are the lone, sonic toolmakers.

And spiders are also soundmakers, using a comb-like part of their body to strum leaves, as well as their own webs.

Through echolocation, blind animals literally see with sound, bouncing reflections to create a mental map of their environment.

Dolphins, bats, and skunks all name one another through song. And, that is exactly the element that has been lost in much human speech, the musicality. This squashing is mirrored in broadcasters' flat enunciation that has decimated idiosyncrasies and regional accents, as in cities like New York and London that have historically sported stratified-soundmakers, sporting spots where previously single street blocks were often definable by the residents' particularized enunciations.

For example, my wife once was able to recognize someone from her father's home village of just a few hundred people, based on the man's accent alone, which differed even from that of the next town's, a few miles over. But those same distinctions have already evaporated across the entire, wider state region among her own television-reared peers.

We can ascertain the more distanced that we have become from nature, by how specific or not we are able to be when we speak about it. Often, city-dwellers will state that the sound they heard was "some" animal, without even the ability to distinguish *which* species. Whereas, those living on a farm cannot only tell you what animal that they've just heard, but exactly what breed . . . and maybe even which exact bird!

27

Aural Culture: Music Not As Math, but Individuation

Historically, music belonged to the community. Concerns about authorship were born out of the aristocratic class and its own sense of "importance" and ownership.

It is easy to forget that before the development of classical music, instrumental music existed only as dance songs (which means in many ways we have come full circle with raves and techno-music). The idea that one would sit and listen to music and not participate is a capitalistic construct that still strikes many cultures as absurd—like paying to go to a restaurant and watch *other* people eat.

Once songs began to be "written" instead of played, a division was created between the notationally literate and nonliterate, designating the majority as a nonmusical class. This, of course, could not be far further from the truth.

Not so coincidentally, following the advent of sheet music, "tone-deafness" arose as a new medical diagnosis. A complete hoax of one: for if anyone were completely tone deaf, they would not be able to communicate orally *at all* since *every* language has pitch embedded in its production, to some degree.

Furthermore, learning a language actually largely involves *forgetting,* since almost all infant's babbling emerges already containing every possible sound humans are capable of producing orally. Babies must be trained to forfeit some of those options in order to adopt their given tongue. When it comes to words, it is interjections (e.g., "Fuck!") that fall outside the acoustic norms of any language and are universal. They are not really *of* any one language and instead potentially belong to all. (And, drunk people all over the world "sing" in the same slurred and shrill *lingua franca*.)

Babies can scream all day and almost never blow out their voices. They are born knowing how to breathe, to use oxygen as their friend.

In the past, choral singers would freely move between speech and song as the moment seized them, embodying that they are both part of the same chain. When people sing together, the collectivity literally fixes one another's errors. This is the original auto-tune, joining forces through communal chorus. Not irrelevantly, joint vocal action also enables social species to mask one another, confusing predators so that they have a harder time honing in on any single prey.

To "read" music proves a bit of an oxymoron as it is something that is usually felt and heard. This paradigm reserves music to the learned and "cultured," christening it as something that you are taught rather than born to do, denying it as an action that can be developed through the doing. The truth is that no one person is without "culture" of some sort, no matter how ingrate it might be.

As cliché as it may be, many of the most exceptional musicians throughout time have proven to be blind and/or lacking in any basic, formal education. But as individual genius and/or inspiration give rise to imitation, idioms are regurgitated, with cultural scavengers hoarding and mulling over the remnants. A lost truth is that many great erudite composers (Mozart, Beethoven) were all *also* adept improvisors. It is mostly those that came *after* them that created rules and were concerned with enforcing right and wrongness. Also, in the last analysis isn't every symphony orchestra nothing more than a hifalutin' local cover band and any production of Shakespeare yet another overbaked remake?

Written scores put the music outside the person and force the player back into their head. Often, what we end up with are recitations, like a grade schooler having been called upon to read in front of the class.

Folk songs were essentially written concurrently, by no one *and* by everyone. Even today, in many primarily oral cultures, authorship is often not literal, but subjective. Songs and stories thereby remain properties of the society. An artist's work is often the tune(s) that resonates so deeply with that singer, that they feel it has *become* their's. Lyrics and melody are tweaked accordingly, customizing that which was already a nice fit. And melodies wander from song to song, region to region, and phrases are borrowed or reborn.

Anytime a different singer sings a song, it inevitably changes. At least slightly. The lion's share of culture proceeds through this sort of generational, Darwinian relay. It is an exercise in attrition, with only the best melodies and stories remaining rooted.

When songs and stories are passed down orally, without the aid of technology—be that writing or an iPhone—memory is strengthened. But, also, more room is allowed for adaptation, for the piece to congeal over eons as a reflection of the evolution of that society.

Preliterate societies have historically been right-brained and matriarchies. But once literacy is introduced, male dominance soon follows on its heels with multipronged efforts to control, rather than allow flow. What is often lost are prelingual elements—voice tone, facial expression, gestures—that provide context. For example, it is said that lipreaders have difficulty deciphering what someone is saying if the speaker is wearing sunglasses, since their expressions cannot be studied, too.

The compulsion to possess and affix has eliminated most of the irregularity from lines of lyrics, something that was previously one of the identifying qualities of folk songs. Freedom has been sacrificed and split into the duality of good/bad, rather than seeking beauty in whatever form it takes.

Similarly, those cultures that have suffered their own languages being outlawed (African American slaves, the Irish, et al) have correspondingly flourished in paraverbal musical expression as an outlet for the emotions that were otherwise censored. It is not so uncommon to find some of the most gifted musicians barely muddling through everyday life in autistic-like states, struggling to communicate even the most basic information, such as ordering a latte. But then, through art, prove able to articulate in profound ways that few humans ever can.

In the end, the greatest stability for any government is not an armed populace, but a musical one, freely sharing and nurturing ideas and feelings.

28

Moving Targets: There Is No "There" There

P laces are moving targets. They change with time—not just with years, but even seconds. An intersection in the moments following a car accident is a far different scene than it probably ever has been before.

Consumers have become conditioned to treat life as a checklist, of experiences to *have*—rather than things to do—and places are positioned as items to collect. When people say they've "been" somewhere, I am puzzled what that can even really mean.

Where "there"?

No two people have ever been to the same Paris or Honduras, guaranteed. Not *even* if they have walked the identical block or corner, from the same direction, at more or less the same speed, during the same time of day, and with the more-or-less same emotional disposition.

My own goal is *not* to go everywhere. In fact, my all-time favorite place is at home, indoors, with a book. The fewer intervals that I am in transit, the happier. Generally, I try to skip hyped monuments within a short jaunt, in favor of just trying to learn from my immediate surroundings—whatever they may be or however drab—which by themselves no doubt contain more detail than one person can ever fully absorb.

Globalization tends to be a binge-and-purge buffet, though, with entire cultural mosaics pilfered down to tradable, colorful trinkets. But, when any of us are bombarded with too much stimuli, it becomes unlikely that we retain much at all, losing most of the finer shadings.

29

Do You Hear What I Hear?

If traveling, we can take time to notice the reverberatory contrast of cities built in stone rather than wood. This can help ensure that we are more oriented rather than dislocated from the reality of our surroundings.

We can attempt to imagine how an animal would hear the same information (. . . and not just a celebrity-animal like a giraffe, but why not a run-of-the-mill, lowly squirrel?). Or what a child's experience in our environment is, knowing that they receive notably more of any signal's reflection since they are so much nearer to the ground. Or how differently our ancestors may have sounded. Were their voices higher, crispier, or lower? The rate of speech slower or faster?

We know without question that different cultures perceive—or at least re-create—sounds divergently. Otherwise, onomatopoetic words like "bark" would be identical in every language, instead of differing.

No two people hear the same. Even identical twins have *differing* neurology.

Yes, we have a mother tongue, but we also have a mother *ear*—acutely sensitive to whatever we have been conditioned to hear. And most of this occurs *pre*verbally. Historically, not only did musical forms differ country to country, but even village to village, and family to family, across which tunings differed, making any jamming together on the "same" instruments quite challenging.

Different people process the same music differently, too. Not just whether they like or don't like a given piece, but which elements stand figure to background for them. Nowhere is this more obvious than on a dance floor, where you witness various parts of bodies sympathizing with unique elements—a left elbow playing counterpoint to a cowbell, someone's head spinning around the cusp of the holes left by the bass-line—forming their own unique orchestration.

30

Playing for Keeps: There Is No Rehearsal

A thread weaving through many of my experiences around the world has been the apparent ease that many poverty-stricken performers have to experiment without notice. Any direction given tends to not only be applied posthaste—without resistance or contemplation—but usually with great improvements on any feedback also. That's cosmos apart from precious "artists" who belabor—usually with greater levity than if the economic stability of future generations depended on their choice—such negligible decisions as to whether they should best cut a verse in half.

In no way has this aforementioned willingness to try things ever seemed to be a deference to westerners. Instead, I have always had the distinct impression that most individuals I've encountered under such circumstances are bemused by and humoring me, in much the same way one does with a child or puppy. Many seem to feel a certain pity to encounter someone up close and personal who comes from a culture without a stronger sense of the supernatural.

Whether with Tuareg posses or Mozambique street-players, handing instruments back and forth—often mid-song, without missing a beat—is a familiar characteristic of cultures that have more of a tradition of active participation in the creative process. Rather than being planned or thought about it, the actions seem to simply be felt. There is little rehearsing, there is just doing—emanating from a space where unity is desired and, in most cases, has already been achieved. The previously mentioned five-person xylophone traded players with greater ease than is usually managed by passengers jostling positions on a subway car.

It was shocking to see the Malawi Mouse Boys—who had never been on a stage of any sort before or even played with electricity—saunter out, seemingly without any nerves whatsoever, and tear the sky off an outdoor stage in front of a crowd of ten thousand. A greater epiphany was to hear them recount afterward how they awakened before dawn each morning to hunt and, if unsuccessful, often were left with only a lone banana as food to share for their entire family all day long. When you face life-endangering hunger, Black Mamba snakes, and packs of wild boar daily to survive, worrying about stage fright might seem not only silly, but not even be a consideration to begin with.

And, the excitement with which they recounted that they were not only fed on the plane en route (which they thought in and of itself constituted a "miracle"), but that they were given *a choice* of chicken or beef could not stand in starker relief to the many of us who are so spoiled that we stereotypically complain specifically about the poor quality of airline meals.

Sadly, though, this triumph was short-lived, as upon returning home after just a few days away, the band was met with the heartbreaking news that singer-guitarist Alfred's father had unexpectedly passed on from this world.

The last time they saw each other, he had walked his son to the bus stop at the start of the journey and told him how "proud" he was of him.

Amid the recurring crisis of seasonal food-shortfalls and with a life expectancy of less than fifty years of age for males, death is an all-too-frequent visitor in Malawi's rural areas. This makes our having once met a vibrant, almost manic ninety-year-old man living in a leper colony in the northern region all the more stunning. He was certainly a living testament to the potential powers of positivity.

Revealing the pretelevision nature of the Mouse Boys' worldview, while on tour in the states, the band met a man named Elvis. When I asked them if that name meant anything to them, they said it did not. When I tried prompting them further with "Elvis *Presley*" and then "the king of rock and roll," they shrugged their shoulders and said they had never heard of either. (And, later when I was attempting to describe falsetto singing to them, it was discovered that even Michael Jackson remained completely anonymous to them, too.)

Not only do they not have a "favorite Beatle." They have no idea who the Beatles are! And why should they really? As nice as a song as "Yesterday" may be, with such a feast of music on earth, why should anyone *have* to hear that one overly prescribed tune (that itself arguably derived from an ancient Elizabethan melody)?

A journalist later angrily insisted that the band was influenced by another more well-known African artist that I knew for a fact they had never heard. But that reality just didn't sit well with his preconceptions and the convenience of his convictions. Apparently, this man had never heard of parallel invention. It is so much more comforting to believe that the world is all so much laundered and explicable than it actually is. This is very similar to extremism of all stripes that offer one easy answer, supposed knowns to ward off the discomfort of having to cope with the unknown in a complex world.

Adult learning and growth inherently require a willingness to admit when we were wrong previously (or, at least, not entirely "right").

As a practice, I endeavor to listen just as critically (if not more so) to my "friends"as to strangers. To not automatically play party booster for them and contribute to that corruption, through the unspoken art mafia blood pacts that often percolate between peers.

In classic misplaced overcompensation, more than once, critics have stated that a westerner should never edit or influence an African musician's work. But aren't these individuals just as deserving of input and an artistic ass-kicking as anyone else? Would treating them with kid gloves be more fitting, thereby doing them a favor?

I do *not* endeavor to make World Music records. I strive to produce candid and raw punk and dusty dance-records, ones that come sometimes from remote parts of the globe. A big city "thug" rapper can rarely hold a candle to the attitude of a rural refugee camp survivor or desert militia member, and most archetypal "angry young men" would crumble in days, facing 120+ degree heat without access to clean water, cable, and with nowhere to piss or defecate but a hole in the ground.

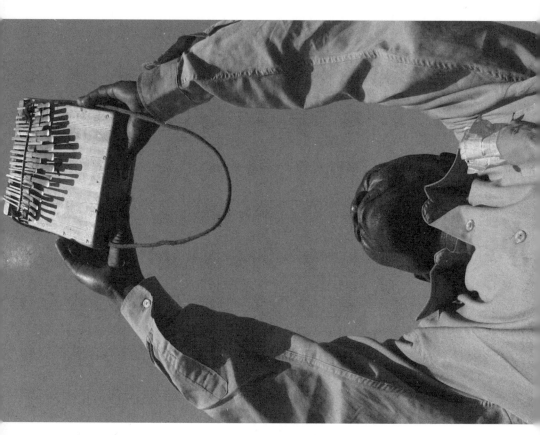

Gaitano from Acholi Machon proudly holds his handmade
lokembe ("thumb-piano").

FIELD RECORDING CHRONICLE
ACHOLI MACHON:
FORMER CHILD-SOLDIER "FREEDOM FIGHTER"

I met instrument-builder Gaitano Otira Tep Yer Yer through a mutual friend in the Acholi tribe who had been abducted and made a child-soldier at age thirteen. A giant of a man—measuring almost seven feet tall and over three hundred pounds, he dwarfed the musician, who walks with a hunched back and prefers squatting to standing, due to a childhood accident where he fell from a tree. These musicians also fancy the greater sound reflection that is generated by the earth when they are nested close to its surface.

They are the "black" tribe. The one that produced the now infamous Joseph Kony. The ones that were designated as a soldier-class by the colonial rulers centuries before and then *forced* into countless battles with their fellow countrymen.

The core of the band, Acholi Machon ("Old Acholi")—a "team" which often swells to fifteen members—arrived riding tandem and helmetless on a dirt bike that had crossed over one hundred miles of bumpy dirt roads.

Singing songs like "Poisoned Food from the UN," "Developing World," "HIV," and "Who Will Build Good Roads for Us?" (the latter of which actually led to a road being constructed in his region), Yer Yer is a topical and prolific writer, but no piece is more revelatory than "I Choose Love."

Enduring war for almost five consecutive decades, first in Uganda and then from the Arab rulers in northern Sudan, the Acholis now suffer one of the highest mortality rates in the world due to AIDS and malaria.

In a region where you are more likely to hear Willie Nelson or Bob Dylan (or Kenny Rogers) on the radio than anything else from America, it becomes clearer how closely connected our roots-music tradition and theirs can be.

"I cannot sing unless there is meaning. The lyrics have to be about something," states Yer Yer. His lokembe and vocal partner, Kornelio Odong Mulili, nodded in silent agreement.

As is their preference, they set up on the ground, beneath a canopy of branches, and proceeded to play for over an hour, without stopping between tunes, their music a tangle of dueling thumb-pianos and dirt-caked vocals.

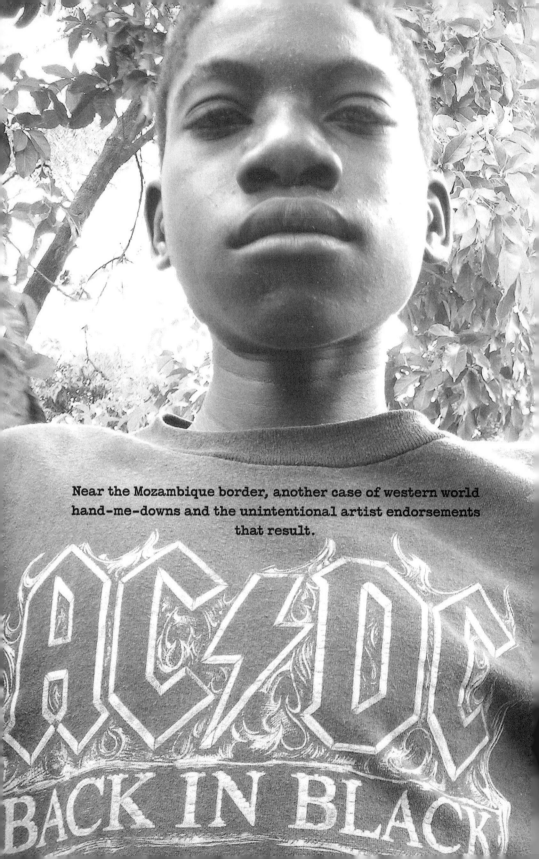

Near the Mozambique border, another case of western world hand-me-downs and the unintentional artist endorsements that result.

31

The Ricochet of Influence

Among my most vivid travel memories was once stumbling upon a cassette-tape seller at a dusty market in Kigali who sold only Rwandan music *except* for multiple copies of Dolly Parton's "Greatest Hits" and Madonna's "Like a Virgin." Or, similarly, while dining at a cafe in rural Algeria that featured a soundtrack of exclusively Arabic music, to suddenly hear Bob Dylan pop out of the speakers.

In an era of mass production, dominated by mechanically reproduced and manipulated sounds (. . . and increasingly images, as well), many have become obsessed with hunting for the "authentic" in art, food, locations, etc.

What often is lost in these searches and debates is that when it comes to culture, purity is actually a myth. Art forms are, by definition, dynamic and in continual states of flux—both providing *and* receiving inspiration from various sources. In order to survive, they must seek fertilization outside their own scant reservoirs.

Ultimately, culture is almost always a smear.

A well-known example is Reggae, which after being born from a potpourri of influences has now bounced back to Africa and infiltrated many local scenes there. (Often, much to their detriment, overall.)

In a parallel phenomenon, most African musicians' only exposure to southern US blues, if any, has come not direct from the sources (e.g., Robert Johnson, et al), but instead filtered secondhand through the more widely distributed artists from England (e.g., Rolling Stones, Led Zeppelin), who themselves were doing their own interpretation of "American" music. Such is the house-of-mirrors of influence that presents severe challenges to the concepts of authorship and ownership of art, to begin with.

The absurdity of trying to catalog what someone *is* has been around for ages. And traces of xenophobia linger. For example, Mexico is a country that many inaccurately refer to as monocultural (and often any and all Latinos in America are misidentified as being "Mexican," regardless of their background). This is in defiance to the huge influence that the Chinese, Africans, and Hebrews played in Mexico's development. In fact, that multiculturalism was so massive that during the seventeenth century, an elaborate *casta* system existed there that attempted to "scientifically" identify every possible racial combination, ballooning to *over* one hundred categories at its height, and spawning playing cards that helped keep track of and determine classifications. Similarly, Jamaica pigeonholed people as quatrain and quintrains (one-fourth to one-fifth "mixed"), in descending order.

That for decades from 1593 on, blacks made up half the population of Lima, Peru, is worth bearing in mind, as just one example. Or that Tango in Argentina was, reputedly, largely pioneered by an anonymous black guitar-player who it is said had a balletic thumb. And still today there are an estimated five thousand Welsh speakers in Argentina, traces of earlier settlers.

Though African American artists have undisputedly played the vital and visionary roles in almost all popular music forms, much of that same music has now meandered around the world, diluting or contaminating older and "purer" musical idioms—for better or worse, depending on your perspective.

Often, faded band T-shirts are spotted in developing countries—AC/DC here, the Spice Girls there. On the surface and at a glance, this might seem to be evidence of the unexpected reach and influence of some figures. Upon even cursory, investigation though, it is more commonly discovered that the wearer has *no* idea of the meaning of or who he or she is sponsoring on his or her torso, but is simply grateful to have a garment of any sort to wear, with no concern whatsoever of its message. Rather than measures of pockets of popularity, these sightings actually attest to *the opposite* usually, that a former fan who knows full well of the artist has now jettisoned them. And, consequently, many less materially privileged are left to wear these trans-Atlantic, hand-me-downs.

Similarly, often the scraps and damaged goods of the monolithic marketing machine are pawned off as quality merchandise and dumped on secondary and tertiary markets (e.g., lesser songs and/or artists being strong-armed into hits on foreign, commercial radio stations). We dump our junk music and films on other countries, to recoup failed investments. And in the industrialized world, the homeless' chests, foreheads, and backs become cost-free, involuntary mobile advertisements, speckling the cityscapes with caps, shirts, and jackets.

Through overexposure, things become familiar and their attractiveness increases. The more something is promoted, the more likely that it will become popular simply by way of the relationship that develops with the information or stimulus due to its inescapable presence. Most "stars" are willed into being, not through superior value, but by sheer promotional force alone.

Nature photographer Ansel Adams certainly photographed inarguably beautiful mountains, but there are many anonymous and breathtaking mountains all over the world. The sights of the American West such as Yellowstone and Jackson Hole became regarded as the "most beautiful" due to his glamorous renderings of them and the subsequent ubiquitous presence of their superstar images. They were not the most stunning, but the best hyped. (Apple recently renewed that feedback loop by naming their newest operating system after Yosemite, also revealing a little regional favoritism since the park is just spitting distance from the Silicon Valley.)

Distribution is power. As lesser quality, mass manufactured items proliferate, "more becomes less." In western countries, largely due to corn-infused foods, for the first time in history, the poor are fat and the rich thin. It now costs more to eat healthily. And most "organic" cuisine is not new, but simply throwbacks to precorporate ways.

Yet, often culture ends up orphaned and adopted, kept alive by other tribes. Rockabilly clubs in Tokyo and Morrissey's near patron-saint status among many southwestern US Chicanos—all despite his Catholic-defying sexual orientation *and* veganism both running counterpoint to the usual party line—are just some of the many examples of this. Then these elements proceed to leave traces, like mineral-deposit remains, often taking root and flowering a new strain. Or they are adopted to such a deep degree that for many they become mistaken as theirs—like a Dutch illustrator I know who grew up watching Japanese anime, believing that they were from Holland. Or the many Manu Chao fans who claim him as Latin American, despite his being a lifelong Parisian, who sings in French, Spanish, English, Italian, Arabic, Galician, Basque, and Portuguese. (Global conglomerates court this kind of confusion by naming themselves with polyglot, made-up words like Nescafe and Nutella, so as to be deliberately vague about their origins.)

Personally, so much of the most fertile fodder I have been exposed to in my lifetime has been drive-bys, nameless snippets of song—strands from a passing vehicle, frequencies distorted by distance—or images that I have probably misapprehended and/or misremembered in some manner. Nonetheless those fragments have acted as seeds and conduits. To think that the web of artists from "developing" countries is any less knotty is preposterous. In most cases, their tapestry of innovation is clearly as rich as our own, if not more so.

And, why would it not be?

SECTION V:

Backin' Up for Some Backstory

32

Transparency: Letting Your Real "Roots" Show

L iterally spitting distance from the Bay Area backyard that gave rise to Metallica, I was suburbia-soaked in the hackneyed, juvenile-male vortex that held music's value based solely on whether it was "hard" enough (something I'm sure that any Freudian or stand-up comic could make a feast dissecting the barely buried subtext of) or even less subtly and most shamefully, the dismissal that something was "gay." And, there was no musical attribute held in higher regard than the ability to play fast(-est). Sadly for me, few aesthetic educations could be further from the intricacies of most non-Western music traditions.

It was considered "uncool" to dance or applaud. So entire audiences stood, fossilized—nigh a head a wobblin', encumbered by fear and judgment.

The prank was often on us, so to speak. That Rob Halford of Judas Priest (who didn't come out officially until 1998) would make his entrance onstage in full S&M regalia and repeatedly shove his microphone up the exhaust pipe of his revving Harley Davidson, before a fist-thrusting, 99.99 percent male audience, must have been one of the great inside jokes in rock history. Or that Queen could've played to stadiums full of fans, most of whom seemed to have never reflected on the obviousness of the band's name, as embodied by the hordes of teenage female groupies lusting after the frontman—to a degree where "flashing tits" to him was standard fair—is another hearty gag. Then seeing Freddie Mercury's hit "We Are the Champions" go on to become the unofficial anthem for alpha-male sporting events worldwide is among the great moments in the history of cultural subversion.

That my peer group of Golden State "natives" detested the Grateful Dead and, rather than appreciating California's unofficial ambassadors, the Beach Boys', more byzantine aspects, found the group weak and frivolous, is another anecdote as to the complexity and confusion of how palates develop. Though we might've lived a thirty-minute drive from the Pacific Ocean, none of us had ever surfed, nor even knew anyone that did. We were landlocked across a bridge and behind the wrong side of a tunnel.

The closest glint we had to a purely aesthetic ritual was holding lighters high in stadiums.

And, when I say "we," I am referring to a specific group of young men: awkward kids who were too shy to speak to girls, casualties of a jock-milieu who still nonetheless reeled from and reeked of that macho ethos. Scared boys, who found escape cranking up self-made mix-tapes while racing against *no one* along desolate frontage roads at night.

It was genuine generational progress when my father—a former quarterback champ/homecoming king—reluctantly relented, telling my preadolescent self that "I didn't *have* to play sports." Nonetheless, the implicit message was clear: there was something wrong with me, if I didn't.

By embracing the "foreign," I am in no way trying to turn my back on my roots. Quite the contrary. My love for music couldn't have been stronger than in those nascent, acne-scarred back days. And, in many ways, it saved me (. . . or at least *accompanied* me) through my darkest hours. Fact is, I made out in the back seat of a Camaro after a Rush concert with a much-older girl who had a marijuana emblem hanging from her rearview. It is hard to come by your white trash credentials more thoroughly than that. We were unintentional, lived cliches—products of our milieu.

Some of the critically derided music I was immersed in then—literally wearing out the vinyl grooves of many albums as a result of so many back-to-back, repeat plays—has stood the test of time or even aged favorably once unhinged from the myopic context of its era. The issue is with the ridiculously rigid and judgmental range of what we allowed to be appreciated.

My maturation and growth have welcomingly, but not entirely, severed the thread of those mass-marketed, corporate-rock beginnings. Instead, that same fervor has been redirected to be ever *more* inclusive, open, and diverse, *including* even the most bubble-gum of pop, if it inexplicably has *that* "thing."

Sort of like the old saying goes, "There are only two kinds of music: good music and bad music." I would requalify that as "honest" (usually positive) and "affected" (*usually* negative) music.

Even the concept itself that there is bad music is an obnoxious one, if viewed in terms of every piece probably being enjoyed by someone somewhere and providing them solace or even an "eargasm." Almost *any* sound that makes someone else feel something—anything—has some worth or purpose. More accurately, the music that the person is enjoying is not "bad," but just not *as good* as it could be due to its lacking the greater breadth that the most epic musical communications possess. Subjectively, almost all music making has value, if for nothing more than the therapeutic release of the performer. And, in some cases, those assembly-line entertainers *are* in fact telling the truth: of their own shallow and materialistic ambitions.

Furthermore, shallow*er* people need music, too. And any scan of the sales charts testifies that they are in legion. But art at its best can help people grow, rather than remain arrested and putrefying. For it is not intellectual deficits that cause most regrettable behaviors, but emotional immaturity. A toddler can far outshine many a distinguished world leader when it comes to compassion and interpersonal insight.

People often speak of posers. For me, nothing makes my skin crawl more than the slew of skaters I've met on the coast that suddenly adopt a dense-Southern drawl when singing "roots" music. *All* music has roots, for fuck's sake. Sing about where *you're* from, wherever that is, not some more storied place. And, through that, help to define that place more clearly, for oneself and others. The only possible way to generate something verifiably rootless is if one tries to deny one's own true origins.

So, for all the haters or art-school slummers out there: Zeppelin still rules, dude!

33

Drawing Random Inspiration from the Inspired: Liberating Influence from the Ghetto of Sanctioned Outlets

My sister was born with Down syndrome, grossly underweight, and two months premature. After varied attempts to save her failed, the doctors advised my parents to bring her home so that she could die humanely with family rather than in an institution.

Miraculously though, she did not perish, but instead, thrived.

She and I were less than fourteen months apart in age. I learned from her the value of nonverbal communication. To forge even the most basic sibling relationship, I was impelled to become better versed in the powers of vocal and tactile relating (e.g., her lexicon of handshakes alone is far greater than most others have in their entire bodily repertoire).

She is clinically diagnosed as severely retarded, but I have not ever known a better listener. With her limited vocabulary, I have come to the realization that she is never *not* in a foreign language environment. The vast majority of what is spoken in English is as incomprehensible to her as if it had been Farsi. And, in the absence of these conscious and literal means of conveying information, in compensation, her skills of observation and emotional-tracking intensified.

(I also learned through her peers and in my many years of working in mental health that each personality is deceptively complex. Just because someone may be mentally ill or disabled, that in no way rules out that they may not, also, chronically act like an asshole, most of the time. They could be just as flawed as the next person, with no relationship whatsoever to their dominant condition, but simply as a manifestation of character. Similarly, I had a dog once that I'm convinced was a racist and a cat that had serious control issues . . . but I digress.)

Two of the most influential musical performances that I've ever experienced were thanks to my sister.

1. First, was seeing one of her grade-school classmates perform the Broadway tune "Tomorrow" from the musical *Annie*, at a school assembly. The singer was so short she had to stand on a chair to be even partially seen over the heads of the audience. With a curly, red wig, lopsidedly covering part of her face, she delivered a piercingly direct and devastating plea for perseverance. The technical performance's lack was completely subjugated by her pure and unaffected poignant potency.

To this day, decades later, I have never seen a studied or professional vocalist even approximate the fearlessness and ineffable depth of feeling that she radiated during those minutes.

2. Second, my sister was inexplicably smitten with TV personality Tony Orlando, during his 1970s primetime heyday. When I later discovered that he had started singing as a way to communicate with his own speechless and disabled sister, the spell that he cast to my own sibling through the television set made absolute sense. Like some sort of secret handshake.

   My sister, Jane, was such a fan, that for her birthday one year, I bought her tickets to see him perform. As it turned out, days before the show, one of Mr. Orlando's closest friends had shot himself in the temple during a drug-fueled mania. Midway through the concert, while standing in the round, there was an awkward change of mood and Mr. Orlando dismissed most of the band from the stage, all of whom seemed flustered by the sudden turn of events.

He then went on to dedicate the next number to his departed friend and proceeded to transform what was an otherwise maudlin song about homesickness into a triumph of cathartic power. Show-business acumen was halted, as the sweat, tears, and snot sprayed off and out of him, his voice hoarse and cracking. It was clear that he was sharing an authentic experience with the audience, never again to be replicated. By the time he was finished, the majority of those in attendance were visibly a-quiver from this unexpected detonation of self-revelation, and after a stunned silence, a lengthy standing ovation shook the room.

What I took away from both of those events was that beauty has the potential to arise, without warning, from anywhere. That if we are truly in search of inspiration, it serves us to remain open and not reliant on prescribed and predictable outlets. That a famous singer's greatest hour, might be his least skilled and vulnerable. And, that an amateur's ability to convey feeling can far exceed any virtuoso.

What is paramount, is the moment. Truth trumps immaculateness *any* day. And, the most sacred expressions cannot be manufactured and duplicated, but are spontaneous and unrepeatable outside the context of sharing that has given them birth.

34

Who's the Boss?

When I worked in the psychiatric emergency room, there was one middle-aged woman with schizophrenia, who would refuse to speak or look up. She spent the majority of her time doing a ritualistic form of movement, in which she would stop at the edge of each floor tile, hover there on one foot, until hesitantly launching herself forward, then rebalancing, only to continue this same pattern at each seam in the flooring.

The television on the ward was kept on in the dayroom from morning to night. One afternoon, for the first time that I'd witnessed, she stopped in her tracks and stood upright, her attention frozen by the screen. The 1978 live footage of Bruce Springsteen performing "Rosalie" was being aired. This patient stood transfixed for its duration. (Mind you, the clip is 9:44 in length.)

When it was through, she remained there, unmoving, and continued to stare blankly.

I gingerly approached her and asked, "Did you like that?" stupidly hypothesizing that she was not a music aficionado.

She turned to me and, for the first time I'd ever seen, made very precise eye contact, much more penetrating than most.

"I *loooooooooooooove* Bruce Springsteen," she said. The spell broken and the point well-made, she immediately spun on her heels and retreated back into her interior world, resuming her speechless, compulsive progression down the hall.

35

The Road from No-Name-Ville

As a kid hailing from a backwater, West Coast suburb, I had no dreams or expectations of ever traveling outside the United States. All that was ever emphasized to me growing up—be it by the screaming-drunk, German expat, factory worker across the street; the Lithuanian refugee up the hill whose house burned down mysteriously one Fourth of July; the first generation Italian American, Korean-War-vet boxer from Queens; the night-shift-pulling Native American postal employee who was my best friend's single mom; my hero-in-addicted uncle who died in his thirties; or the couple that suffered through the Japanese internment camp together as children in the central valley—was survival. Most were reasonably comfortable, but without having much financial cushion, the omnipresent result was a general, collective sense of unease.

Where I came from you weren't a success if you became a doctor or lawyer, but if you had a job. *Any* job.

I started singing as child, not to try to be a star, but as a way of communing with myself. It was done also in the hope that it would somehow save my soul or at least help me to try to find out if I at least had one.

But, that community was nonarable ground in terms of aesthetic models. Corporations had already mostly seized music making and divorced it from daily routine. Music had become something mediated and sanctioned, to be emulated, reflected, and bought, rather than embodied.

And, that compartmentalization and discontinuity is the key demarcation from societies where music remains immersive. Art is not a "thing" you pick up and put down, plug in or shut off at will, but instead is a constant. As ever-present as your own heart's palpitations—and even directly linked to them.

I remember being locked in my room, laying on my bed one Halloween, after shredding the shrink-wrap to listen to Side 1 of "Darkness on the Edge of Town" on repeat play, as the trick-or-treaters rang our doorbell, unanswered. It was a baptism of sound. The howl contained within those grooves seemed to call out like a spectral guide, revealing the forepangs of a future awaiting me someday, beyond the close confines of what I'd known. There are certain places that only the invisible spaceship that is music can take you.

A good record should place you amid the musicians, as if they are there with you. It should bring you *there*. Not as if they are specimens pressed behind glass— taxidermy, to be appreciated only from a distance. To this end, different micro- phones can be the equivalent of lenses for cameras, narrowing or lengthening the field to create a more varied and enveloping experience.

Records were sought out as road maps to a better life, prisms that could enhance sight. During an era where the modes of distribution were so scarce (and correspondingly the goods, more expensive), each find carried tremendous weight—a potential Shroud of Turin—and was granted commensurate, though often unwarranted, concentration.

I have images of being a preteen and the cheers we all gave when a local glam- band's guitarist would tip his Flying-V guitar sideways and simulate cunnilingus, a stock "highlight" of *every* one of their shows. No matter, the countless times we saw them, the stadium-size choreography was unchanged as they postured from the civic rec-hall riser to the imaginary throngs.

Or the time a speed-metal, lead-barker brought onstage his two pet Dobermans, frothing at the mouth, and then unleashed them on the mosh pit—with the scant fans in attendance seemingly liking it—as *un*funny of a Spinal Tap moment as you could imagine.

As a lifetime of politeness came uncorked, I remember the violence of an acquaintance breaking someone's nose with his elbow as his way of showing appreciation down in front for the "best show ever." And I shiver at the thought of a family friend who tragically paralyzed another teenager while stage diving (an event for which I thankfully was not present).

And, I remember being held against my will for hours at an audition in the practice basement of a Satanic outfit whose bassist greeted me at the door with no shirt on, tiger-print leggings, and knee-length, pleather moccasins (in hindsight, all sure signs that I should've bolted right then and there). The room had taped-shut windows, a padlocked bike-chain across the double-strength steel door, and walls adorned with torture-dungeon equipment. Somehow fortuitously, I escaped, unharmed. (And, by the way, in the end I wasn't deemed "heavy enough" to be invited to join the band anyway—a snub that still stings to this day.)

Or the rehearsal room in the shuttered factory where possums would scurry along the floor, through the cracks in the walls, seemingly bobbing their blind heads to the groove as we played. Or the night on tour when I slept without cover and literally under someone's dripping kitchen sink since there was no other space for the eight people in the studio apartment that we were crashing in, and I was forced to play dead as two of those present—to this day I do not know which of them—tried to sneak sex, undetected, just feet from my head.

Or the flabbergasted choir coach who yelled at me to "relax" almost every time I opened my adolescent mouth to sing.

But I alone was my own biggest foe.

My obsessiveness as a self-taught-by-ear preteen and teenager—to practice guitar every waking hour possible, often falling aslumber seated, while drilling scales up and down the neck—in many ways only entrenched habits that I had to later attempt to *un*learn. Too much practice can unwittingly reinforce rubbish methods. That is a primary error that I made as a developing musician, one of quantity (the number of hours clocked) versus quality.

Later, the auteur model of Prince drove many of my generation to microman-age every detail of a recording. Rather than encouraging collaboration, I charted every last note and part, and then demanded that living drummers re-create those beats with exacting faithfulness.

The predicament was that my talent was not remotely of the caliber of a rare someone like Stevie Wonder, who could actually pull off such a feat. And, this was a reality that I was *completely aware of* at the time, by the way. But that still didn't curtail my self-defeating compulsion. Such is the power of fear. I was so concerned about failing, I induced it.

And even now I still occasionally face the temptation of any recovering per-fectionist: to become obsessive and controlling, if allowed the chance.

If any good came from these excesses, it was my learning how *not* to make music. (Also, as a side effect, I did become versed in many aspects of traditional arrangements—drums, bass, keyboards, harmony vocals, et al—that have on occasion come in handy.)

I am tormented by the time where I burst impromptu into a song during a rehearsal and the rest of the members, slack-jawed at my sudden extemporaneousness, soon jumped in. It was, by far, the most inspired thing I ever wrote hookwise, as well as the best the band ever sounded. For the first time, we were open and vulnerable with one another and truly unified—not just at the start and end of the song, but throughout and in-between. The rapture passed though as soon as the song concluded. When it was through, we snapped back into the routine, slunk back to our respective corners, setting aside and forgetting the tune (mind you, this was a pre-iPhone age, where recorders of any sort were rarely easily on hand), and we got back to working on our "real" set for the umpteenth time.

I still shudder at witnessing an alcoholic, loudmouth drummer I played with berate a diminutive, Goth female bass player at an audition. He was clearly threatened that the men's club was being crashed, and I lacked the conviction to intervene against the this antagonizer, who was much older than I, and be brave enough to swim against the misogynistic rocker tide during that sad twilight when the few women allowed in bands at all were still usually relegated to singing roles only or possibly, if they were *really* lucky, a token tambourine, too (or in some cases, if they had the chops, they were allowed a fellatio saxophone solo). (All of this, of course, was in direct ignorance to the fact that the first song ever titled "rock and roll" was sung by the banjo-playing trio the Boswell Sisters, a full *twenty* years before Elvis' debut. Not to mention that in the 1920s Bessie Smith was the first "dirty talk" pansexual god of the recording era—male *or* female—fronting up to a forty-person outfit.)

And, I remember the exact instant onstage after decades of performing publicly since age six, when before less than a half-dozen disinterested people at a coffeehouse, I finally found some semblance of my voice: by simply surrendering to the sound.

None of this is to scorn anyone above. All of these folks in their own way were searching for the same thing. Groping in the dark for a deeper meaning, a birthright that had been stolen from them by the mechanization and individuation processes of the mid-twentieth century.

I am old enough to have experienced how the Beatles (along with co-aligning forces) began to change the way the common man moved and spoke.

Even as a small child, within that short lifetime frame of reference, I could feel the destabilization that sounds helped create. (It is worth noting how much the Beatles' indispensable producer George Martin looked more like an accountant, than anything even remotely bohemian. He had no tattoos, no attitude. Just a button-down, all business demeanor. But he sure delivered. In much the same way that so many bespectacled and chino-wearing early civil rights activists resemble today's "dorks," but quite radically risked or sacrificed their lives to change.)

The 1980s gave way to plasticity. The pulse slowed and the beacon flickered. To grow up amid that wasteland of truth was to be robbed of many basic nutrients of imagination.

Within a span of six short years, punk had been reduced to boys-only, and all of its skeletal complexity shrunken to adrenaline-seeking, slam-dance and razor-blade fistfights.

A case in point of the stagnation of that era is that I once witnessed the greatest rock band of that period, the Replacements, play nearly four hours of jaw-droppingly exciting, train-wreck music to a sparse club audience. Meanwhile across town, the Who had sold out two nights on what was already their second farewell reunion tour (!).

When as a high schooler, the quad was overrun at lunchtime with lollipop-blue, Styx-concert baseball jerseys the day after their concert, I felt as if an alien invasion had occurred, making corporeal an even more distinct sense of "alienation." More sadly, I came to realize that it was all just a sort of Rorschach test that I had failed (or passed), and the merchandise had simply renderedisible what I had previously been blind to, but had been there all along.

36

Premature and Promiscuous Championing

The grind of working in locked, emergency-psychiatric facilities led me to realize that one concrete way to demarcate whether someone is from a truly privileged background or not is if they've ever had to punch a time-clock, and had their life siphoned back minute by minute to czars.

Music was always my obsession. More than anything, for me it was a vehicle for words. I figured almost no one read poetry anymore, but nearly everyone had been exposed to the couplets of Bob Dylan . . . whether they knew it or not. Yet, the rare few writers of the rock era that even neared passable writing (Tom Waits, Paul Simon, Paul Westerberg, Shane MacGowan, Chuck D, et al) only did so on sporadic occasion, for a verse or line, here or there. The collective quality of pop lyrics is so low that an entire career can potentially be hung on one brilliant couplet. The fact is, though, that the bulk of even the most lauded songsmith's output would be laughed out of almost any routine creative writing workshop, anywhere.

Paul Simon probably wouldn't have escaped with his life if he'd dared utter, "And a rock feels no pain, and an island never cries" before a roomful of aspiring scribes.

While it is unthinkable what the Boss's fate would've been putting forth, "Two hearts are better than one/Two hearts, girl, get the job done."

The law of contrast allows for this lowering of the bar, though. As a result, since fashion models are expected to be daft by many, they are more easily regarded as "smart" for any nonfailure intellectually (e.g., "She knows who Jung is!"). And a hardened criminal is often classified as "sweet" by their caretakers if they have managed to demonstrate even a modicum of civility.

In general, the contributions and abilities of the famous tend to be overestimated, and of the unknown, dismissed. For example, when it comes to Spaghetti Western music, film director Sergio Leone is often spoken about synonymously with the form. The more studied instead refer to the music's actual composer, Morricone, as being responsible. But, in actuality, the person who performed the somnambulistic surf-guitar parts *and* the forlorn whistling—the two elements that are the indelible trademarks of this musical style—is the barely known Italian musician Alessandro Alessandroni.

37

Pain Dues, Dude

As a long-haired, uneducated eighteen-year-old, I was *so* persona non grata that a small hospital refused to hire me for a minimum-wage, part-time position changing bedridden people's diapers on the night shift. Eventually, I found another suitor for an equivalent position—a shit job, for shit pay—literally starting from the bottom(s).

This all came back to me in a flash when a band I work with, who lives without running water, were on their first tour and called me to one of their hotel rooms hastily at 4:00 a.m. They had plugged the tub, overflowing the tiles with water that was the consistency and color of coffee grounds. When I saw the horror with which the man's other bandmate cautioned me to not stick my hand into the water to fix the problem, I realized the true gravity of the situation. Looks had not deceived as to what might've caused the stoppage.

But duty called, so taking a deep breath, I plunged in, up to my elbow, as the others gasped in revulsion. From that day forward, their leeriness seemed to drop slightly, and they related to me increasingly as a peer who was "down."

This was not so different than the time when I had to surreptitiously take a musician into the hallway during a "live" BBC radio broadcast, so that he could hurriedly relieve himself into a water-bottle I was holding (since we were literally locked in the studio, with no access to a toilet) seconds before he was due to perform. I then had to hide the brimful container in my pocket and carry it throughout the post-show, meet-and-greet schmoozing, to then be discarded later, with no one aware.

To have a knife pulled on you by a drunk Norteno gang member at 2:37 a.m. as you guard a stage in a Mission District park must count for something. The days of preparation for the free concert featuring Fugazi had been filled with all the wonders of positioning porta-potties and trash bins, while the morning after was spent side by side at dawn with a complaining city gardener, cleaning up cigarette butts and refuse left by those who had gathered, as if I were working off court-ordered hours for unpaid parking citations.

As always, the producer's code is to take the heat if anything goes wrong (even when it's not necessarily your fault), and to watch others steal (or question) acclaim, if proceedings are at all a success.

The storied songwriter kept us waiting more than two hours in the posh hotel lobby that he had chosen as a meeting place.

Word was that he was brain-damaged from years of alcoholism, and was incapable of even holding a basic conversation, let alone writing new material anymore. I was warned repeatedly that I was wasting my time.

When he finally arrived, it was with much fanfare. He wobbled in, wearing sunglasses at midnight, and knocking over a marble end table as he missed the few steps down.

Once seated, a gigantic stream of green snot was birthed from his right nostril, snail-like, catching there in his wiry beard. He then proceeded to conk out in the chaise lounge, his head reeled back, and the mucus sucked in and out with each inhalation. In those pregnant moments, as I stood spectator to a living legend awash in his own bodily fluids, nodding off to la-la land, any remnants of the glamour of the entertainment industry were obliterated.

My past was revisited in a harrowing way, when a now-homeless former rock star was brought into the ER by police so that he could be interviewed as to his need for treatment. He had been a role model for me during my preteens, but I never let on to the man that I knew who he was. His band had largely been forgotten, and had never fully "made" it. But for local kids of a certain period—as we faced down the void of their futures—the band's members were heroes.

I nearly did not recognize him, though. Were it not for his name, I might very well have never realized it was him. What was left of his once-fierce mane had turned a milky gray. But most disorienting, his nose had been eaten away to just a nub from cocaine abuse. He sat, crestfallen, a walking testament to the perils posed by a life in the fast lane.

A short time later, two of the most gifted songwriters I'd ever know, personally or otherwise, killed themselves. One on Christmas morning, the other a few weeks later. Neither had ever been well-balanced individuals. Both gave their all, though, to music and lived as if their life had a pure purpose that could not afford to be hindered by the demands of the daily grind and such trivialities as physical survival.

38

Amateur Hour: "Real Musicians Have Day Jobs"

Music is a strange aspiration, being one of the only professions that aspirants are unabashedly discouraged from pursuing. It is difficult to imagine a well-meaning uncle attempting to convince a teenager that they shouldn't become a plumber or a teacher because "it is *really* hard." But it is a rare artist who has not heard this refrain *ad nauseam*, even *after* achieving identifiable success.

Furthermore, no matter how disinterested or casual a participant is, due to the simplicity and subjectivity of popular culture, nearly everyone feels they are an expert in this area and will freely dish out offhand and brutal criticisms about a novel, film, or song, in ways that they would never dare venture to confront more respected vocations such as attorneys or vascular surgeons, unless those had made the most grievous errors. Instead, to more respected occupations, many would often, contrastingly, even demonstrate blind and undeserved deference to them, even in the face of continual incompetence.

But pop music is also one of the only occupations that verifiable amateurs are potentially allowed to make careers in. You'd be hard-pressed to find a medical doctor anywhere who could not explain basic anatomy or a mechanic who cannot quickly sort out an engine's basic configuration, yet the majority of post-punk pop musicians would struggle with such basic questions as what is a sixteenth-note or the relative minor to the key of A. The rock-eras worshipping at the altar of idiot savants has ushered in many nebulously qualified "professionals."

It is true that post-modern art is post-technique. But with folk forms, this has always been the case, that technique is secondary. The difference is that before recorded music, folk forms were never largely commercialized—save for the begging of starving, wandering minstrels—but instead were mostly maligned.

The next time a cooler-than-thou haircut tells you they are a "guitarist" or in a band, quiz them casually to clarify the differences between a five-, eight-, and twenty-two-tone scale. Don't worry if you don't know the answer. Almost guaranteed, they won't either! You can have great fun watching them blankly try to confabulate an answer, before darting away or changing the subject with the cop-out that, "some things are better left unexplained, otherwise you risk chasing the vibe away" or the all-purpose, "I don't know. I'm more of an *instinctual*-type player."

Those same individuals no doubt play music, but *being* a bona fide artist or maestro is a whole different thing altogether. And any of these such titles are ones that cannot credibly be bestowed on oneself (as much as the self-help gurus may claim otherwise), but must be decided by those with more distance and objectivity.

I'm not sure whether I am a "writer." I only know that I write. Verbs and adverbs are concrete, nouns and adjectives can be a treasure trove of subjectivity.

Music must choose you, though. For it to be an avocation, it must be treated with great respect and not toyed with and set aside at whim. Truly gripping artists are lifers. The drive is caught young, like a fever, measurable by the haunting, relentless quest to express, learn, and share. Art is not something to "try" (and then ditch), but to *do*, regardless. One can't really select what sets us afire. But it is undeniable when it occurs.

It is not enough to have always "thought" about playing music and/or wanted to. Almost every maintenance-alcoholic from the social set will tell you they plan to someday write "the great American novel," as if that were something that can just be squeezed out after their retirement and between rounds of golf and ski vacations.

Ironically, though, unlike other fields of expertise, music is not becoming more complex, but simpler—from rock and roll to hip-hop to electronic music, the elements involved have become fewer, with harmony and melody largely being left by the wayside. Therefore, to be part of this shamanistic caste is now based on appearances and personality rather than actual output, since the entry-level ability is so damn low. (And, an additional drawback of this is that if massive success is so easily facilitated for some, then it is almost inevitable that they end up blasé and unappreciative of their good fortune, since from the get-go they didn't work very hard to achieve it. It is hard to value something that is given too easily.)

In the west, we boil down Harry Patch's forty-three-note scale to a mere eight tones from which the pentatonic scale of folkloric forms uses only a measly five notes (and, not so coincidentally, the oldest known instrument in the world is a forty-thousand-year-old bone flute from Germany with five soundholes that form a crude version of that same pentatonic scale). Our cavemen cousins were jamming the blues, too. And all of this is out of the possible seventy-eight intervals found in a single octave (a number that some even claim is actually as high as 231 intervals), *none* of which are perfectly "in tune" by nature.

The by-product of scales is a xenophobia of sounds and a bigotry to alternate aesthetic concepts. And, in many ways, this imposition of limiting options as to what are "legal" sounds (4/4 rhythm, major and minor keys) is merely a continuation of Eurocentric equal-temperament tuning that is rooted in the Baroque period.

As an outgrowth, at their dawning, bebop pioneers were often misunderstood. They were dismissed as bungling and spasmodic, though what they were actually doing was a very conscious attempt to break free from the constraints of Eurocentric structures and confines. In eras where it was constitutionally impossible for many races to have such freedom socially in everyday life, it could be achieved musically. To think that their music has gone on to become synonymous with unpronounceable cheese and Chardonnay wine tastings is yet another example of how delayed assimilation castrates.

As far as soundscapes, if we *all* accepted more culpability for what we contribute to our collective sonic-habitat via our voices and movements, then the thin layer on the surface of the planet that we inhabit would become a bit more livable—a more dancing *and* danceable space.

As I floundered through the decades, working as a learn-as-you-go, front-line counselor in locked psychiatric wards, people would often state, "But I don't understand what you *do*," or would dismiss music as a hobby for me since it wasn't what I did full-time (though in actuality I was always doing it *more* than full-time, in the off-hours). What these privileged gents were unable to recognize was that I was mortally scuffling for my very material existence on this planet in the only manner I was able and knew how to. Creative projects occupied nearly 100 percent of my heart and consciousness. But my workplace drudgery left less time for them than I had ever dreamed possible, even in my ugliest nightmares.

Art at its most matchless becomes a part of the fabric of people's lives and enriches them. It can act as a life raft to carry people through the roughest times, and rather than "creativity" being the pastime it is often dismissed as, at its most realized, there can be few more noble acts.

Some "music producer" from California.

39

Bittersweet Dreams

It is hard to ever look at a five-dollar cup of coffee the same (not that I ever thought it wasn't absurd), knowing how many musicians I have known that get by on less than that in a week . . . and that's if they're lucky.

There are increasingly times now that I lie awake and remind myself that many people I know are sleeping on the ground, faraway somewhere, without locks and only partial shelter. In homes that I've visited, but never had to live in.

Or, on occasion when I am partaking of the miracle of instantaneous hot water and night-defying lights, I shudder with shame at my underappreciation for my dumb and unearned luck in these material matters.

I am repentant by my failed attempt to satisfactorily answer the members of Acholi Machon that the monstrous buildings crowding the freeway outside London were storage-units built to hold things that people owned, but didn't use anymore or even want. Their inability to make sense of this excess was far more articulate than any metaphysical argument that could be made against it. Such was watching Stani from The Good Ones hold up a chunk of steak on a fork while seated at a booth at Denny's. He contemplated that one bite of meat for minutes, and then declared under-his-breath, "At home, just *this* would be our Christmas meal, our feast."

There is really no way to make peace with it. How to live on the winning end of a bad deal, globally. Knowing that a half brother by marriage died in his thirties, homeless and of AIDS or that my mother-in-law's formerly prosperous village has fallen into disrepair, out there where the almost endlessly branching dirt roads, assemble and literally fall into Lake Kivu, a spot where it feels most like being abandoned on the precipice of the moon. The inequity of my material advantages and waste is simply wrong. There can be no justifiable buts about it.

What I do know is that there are so many, countless others who have done *colossally more* than I to make the world a better place—whether it be the Sicilian woman I know who left her life behind to start her own orphanage in Malawi or the numberless others like her.

For me, one of the most heart-wrenching occurrences when traveling to more remote areas is to witness how acquiring even a single European or North American phone number is held as such precious a commodity. It can be simply crushing to see the hunger that so many have expressed for having even the slightest lifeline of connection, however tenuous, beyond their own borders, and the elusive hope that lends them. Or how when I call someone in remote, rural areas—even if it's been years—they usually instantly know that it is me and greet me by name before I've even said a word of hello.

It is haunting hearing people in industrialized countries assess themselves as "down to earth," we who've already been given treasures in this life beyond the wildest hopes of the many.

I carry these people with me, so many of those that I've met.

Steveria, the woman who was wandering past, and walked up to the mic mid-take, uninvited, and added sepia-saturated vocals to the Malawi Mouse Boys' first record. Then adamantly refused reimbursement of any kind. For her what seemed to matter was proving that she had something to contribute (. . . which she *very* much did).

Or Abuba, the three-year-old prisoner at Zomba who lost his mother there. He carried himself with the weariness of someone at the end of a long life. When people claim that they are "strong" people or "survivors," his granite-and mud-crusted face comes to mind.

As I spoke to this nonverbal boy-man during the last moments we were there, I tried one final time to make some small connection. As we were walking away, from one hundred yards away for the first time in those weeks, he acknowledged me—springing to his feet, lunging forward, rocking on his heels infirmly as he raised his left hand, and wagged just the pinkie almost imperceptibly. But it did not feel like a victory. Instead, a tidalwave of sorrow bore down on me, one that is hard to ever again break the surface of.

The leader of Tinariwen, Ibrahim, once knelt me down beside a Dumpster teeming with rotting food on a loading dock, out back of a nightclub, and then pointed upward at the sliver of opening between the buildings looming above.

He was showing me the sky.

Regrettably, despite having helped more than one musician to gain better means to feed and clothe their families, and having had an artist of such gifts as Nelson Mulligo write a blessing song to tell me that I had helped make him a "rich man"—and even after having helped a few innocent people gain their freedom from prison—I have no doubt that spiritually it is *I* that have been the primary beneficiary, once again getting the better shake, and somehow coming out ahead in the exchange.

Far from a messiah complex, this is not yet another enactment of the "white man to the rescue" syndrome, but, if anything, more a case of a white man *being* saved.

My only hope is that I will *never* grow comfortable with the feelings of discomfort and accept any of it as normal. That I will always remember that none of this makes sense and more than "just the way it is," poverty and exploitation are a curse visited upon the innocent. Yet, they are ones that afflict us all, more than we can ever fully know.

A sign that speaks for itself, in a country with one of the
lowest life expectancy rates in the world.

SECTION VI:

Beware the Traps

40

Living in the Moment, But Keeping an Eye on the Horizon

T he very concept of a "controlled" environment indicates the conundrum that exists due to this approach's limiting, rather than encouraging, freedom. If only recording were as easy as just having to buy the "right" microphone. But there are just far too many variables that go into the recording process. And the one thing you can't buy are the intangible elements—the emotion and life, and sometimes downright "ugliness"—that make or break it, after the shouting is all over.

No one but a techie-nerd really cares about the process. Listeners are concerned almost exclusively with the end results. More than what something sounds like, the timeless measure is what it *feels* like.

When buying music, I have never once heard someone ask if a record "sounds good," but instead if it *is* good. If they like it, how it was recorded technically is of no consequence (though, if it's really special, they may have interest in the backstory of what were the *life* circumstances that it emerged from). When all is said and done, if a record does not evoke a visceral reaction of some sort, then it is next to worthless and the process was wasted. What attracts people universally and what they hunger for is something that produces a reaction, a sense of aliveness inside, be that from food, music, fabrics, or other.

The flood of recent technical advances has led to the flipside of some fetishizing tape, going to great lengths and expense to "warm-up" the sound by recording on analog equipment, with often debatably different results. And yet again, being overly reverent of iconoclasts' proven methods seems to be an instant contradiction that many find false comfort in, rather than forging ahead more blindly into the void.

Trying to make the "best" or perfect record are goals, precursed. One is doomed to fail, since such outcomes do not and cannot exist. Instead of sitting at mix-desks as if manning the spaceshuttle controls, just let go and hit "record"…it will be okay. The methods ultimately evaporate and all that's left is the air that the resulting vibrations are carried on.

41

Sonic Prisons: Getting Off the Grid

Almost all recorded music now is filtered through one computer operating system, which itself acts as grid.

This creates sonic prisons, whereby purviews are set over that which has historically been wild and free. What is better emphasized musically is not one standard of what "is" right (with any deviation from that being labeled an error and auto-corrected), but, contrarily, what *feels* right.

Grids encourage conformity to standards and sound becomes domesticated. Yet, it is the rough edges and accidents that provide grain and tension. Without at least some passing acknowledgment to death, most actions lack depth. Each sound should be allowed the right to be itself and retain its own identity.

Rather than attempting to fix flaws and mistakes, we can, instead, celebrate them. With recording, it is well known that any musical error that cannot be eliminated should be turned *up*—to "hide" in the open through unveiling—which usually works far better than trying to bury it. (This is because we customarily perceive that which recedes as "voids," but that which advances and protrudes as valiant and strong.) Or, in a live pickle, unintentional phrases can be repeated until a deliberate pattern is created and is no longer detectable as an error.

Any failure just awaits giving birth to a newfound style.

Also, misdirection can best be created by masking sounds with something louder and distracting, just before or after, rather than exactly at the same moment. This works much more effectively than two sounds occurring simultaneously.

As in cinematography, where often a soft focus is more beautiful than a precise one, a deliberately flattened note or a wavering, reaching tone can convey so much more than exactitude.

It is almost impossible to imagine what would have been the course of musical history if "blue" notes had been banned.

It is a commonly claimed myth that music is algorithm. But living music is not incremental with precise, discrete stations, but is built on a continuum. Rhythm and pitch rise and fall with variability. Within this imperfect—but still nonarbitrary and unrandom variety—is where individual expression is found: the one consistently flatted note of a singer, the drummer playing in some "sweet spot" just behind the beat on the snare while simultaneously pushing the kick, or Frank Sinatra toying with micro-time to create an otherworldly and timeless floating sensation, lingering around the brow of each note.

The trick is to play on the edge of wrong in some sort of composed chaos. Whatever notes we can't reach, to at least point to them, to acknowledge that something more might exist.

Rhythm is not only linear, but also has a vertical element. And that is the sway and swing, where the sexiness tends to hide. In that centrifugal motion, like a rider weaving side to side atop a camel. It is there in the hesitations and pushes, without which we would move like robots (. . . or venture capitalists trying to let loose and "get down" at a bro's wedding). It is through the gaps within a pattern—what isn't played, but implied—where we find the space for our bodies to inhabit.

Rhythm has greater depth when it is based on the internal relationships and relativity within the song, and communal music has almost always sped up and/or slowed down naturally as a direct by-product of the emotions being lived moment to moment by the players, as they collectively experience time.

Embrace randomness and "chaos." Celebrate freedom, not precision. Machines are exacting, humans sloppy. But in this unpredictability is where we evolve and flourish. Accidents enable us to try to achieve new things, and generate new paths that can potentially elevate us.

As music making becomes less physical, the dependency on equipment and electricity grows. Historically, musicians create music by the way they touch an instrument—striking, grasping, pulling, sawing, releasing—and these actions can make almost any physical matter sing to some degree, where emotions are radiated through the fingertips.

When we strike something, everything sonically is decided by that one action and moment. It is a hit-and-run. But when we bow and stroke an instrument like a violin or our own vocal cords, there is the potential for continuous, minute changes in even one held note.

It is hard to imagine those who have never made music outside of a laptop screen and keyboard being able to independently generate much natural sound with their primary motion—the tap of a forefinger—except if interfaced somehow.

Since singing and dancing are the genesis of all music, it is an odd development how much music is now made while sedentary, hermited, and in near silence. (I once walked into an early music start-up in San Francisco with around fifty workers crowded at cubicles in an open floor plan, and you could hear a pin drop—a "rock" company that was more hushed than a monastery.)

Furthermore, electronically generated sound does not exist in nature. It can only gain life *through* machinery and remains trapped within the technology, having no independence outside it. And inside that computer, all information is indistinguishable—be it an orchestral masterpiece, a third-grader's essay on carrots, or an embezzler's ledger. It all has been reduced to numbers.

A blackout need not be a soundout, too. In fact, such a time should be when people become *more* vocal, to stave off the dark. If any population's electrical system is taken away for long, rest assured that they will learn to *make* music in astonishing little time. And, similarly, any time lights are unexpectedly cut off, almost always the first reaction are screams into the shadows.

42

Personalities Displacing Spirituality

Recorded music, by literally freezing life, is an act of conservatism. And these conservative units—in exponentially increasing aplenty—position us awash in noise that, for all its bluster, is little more than rote, reinforcement of the "same old, same old." The dilemma is when that investment toward some invisible, eventual audience becomes the sole focus, and nearly all life is drained out of the moment.

Rather than the reciprocity of live-music situations, where performer and audience exchange and influence one another's energy, recordings are made in a vacuum. Taping is an estimate, a projection of something imagined and hoped for, rather than a reaction to something real. And those who are the best guessers often have the biggest hits. (Contrastingly, in the past when crowds called for an "encore," it was a demand for an *immediate* repetition of that exact song. Often, singers would repeat the same tune multiple times, each time with the pressure that they would not replicate, but would top the previous rendition. The goal of live performance was not reenactment, but *reinvention*.)

In a fully participatory music happening, a performer is only as good as the last note out of his or her mouth, or the last song or set. They are forced to live on the ridge of that truth, with it pushing them mercilessly forward.

In the age of auto-tune and lip-synched National Anthems, it is sometimes hard to imagine that there ever was a time not so long ago when artists' careers were at stake if any such falsity was uncovered. But now we live in a post-hi-fidelity age of *stereo*-oids. Stars are made and enhanced through these forms of vocal Botox.

Today, it is almost laughable to imagine that the 1970s chart-toppers ELO's peak was stopped cold by the revelation that they were backed at stadium shows by prerecorded tapes and not an actual orchestra, which was the trademark of their sound. (Was this the first known case of "air oboe"?) This amounted to front-page, international humiliation that altered the course of their career, from playing arenas to crashing and burning. The public was aghast and outraged by the deception, angrily demanding refunds. Audiences back then expected to receive what they had paid for, not a simulation of it, and lawsuits flew back and forth. Such was an innocent and purer time.

A decade later, the European male-model duo Milli Vanilli were stripped of their Grammy when it was later uncovered that they had not actually sang a note on their own record (a controversy that resonated years later with one of the two suiciding). They now look almost like accidental prophets for an era of front-people's truly "fronting" becoming the accepted norm. The stark reality is that we've now reached a point where the vocal skill-set demanded of your average small-town, karaoke-bar patron is far *higher* than for most pop divas and divos, since the amateurs are actually audible.

For decades the primary complaint by fans was that records weren't as good as the band was live, but with the advent of multitrack manipulation it all flipped and live performances became disappointments since they were not as good as the records. And now with digital correction, the wagons have been circled and what is heard live *is* the record, to which the artists dutifully sing along or pantomime to.

This trend has deteriorated to the state of having a pop superstar boast as if it were an unprecedented accomplishment that she planned to "sing a lot of my performance live" during her two-song live set at the Super Bowl. In what other profession would this be possible? An Olympic champion bragging that they would actually be running for *some* of the race? A carpenter boasting about having actually hammered a few nails?

Increasingly, we have performers wearing someone else's voice (e.g., wannabe-thug actors scraping and probing the basement-register, vocal fry of their tone to try to sound convincing), stringing together cliches and hyphens as "self"-expression. They are heard by millions, but ultimately matter in no lasting way to anyone, for they do not attempt to speak to *any* specific individual, but to "everybody." They are unclear as to what message they wish to convey, other than that they furiously want to be seen and "matter." It is a superficial basis that cannot penetrate deeply, past the surface.

Commercial singers are, by nature, throwaway and tradable. Cult artists instead are irreplaceable to their followers. That is why many of those with multiple #1 singles often struggle to lure audiences to live shows (and then have to rely on armies of Vegas-y showgirls and pyrotechnics to barely hold interest when they do appear, not to mention casts of thousands being featured in their videos), yet others with no mainstream muscle can grow, over time, to fill arenas, completely under the radar of the mainstream (the Grateful Dead model). This is because people care about what the latter does and don't just merely like some random hook or think that the band are "okay." Iconic artists enter people's hearts *through* their ears, connect, and move them profoundly somehow, an accomplishment that the eyes alone can rarely do (e.g., a supermodel is not likely to ever create a wellspring of mournful emotion, no matter how physically beautiful she or he may be; yet, rare is the person who has not been brought to tears by a song).

One of music's functions is supposedly that of liberation—a heightened form of communication that allows for the expression of thoughts and emotions that are otherwise generally restricted in daily life. By design, it picks up where ordinary speech no longer suffices and has left off. But now, rather than pointing to the possible and helping widen our potential interpersonal vocabulary, redundancy and sameness restrict and limit.

We are fed scraps: pilfered angst, soundtracks for corporate domination. And all the lip-piercings and half-naked, sneering selfies in the world are nothing more than a smokescreen.

What greater act of conformity could there really be than simulated subversion?

Historically, performance always came first. No copy could be made until a seminal musical action occurred. That is why the earliest stars of recording were already firmly established live performers, like tenor legend Caruso. Today, instead often performances must be brought to life after the fact, from pieced-together and doctored, punched-in recordings.

What remains are personas more than people. Live concerts transformed into promotional opportunities, rather than musical experiences. And, instead of creative acts, we are given *re*-creation.

Devotion to superstars is not so different from believing in Santa Claus or Bigfoot. That the peak musical experience someone can attain is to pay hundreds of dollars, just for the privilege of sitting a football field away to watch preeminent specks posture onstage, is a fable.

Contrastingly, authentic emotional experiences are rarely one-dimensional, and are almost always blends of feelings (e.g., anger mixed with fear offset by guilt tinged with sadness, etc.), just as any one note actually is made up of various overtones. Presentational artists offer only a thin veneer—contrived displays of cliched emotional reactions of how they are "supposed" to feel or act. Monochromatic, cartoon versions of a preset role (e.g., a "real" man). Instead, finely tuned actors often "play opposites" and utilize secrets, to provide each moment more unpredictability and expanse. They break patterns, rather than follow them.

True emotion almost always manifests as chords, not melody lines traveling in tidy sequences.

FIELD RECORDING CHRONICLE
ROUGH ROMANIAN SOUL:
THE ORIGINAL COWBELL

> "Tell me which leave it is
> that moves on a tree,
> when there is no wind."

The irony was not lost on me of being steps from Dracula's Castle, during a full moon, while being fed a local diet heavy on garlic. And, when a sweet Transylvanian grandmother cradled my head and petted my hair, and told me she liked me so much she wanted "to eat" me, the choice of words did take one aback.

With vibraphones as the lead instrument, the band Zmeitrei takes its name from legend of a dragon that often fails and is flawed, a more humanized myth.

We recorded at the end of a road so steep the van stalled and barely made the pass. The area is called "the saddle of the out-law," because an eighteenth-century bandit used it as his escape route each time he terrorized the villagers in the valley.

The group wanted to set up in the attic, where they thought the sound was "dead" (. . . and that *that* was a good thing). Instead, we opted for a children's playroom downstairs, amid the toys with the vocal mics positioned so that the singer Paula could look directly out the window at Mt. Omo ("Mount Man," since it is claimed to look like a person lying in repose) as she sang. It is the highest mountain in Romania, and the one from which the purest waters in Europe reportedly spring.

In that room, the pipes from flushing toilets would occasionally flow down from above. But water sounds can be good. They are always "fluid" literally and patterned.

Drums were and are made from animal skin. And, in this case, the percussionist played his own skin (chest), "like the Gypsies do in the villages."

Later we set up in a field with two grazing utters, literally with bells on—the original "I need more cowbell."

Paula and Mihai said they always had a "block" when it came to writing. We experimented with them returning to the back-to-basics of how they'd started the group—as duo, with him on classical guitar. After only a few minutes, they were ready to scrub the attempt to write a new song on the spot. But with encouragement, they persisted. Paula then committed and opened her mouth like a wound. Within ten minutes they had written "I Will Find," which sounds like an instant minstrel anthem. Having claimed to "not be a songwriter," she went on to pen six songs in three days, the melodies pouring out of her.

One of those songs was written, by forcing the "leader" of the group to play blindfolded in a room where he could not hear the band, but they instead could follow him, as a way of freeing up the power structure of how they'd always operated.

Paula is a recovering operatic mezzo-soprano having to "forget how to sing," in order to begin again. "But if you know how to breathe, you can do anything"—so her formidable technique is now enlisted to earthier use.

In an attempt to boost the size of the work force, the Romanian dictator outlawed abortion and contraception in 1966. They even created incentives, where if a mother reached five children, they were given special benefits. And if they produced ten kids, they earned the official title *heroine mother*.

Consequently, scores of offspring were abandoned and put into orphanages. Due to the government lacking resources, the children were housed with the mentally ill and disabled, and subjected to abuse, sometimes chained to cribs from birth.

Paula recalls a childhood of sneaking sips from Coca-Cola bought on the black market in the night, literally making one small, stale bottle last for weeks. And television that broadcast only the dictator around the clock.

Horse-drawn carriages are still a main means of transportation for many. And as a work incentive, many farmers often throw bottles of grappa (i.e., moonshine) ahead of themselves into the field, as a prod to continue harvesting with a scythe until they find the bottle and take another shot as a reward.

Little dogs are nowhere to be found. Farmers value big animals to help ward off bears and wolves. Only usually in cities globally do pets of any kind begin to be brought inside, out of necessity, as the available space shrinks (e.g., there is nowhere else for a Labrador to roam in a studio apartment).

In the village, those who suicide are buried separately, abolished to outside the cemetery in the trees. A deeply religious community, there are five churches for less than one thousand people, and in the Orthodox church, there are designated cantor singers ("dascal" as they are called in the south of the country). So it is little surprise what a rich vocal tradition there is from the community.

43

Self-Sabotage and the Unconscious: Subjectivity's Quicksand

Artists are masters of self-sabotage and habitually are their own worst enemies.

The same feral and often arbitrary sense of invincibility that makes it even possible for an individual to dare put a pen to paper or step onto a stage and be scrutinized acts as double-edged sword that can limit what they are able to actually accomplish.

All such dead ends as these lead back to fear, driven by a need to protect the ego.

A small degree of success, ironically, can limit *greater* success. The desire for continued accolades, of any sort, tends to discourage risk-taking and, despite rebellious personas, artists become stolidly conservative in defending their status quo. (And at the bottom of the cultural barrel, we see unknown, middle-aged holdouts defensively battling for their tiny piece of the pie in local scenes that they have sanctioned as their own.)

The trade-off for *some* success is the issuance of a self-imposed ceiling that cannot be surpassed due to overly referencing idioms and precedents.

A healthier orientation is when we are more stirred by the future—the unrealized possible—than the past. When we listen *forward*. Somewhat paradoxically, our memory actually exists primarily to prepare us *for* the future—what might lie ahead.

Following the bi-revolution of Bob Dylan and the Beatles, where albums versus singles were introduced as the main musical products, the merger of singer and songwriter brought about a level of grandiosity rarely before seen.

The model that . . .

a) The best singer and best songwriter could coincide in the same person (which has about the same mathematical odds as a person with brunette hair being automatically adept at badminton) became the new norm.

b) On the rare occasion that such a gifted person even exists, their talents should *also* be abundant enough to supply not just one amazing song—a wondrous deed in and of itself—but an entire's album worth of material, and in most cases, a body of work stretching out over decades.

. . . is that it completely misses the point that, all other factors being equal, the majority of even good musicians' abilities are just not of that level. Not even close. A Bob Dylan or a John Lennon only comes around ever so rarely. They are mutations, like Shakespeare and Einstein, leaping forth erratically only every so many generations to help the entire species make a giant leap forward.

In my lifetime, I can name near to a hundred songwriters I know of that have been touted as the "next Dylan." And you know how many of them were?

None! (Though some—like Shane MacGowan and Jason Isbell—have been quite good, on occasion, in their own right.)

The "best" songwriters of an era, would usually be more accurately defined as the most-promoted and -distributed quality artist of their time. For every classic song, there is a twin (or quintuplets) lost somewhere inside someone's cranium or fallen on deaf, drunken ears at some local dive. Not to mention, the vast potential that is never given an opportunity to prosper among the 80 percent of the world's population that live in poverty and whose energies are forcibly directed toward the hand-to-mouth grind of daily survival.

Just because someone is lucky enough to have once in a lifetime tapped a vein of the universal hymn and ridden it successfully for three minutes (give or take), should not then vex us with the rest of their dim-dribble aftershocks of output for decades to come. More than gifted, most one-hitters just had blind luck and will never again reach near those same heights. Particularly, since they usually have no clue how they did it in the first place and/or have, through its expression, *already* exhausted the finest articulation of their vision in that one, simple little tune's package. Thus, that one song's power.

But instead, truckloads of self-plagiarism are heaped on the public as if they were the Holy Grail of pop. Fact is, most "songwriters" are more rearrangers than anything else, anyway. They are assembling pieces from existing shards and frames, and then hanging nominally new words on them.

For most great visionaries, their's was an accidental aesthetic. Born out of their own "shortcomings." That is why those purists trying to get to where their heroes did by retracing the same external steps are sleuthing down a dead end.

But the marketplace demands a tag team of the artistically unmerited "next big thing." This is due to there being established voids and slots to keep stocked. The cycle becomes vampiric, needing new blood and the conveyor belt keeps raging twenty-four hours a day. This literally retards progress, warding off change until every existing pocket is fully mined.

Often music as a profession can become like a form of welfare, where performers feel a living is henceforth deserved to them, rather than bowing out honorably, and taking their place at the back of the line along with the rest of us after their halcyon moment has passed. Voluntary self-cancellation of furthering their own voice would be a most courageous act—a graceful bowing-out, an artistic Hari Kari, if you will.

Awards like the Oscar or the Pulitzer would have far greater significance if they *refused* to name a Best Picture every year, but only granted the award on the rare occasion that a work truly called for such mighty of a tribute.

44

The School of *Soft* Knocks

Tip-offs of unseasoned artists are:
1. Becoming married to every idea and not realizing that often the genesis of that idea may just turn out to be the caterpillar to the butterfly, and must eventually be let go of and shed.
2. Not possessing the restraint of allowing ideas to speak for themselves. Every idea is turned up to a conscious level, despite parts often packing more punch if they are left subliminal and enmeshed.

Amateurs hamstring themselves by not trusting audiences. They leave nothing to be revealed. It is akin to soap opera actors who indicate emotions in the way they think they should happen, rather than celebrating the unpredictable outgrowths and embroidery of real experiences. Even the most base terror or erotica practitioners know that a little mystery can be by *far* the most titillating due to its piquing the receiver's interest and harnessing their imagination as an accomplice.

It is the audience that is the final author of any work, anyway. Whatever they think it means, is what has been communicated, regardless of the intentions. The more there is some suspense and the listener can be let in to discover secrets, the more active and engaged they will become as partners in the process.

So often, the song they heard was so much better than what was composed, and due to whatever unmet needs that they have brought to an experience, the show that they witnessed can seem much stronger than that which actually took place.

Do not overemphasize. Invite listeners in with nothing to prove, but instead something to share.

45

Hearing *Lost*

For the most part, with recorded music, people are exposed to idealized sound. Technology allows engineers to micromanage the experience.

With the dawn of the twentieth century, as machinery that ran under its own combustible power was interlaced into our existence, the oscillations of life altered to align themselves with the mechanical and, ironically, the increase in overall volume from industrialization resulted in our being able to hear *less*. Amid the constant cacophony of urban environments, not only have rest and silence been obliterated, but finer details have been lost in a wash of sound. Thus, we tend to use our hearing mostly as a filtering device rather than attending to finer intricacies.

Quite symbolically, many of us—myself duly included—suffer hearing loss *as a result* of the volume of the excess of what we've listened to.

We fell mute before mechanization's grind, silenced by sound. Previously, singing was so important to group labor that not only was singing *not* seen as a distraction from the tasks at hand, it was often *mandatory,* with the best lead-singers being paid more since it was found that workers were usually most productive when the pace was set by choruses sung in unison.

But today, almost all people now emit as a default keynote (i.e., the first note that comes out of their mouth spontaneously when singing) the steady tone emitted by the respective electrical system of their region, a droning that actually helps stimulate a theta brain wave, a trance state in those exposed.

Train rhythms squired jazz into being—as well as easing its diffusion, the telephone's invasiveness facilitated greater fragmentation and abbreviation of social and family life, faster cars propelled rock 'n' roll's birth, and interspace rockets being launched led to more explosiveness.

In no way is sonic manipulation something new. The earliest gramophone users in the late nineteenth century were instructed to point the horn toward the nearest wall to up the bass frequencies, and escaped slaves would speak over pots of water to drown the sound of secret prayer meetings.

But the more that people listen to inauthentic sounds, the more difficult it becomes to articulate genuinely *and* even to be able to detect genuineness. As a corresponding measure, as a culture grows more synthetic, the more that the tags "natural," real, and organic get used as a selling point to mask the artificiality. Gestures are reduced to formalities and lip service triumphs over simple, unpracticed, and spontaneous nonverbal or vocal emotional expressions.

Chosen sounds best not exist to hypnotize, but to awaken us from our stupor and heighten our senses.

46

"Free" Samples?

Ever since the advent of the Industrial Age, man's rhythms have been altered to fit machines' dictation. Yet, technology's purportedly labor-saving advantages often prove more labor intensive, such as when it comes to the need to infuse back in a simulated naturalness (e.g., hiss) and believable "disorder" that would have already existed without the aid of these said mechanized advances in the first place. Even when a balanced and believable asymmetry can be achieved after the fact, it will have occurred via calculation and cunning, not intrinsic and spontaneous motivation. It is through this that the creative process has been inverted to where the art begins to serve the appliances, the artist becomes ruled by tools.

A drum machine or click-track are the map and not the territory, to borrow a phrase. They regiment a deathly sameness. It is a perversion of priorities for entire recordings to be built on this faulty foundation—man playing to a machine—and smacks of the illogic of putting the cart before the horse. All the decoration in the world still cannot possibly "shine a turd," as my Kansas kin are fond of saying.

To flip the saying: we should love the playa', *not* the game.

Inflexibility is the hallmark of stasis as well as making a system more prone to trauma since the energy is absorbed and has nowhere else to go. This is why a suspension bridge that swings and bounces and "looks terrifying" can survive an earthquake, but one that is stalwart and strong will often collapse due to its own inertia and lack of accommodation.

Contrastingly, the genes of awesome songs are immutable and the awe cannot be squashed out of them. They can transcend miserable production. In contrast, studio trickery alone cannot entice a listener for long unless there is enough melodic and/or rhythmic meat on the bones.

What mathematicians delete is the disorder and inconsistency that cannot be chopped into sockets, but that makes the functioning of living beings possible.

Heartbeats ebb and flow, and our walking pace may entrain with another's or plateau, but movement inevitably rises or falls depending on the context during different stages of a journey. And what is music, if not a passage? Art played out in real-time and not fixed in place, nor frozen temporally, but unlocked.

Not all things can or should be reduced to mere computation.

The slippery slope is when what begins to be produced is what the technology *allows,* rather than that which is actually possible.

Sampling: The convention of sampling is akin to taking a single photo of a location and deluding ourselves that is the same experience as actually being there. That nearly every musician and engineer is now manipulating sounds from the identical, thin pool of samples only narrows the sonic scope further. And, the result is a slow-onset paralysis, creatively. Or, in the least, a progressive shutdown system-wide.

What is absent are the overtones and the random variables that occur in performance. No two cellos sound exactly the same. They each have their own "personality." And no two cellists produce identical tones, even if playing the same instrument. On top of that, each environment interacts and becomes a partner in the sound—indoors, outdoors, wide, tall, post-rainstorm. And the louder anything is played, the more we hear its overtones. Furthermore, not even recorded sound is ever exactly the same when replayed, as it is affected by its immediate, relocated environment.

Each physical instrument contains its own inert secrets that individual players unlock through their idiosyncratic interaction with it. That's one of the reasons many wealthy and successful musicians amass so many guitars: because they know that they will get at least one good song out of every one of them.

Stored libraries of sound can never offer close to the almost inexhaustible inherent variability of a single handclap. Most importantly, microchip-manipulated sound excludes the bodily exploration of the environment, that in its very physicality, demands greater involvement and commitment of energy by the person (e.g., striking a snare drum with your entire arm or a flailing windmill guitar-swipe). To play good old mechanical instruments, one must dance with the music to some degree and let the body "speak." It is exterior by nature and limits self-absorption and containment. This can stand in sharp contrast to computerized sonics, where statue-like postures and countenances are often only betrayed by the faintest head-bob and/or typing.

Anyone disputing the importance of physical attack to the acoustics of a note must examine the fact that most instruments are defined almost entirely by the onset of their sound—how quick they are to voice—and that if the front of this envelope is clipped, instruments become often indistinguishable from one another.

Music made on computers never enters the air and breathes. It remains strictly confined and is transferred internally, underfoot, by mathematical systems alone.

Samples encapsulate sound. They dumb it down and restrict it, reducing its subtlety in order to manufacture templates in its place, so that these can then be traded and bought and sold. They are the audio equivalent of reductionism, a sonic prejudice that oversimplifies what it allegedly represents. A distant cousin to a racist stating, "I can't tell any of them apart. _____ all look the same."

Undoubtedly, musical tradition has always been based on real-time sampling—a chord progression being recycled *ad nauseum*, an archetypal melody reapplied. What would Nashvillian writing be anyway without turns of phrase?

But similar to puns and parodies, sampling is always feeding off the corpse and fumes of someone else's more direct creative action and labor. By nature, it is cannibalistic and can only result overall in successively diminishing returns. Rather than paraphrasing, it is a direct quote. Relatedly, the word echo itself derives from a mythological figure that was damned to never speak first, but only to repeat what others had already said.

Pop music has gone from copying and homage to, to full-on cloning.

Much of the history of creativity in folk cultures has been the unintentional miscalculations in copying that lead to something altered and new—the painter that thinks he's painting an orange, but due to a deficit in skill, it comes out looking like an apple. Part of the beauty of this are the errors in transmission, the data loss *due* to human error. That is why idiot savants usually cannot ever again even approach their peak work: because they have no idea how it happened in the first place!

The difference with mechanical sampling is that the natural drift from source material is lost. Yet, most lasting epics have actually been great collective ad hoc projects, revised and updated through the ages. There are invariably gradual alterations that occur, both intentional *and* unintended. Computers eliminate those happy, sometimes cosmic, mishaps. And any brief study of history demonstrates that many of the world's greatest discoveries were made by accident, usually when great attention was being paid to something *else*, and through that attention another, even better, thing became recognized. To lock in communication is to lose all other expressions that can only arise from "the wild."

In the highest-end marketplaces, people today still value items that are hand-made, "one-of-a-kind," for no machine can compete with the subtle sophistication of a pair of hands. It can only crudely replicate that which has already been formed.

Loops: They are the embodiment of being stuck and trapped creatively. Not only are they parasitic to a preexisting work, but they also are unable to move forward from themselves and what already exists. So this has led to music that is not only made from a limited number of identically manufactured instruments, but also now has the exact same sounds reused, in lieu of new ones. And then repeated in said songs! (Though ever escalating and in dispute, to date, "Amen, Brother" from the year 1969 has been used on almost two thousand occasions, more than any other recording.)

Samples create an illusion of progress, yet perpetually remain back in the same place. Obviously, there are appropriate applications for this—a metaphor for a basic sensation of a disenfranchised group via a "nonmoving" music—but on a broader level it embodies a culture that is literally feeding on itself. Ideation becomes limited to that which preexists in tangible forms, rather than to whatever else new there is that can be envisioned.

Discontinuous sound: No matter how big the file, digital sound is a string for fragments. What this translates to is a waveform that is different than any other we receive in the natural world.

Analog sound is continuous, an unbroken stream. This is in part why so many still claim its "warmth." It is a direct, uninterrupted transfer of energy, which is retraced by vinyl records as they circle in one continuous wave from the outer to inner rim of the disc.

Digital is an entirely different species. It is fissured. There are holes in what we are hearing, since there are always gaps where parts are missing. The wavelengths end up jagged, rather than flowing. What the ear thus receives is a pattern that resembles a saw, not a line. And its unnatural effects are alien to and tiring on the ears.

With analog, if we choose to use an excess of signal, distortion blossoms. Overtones can take over the sound wave, sometimes even regally. With digital's either-or format, though, there is none of this. Instead, any time there is overload, the signal simply clips or flatlines. Rather than more or too much sound, all details are voided entirely.

Ironically, now after over a hundred years of pursuing cleaner sound, it is common to have more electronic process audible than actual source, and to have noise *put back in*, as with the cliche of scratchy-vinyl being used (second only to microphone feedback occurring in films as the cue for any awkward public speaking moments).

When we compare tape or vinyl to CD, the real issue is quality versus quantity. Digital gives us more *of* less by coagulating certain elements in lieu of others that are skipped entirely. With MP3s, it is a guess made from less than 10 percent of the original information that creates an illusion which we must later sound out.

The irony is that film images have always been chopped—twenty-four still frames per second—an illusion *of* an illusion, that our brain completes. And so it was the analog audio that was used to accompany those sputtering images and provide more texture.

Guitar: As the most overplayed instrument of all time, it would be remiss to not include it here. Similar to the "guns don't kill people, people kill people" argument, any technology can be used for good or be abused. It's all in the hands of the technician, so to speak. But, certainly, the exploration of this instrument's possibilities has neared a point that is close to complete collapse now, and dulling repetition is by far more common than innovation.

The instrument's portability and relatively low cost gave rise to its proliferation as the folk instrument of choice, emanating from seventeenth-century Spain and having its continued popularity to this day. Piano had helped to start the schism socially where harmony could be created easily at home, without the aid of others (e.g., choral singing, string quartets), and guitar furthered the hemorrhage. The highly visual characteristics of the fretboard (i.e., itself a grid) make some choices like hammered-on whole notes at the second fret and scalar walk-downs to open-strings nearly behavioral inevitabilities.

An example of the value of non–mass-manufactured instruments is that the Malawi Mouse Boys were highly resistant to bringing their self-crafted, salvaged-parts, four-string guitar on their first tour of Europe. They were ashamed of it and wanted to play "real" instruments instead. It did not take them but one gig, though, to appreciate that the rudimentary piece of equipment that had earned them so much castigation at home, instead, leant a certain cachet overseas.

Seeing fans line up to snap photos of their handpainted, tree branch "axe" as it rested alone against a wall following their inaugural show only solidified their newfound appreciation of such a dowdy instrument. So much so, in fact, that when we next returned to Malawi, the band had sold most of the western factory-made guitars that we'd given to them as gifts and used the money instead to construct a mini-armory of funky, one-of-a-kind scrap-metal playthings.

Ultimately, any instrument is merely a vehicle, a means to an end.

SECTION VII:

Welcoming Magic: Heeding Wanderlust's Call

47

Following Existing Currents

A s a practice, I do not have musicians wear headphones in the studio. This nakedness besets people to listen in context. Ironically, headphones actually can reduce people's awareness musically.

The players are forced to fall back to old-school technology—gestures, pointing, winks, a nod of the head.

Also, I believe that in whatever manner a band is accustomed to playing, that is how they should be recorded. If they normally sit on the ground, or play Autoharp and sing at the same time, then that is what should dictate. (Otherwise, the foreignness of the proceedings only adds additional disorientation and anxiety, much like when for a special occasion people get a whacky new hairdo or fancy shoes or an outfit of a type that they've never worn before, and then they end up feeling uncomfortable rather than being at their "best," as they'd aspired to be.)

If piggybacking on the existing tendencies and practices is not done, the upshot can be a runaway-train live band sounding as proper as an altar boy on his finest behavior, exhibiting all of the same strained insincerity that happens during posed pictures where people are pestered to stand in a certain way, "*act* natural," and smile for the camera. Without fully thinking it through, we tell each other to "freeze" for photos, as if a pistol has been drawn.

This point was brought home to me again when a group I work with insisted on deviating from their operating mode by no longer playing an instrument whenever they were singing lead. They wanted this change so that they could perform "better" live. But their formerly stellar vocal pitch suffered dramatically as a result of this uprootedness, a shabby new state of affairs that was instantly restored the moment they returned to their usual practice of playing and singing simultaneously. It was like an on-off switch for quality being flipped back and forth.

Certainly, forcing musicians to "hold still" is antithetical to the sense of freedom that is aspired to. And, separating musicians and making them play apart in different rooms is an unintentional case of divide-and-conquer, a pushing away.

This spills over into the recording process itself. Where every player feels they needs their *own* channel (or even *multiple* channels)? What, you can't share?

The act of recording itself alters performance. In the earliest stages, this was due to technological concerns like not standing too close or too far from the microphone or the prohibition against singers being *too* dynamic. Often, musicians were even wheeled back and forth and around the room by "engineers" who were repositioning them on makeshift dollies and rolling them up for each solo, midtake. But even today, in our media-savvy times, people speak differently into a phone than face-to-face. That is why phone conversations in public places often disturb others so much: because the speaker literally is not there, but is projecting themselves somewhere else.

On a strictly practical level, what should not be lost sight of is that being fully ourselves—whatever that may be—is the most reachable goal. We are already "there." It is the thing we are usually best at, to a degree that no one else on the planet can ever have a shot at doing, so precisely. Even the best celebrity look-alikes never quite fully reach their mark, despite all of their effort and straining, and even their sometimes resorting to plastic reconstruction.

The matter-of-fact method is not unlike the Italian neorealist directors of the 1950s, who believed that if the character was a truck driver, then you should simply cast a real truck driver, not an actor. The advantage is that energy is not squandered laboring to enact details that in some people *already* exist effortlessly (e.g., instead of learning and having to think about an accent, some people already *have* that accent). On the other hand, being forced to concentrate on exterior details can actually emancipate rare individuals to get out of their heads and be more expressive, as David Bowie so famously did with his 1970s characters.

In general, it is the rough edges that tend to be glossed over. But it is these things about ourselves that we disown, that actually usually give us our distinction and texture. Recording tends to tame music, to literally bring it indoors, make it stand still, and "behave" rather than bravely wrestle with demons. Then afterward, in hindsight, there is much head-scratching and theorizing about why something is missing. If the bodily attitude of a musician is bored or fatigued, how can invigorating results be expected? Two different "superstars" I know run sprints before going onstage and hit the stage not just warmed-up but "hot" and already oozing sweat from the first song.

Sound itself cannot be stationary. It is always in more than one place at once. It is born to travel. And echo is its shadow.

One of the reasons why songs with matching eponymous dances often become such massive successes (e.g., "Macarena," "The Twist") is that when people involve their bodies, the power of memory and recall increases. If people are moving, they become "moved" and something is bound to change inside them, literally. This aligns somewhat with tales of tribes that force students to stay up for days at a time listening to the same song so that it can then come back to them later—spontaneously, without ever actually having played it—as if always there. Or teachers that sing songs into the mouth of the apprentice or beat rhythms onto their chests.

Bay Area pop-punk producer Kevin Army used to remove all of the chairs and stools from the studio and make bands jump around as he taped them. To dance is to animate sound with our flesh and bones, physical materials which themselves are direct outgrowths of our brain. They are mere tools.

Bono, who's known to have recorded his entire career on the most basic of handheld microphones, reportedly had an intern fired recently for attempting to advise him to not move and use a "better" mic. (There seem to be at least two possible lessons here: First, meet any artist where they are at, rather than trying to mastermind a one-size-fits-all, proper approach. Second, when working with someone of such stature, "yes" and "okay" are probably the most appropriate responses, at least until a whole load of trust has been established.)

Above all, don't try to be good. Don't *try* to be anything. Just be.

48

Put Up, Don't Shut Up

If true innovation were to occur, the entire idea of what is a drum should be inverted. A radical act of creation would be to play everything *but* the prescribed instruments.

Ultimately, *you* are the instrument.

This deeper structure is demonstrated in that microphones and speakers are interchangeable and reciprocal, either one can be used for its opposite purpose—receiving and sending are just two sides of the same coin.

Rather than beat down the same overtrodden paths, all alternative sources could instead be explored. And these are nearly inexhaustible. The recycling of identical patterns—time-signatures, melodies, nonspecific stock-phrase lyrics, sonic settings, and choices—is not only counterproductive for culture, but this repetition is also destructive neurologically by overemphasizing already well-developed pathways in exchange for the attrition of other possible networks. These rubber stamp "creations" limit the imagination rather than aid it and are staunchly conservative rather than celebrating change. We literally use less of our brains when processing the familiar, and instead have renounced cognitive options.

The same formulas get reinforced, and formerly diverse genres entrain to clone-like rhythms and structures, only distinguished by triflings like whether the song is sung in Japanese or if a cowboy hat and faintly mixed fiddle have been added as a cherry-on-top afterthought.

This is a far cry from the musical deconstructionists that fought to break out of the straitjacket of existing harmonic formulas. Rather than liberating possibility and celebrating exploration, the nonlive broadcast system restricts musical expression to correctness—narrowed to a right or wrong way of communicating, lording over the channels of distribution like uptight mavens of etiquette.

The goal is to train our attention *away* from sound that has been bought and sold, and let the world speak openly. To hear more of what is volunteered.

Most new technologies don't necessarily replace preexisting ones. They in fact usually just augment them as yet *another* additional channel. (For example, radio did not kill off phonograph records, as feared; television did not end radio, etc. In fact, in many ways, they've only inflamed one another.) But inevitably they displace and alter the process and interactions for making music or film, etc. Logically, less tangible equipment—like that of digital nature—invariably produces a different experience for the user than something with physical parts, such as "the feel" of a printed book.

Not to sound too haughty, but regularly witnessing adults on public transportation playing retro kiddie games on their phones makes me wonder what "progress" we've really made.

When people begin to move in lock-step, we know that is a precursor to fascism. And, what could be more opposed to the liberatory potential of dance than marching? Imagine how much would be humanity's loss if every culture prepared their meals with the same ingredients. How is not the dominance of misplaced "black" inflections or backbeat-heavy 4/4 time, not at least somewhat the same?

Liberals who reflexively lean on relativism to dismiss these types of concerns sound spookily (and ironically) like global warming deniers. Apologists who reference "it's *always* been that way," recent-history arguments, deplorably bask in their own comfort and staunchness. If one-of-a-kind instruments are increasingly traded for and perish in favor of guitar-bass-drums formats, how can it not be that the audio palette is shrinking, the colors thinned?

Quôć Hùng plays the K'ni, an almost extinct instrument, with which a rare local dialect is spoken through the string and the player's skull acts as the resonator.

49

Beneath the Words

Once a piece of music is sold *to sell* products, its meaning changes to some degree. And if music is fashioned expressly to sell something, then it is marred at its very inception.

The expectation that artists must now be glad-handing politicians and/or organized "business" people with a minute-to-minute mastery of their online avatar defies the history of eccentricity and sometimes downright antisocial behavior that occurs as a by-product—though, not the *cause*, as is sometimes mistakenly believed—of great art.

Sometimes you have to be an "asshole" for your art. To uphold something larger than the demanded nicety of a single cordial moment. I myself have struggled with this, due to having been raised to be a compulsive people-pleaser and caretaker.

There is so much lying in social life, where denial of feelings is almost obligatory. Art is one place we can potentially be direct, clear, and free. Sociality stands as the smallest, but often deciding factor in the outcome of creative projects. An individual being too concerned with hurting an immediate peer's feelings and/or their own fear of confrontation, leads to details being let slide—fear of confronting an intern and asking them to leave the room, if they are superflous and whose leering presence leads a flawed feeling in the work itself. *No one* will remember (or care) if _____ got a bit steamed and bruised from being asked *not* to play on one song, but the resulting ruined or corrupted track, will live on in infamy, as testimony.

During wheelchair-bound artist Vic Chesnutt's first tour, I secured him a gig at a Fresno bar. Using his specially fitted van, he drove himself five hours up the agricultural valley from LA. He then had to be hoisted onto the six-foot-high stage, since the building lacked a ramp or any legitimate accessibility.

As he sat alone, setting up in the dark, a gang of Christian rock frat boys in the back began heckling him and pointing. Vic stopped what he was doing and proceeded to stare the young men down, toking on his cigarette with increasing agitation. After approximately two minutes of this animosity-building exchange, Chesnutt yanked the microphone down to his lips, squinted his eyes, and drawled, "What the fuck are you looking at?" After a moment's shock at having had their bluff so boldly called out, the three strapping young bodybuilders scurried for the door, hurrying to escape a man who was paralyzed from the waist down, had only partial use of his arms, and weighed just over one hundred pounds. That moment gave a whole new definition to someone taking ownership of a stage. The fact that he is one of the most idiosyncratic writers of his time can't be too far unrelated from that demonstration of courage and abandon.

The energy and time that are required to produce one suite, performance, or poem are incalculable. It is the gestation period, more than the act of birth, that often matters. It can take an entire day's energy to cajole some seemingly minor detail into consciousness. Works of art exist as the fruits of entire lifetimes. And the greater the depth of an artist's commitment, the stronger the likelihood that something will have to give way somewhere else in regard to the person's ability to function or manage other areas of their lives well. Many of the greatest vocal performances sound very much like sung suicide notes, a person letting go of their spirit in one last pivot and wave good-bye to this earth.

A stellar example of this is Lorraine Ellison's "Stay With Me, Baby." A diminutive R&B hit in 1966, it stands as one of the most stupendous performances ever printed. It was recorded live, on a whim, with a forty-seven-piece orchestra after Frank Sinatra had made a last-minute cancellation for a session. When Ms. Ellison launches into the final chorus, it feels almost like some form of flight is taking place and she seemingly pours her entire essence, her very being, into those otherworldly three minutes and twenty-nine seconds. That one of the most exposed-nerve, daredevil vocals ever recorded only happened because of a void created due to perhaps the world's most legendary singer having flaked out ("*The* Voice," as Mr. Sinatra is often called) only adds to the aura and irony of it all.

Great performances act almost as holograms or DNA, where the entirety of the person can be found in that lone fragment, revealing a presence that induces vision(s) and is palpable. We should always be able to learn something about the artist, their history, just from the sounds that they share. And, through that, be reawakened to and dazzled by our everyday surroundings and experiences. Instead, too often, pop singers leave no trace.

The most emotionally raw artists often offer themselves up sacrificially. Due to addiction, depression, abuse, and/or other factors, they may have lost hope in themselves, but still not *yet* in the world at large. Their intention is giving rather than taking, like a soldier throwing themself atop a hand grenade before it detonates, in order to shield civilians from the fray.

Acting as spiritual guides, their aim is not "love me." Not even "look at me," but "look *into* yourself." Full transcendence can only coalesce when and if we are able to fully forget ourselves, and become so immersed in a state of transmission that we grow lost within it—to dissolve into a song.

A performer at his best is concentrating a day or a week or years' labor into a single ninety-minute burst. Almost any art worth its salt requires breaking a sweat and a willingness to get dirty in the process, to risk the injuries of being an emotional athlete.

Between takes, Said and Eyadou from Tinariwen let show how exhausting work recording can sometimes be.

50

Breaking Patterns: Creating Creativity

The solution to inertia is action. *Some*thing must be done to unlock the paralysis. *Any*thing is better than nothing, in such cases.

If one is stuck, experimentation is usually better than rumination.

With writers block, maybe it is best to go in a different direction entirely—to look up, around, behind, to chart a new course. Forcing yourself, without stopping, to fill both sides of a sheet of paper as rapidly as possible with an unbroken string of words—throwing logic to the wind—will almost always take us out of our head and to another place.

Painters can try to compose a song. Musicians to make a short film. Novelists to pen haiku. This sort of artistic immigration can be mind-stretching.

It is much easier to continue than begin, so bypassing procrastination's temptations and jumping in *some*where is vital. (And, certainly, knowing when to stop and curb our own compulsion to tinker once the inertia is reversed is its own separate art. Like so many things in life, this hinges on finding and maintaining balance and thereby, grace.)

We have to find some way through, and often inversions are the answer: turning things upside-down or sideways—if it's a loud song, play it softly; if it's fast, try it as a dirge. If you normally sketch with your right hand, use your left.

Similarly, picking up and experimenting with an instrument that you do not know how to play can open new worlds. Forcing yourself to write even a few lines in a foreign (or made-up) language often unveils more unconventional ways of communicating *due* to the limitations.

When space itself is valued, there is more room for contrast—sonic close-ups and long shots. Otherwise, we end up with everything generalized, a head-and-shoulders, low-budget television framing where all elements become generalized.

Attention is best paid to using admixtures of sharp, spike-like notes with smoother waveforms (bowed and sustained versus plucked, struck, or blown tones).

Many people have to write the "rot" out of their system, detoxing from bad or too dominant of influences and concepts. This can literally take years or even decades . . . and sometimes even a lifetime is not enough.

Rather than waiting for inspiration, assigning yourself a time to write every day can produce better results (e.g., the Tennessee Williams approach) or giving yourself an assignment, such as to create twenty new pieces of music in a single day, can often relieve pressure through the absurdity of the demand.

The rumor is that Prince records and completes about a minimum of one new song nightly in his home studio, most of which are tracks that have never been released. And reportedly, he is known to *permanently* erase some of his best work the second that he has finished it. They act as personal artistic exercises (and/or purifications). Such is his courage, commitment, and sense of disobligation.

In place of starting always at the beginning and proceeding only linearly, commence at random somewhere in the middle. This too can be a remedy.

As a point of view to consider, in some music traditions, players synch only at *the end*, not the beginning of phrases, and the rests between notes are the most impregnated with meaning.

Discrepancies are what often make interlocking parts interesting. How is a song punctuated? Where is the homebase that can act as the ever-present and fundamental drone parts do in the Middle East?

Or sometimes, when overdubbing, good results come from someone improvising to a totally unrelated song and then importing that track into a different session to see if anything cosmically coincides. Or if we start by playing along to an existing piece and then keep recording after that song has stopped, it is sometimes possible to find some new, looser pocket in free time. Accompanying a song while it is playing in reverse can also accomplish results that would be difficult to arrive at, if playing "competently." This is not so different from the ancient Samurai tactic of walking backward daily to rebalance energies and sharpen perception.

Arrangement-wise, making the end the opening instead is often the trick, as film-editor Walter Murch so famously did with *Apocalypse Now* (i.e., rather than a crescendo, maybe a decrescendo is called for). As jazz drummers were able to do when they tipped rhythm on its head by moving the beat up, higher to the cymbals and using the kick drum, not for timekeeping, but instead just for accents.

Many people squabble that fading-out or -in a song is a cop out due to not committing to a finished form, but it can be used to create a sense of the eternal, that we are visiting some unending song that seems to be continuing on in a distant, parallel place without us.

And, whenever in doubt, cut. "Less is more," as they say. The letting go of attachments to what something is, can in and of itself be freeing. In fact, true mastery is the ability to *intentionally* reduce what we do, to shape it by choice. To be capable of more strength, but to apply it only as appropriate.

Creating even the slightest asymmetry in a pattern—dropping one random note occasionally—often enlivens the whole. The absence refocuses listeners. These little surprises and rewards to attention can keep people guessing and wondering.

The attempt is to build a sonic architecture, a structure for the listener to enter and inhabit.

In terms of frequencies, what is most commonly missing are space and respite, to allow the ears time to rest and cleanse. As far as the range and spectrum itself, adding even a single upper-register instrument (e.g., a triangle hit) to dense low-end mixes can massage the brain and reawaken awareness. It helps reset boundaries, widens the frame of reference, and literally lifts us out of the bulk of midrange clustering.

When someone is talking, the modulation rate is about four or five changes a second. But when someone is screaming, it can leap to in excess of one hundred changes a second. These emergency communications use a specialized patch of the soundscape to create "roughness" that demands our attention, a communicational sphere that is not otherwise utilized. The key with storytelling is contrast and build. If a singer does nothing but yell, they have painted themselves into an expressive corner to which we gradually acclimate and the firepower is deflated.

Actively brainstorming the most ludicrous solutions and welcoming any and all suggestions challenges our minds and recasts the scale of what is possible. (This technique of "entertaining the absurd" is also a primary antidote to depression. Similarly, a treatment for paranoid people is to encourage them to try to act as "ridiculous" as possible in public and consequently experience how little most people even notice or care.)

Some other experiments: Try detuning instruments. Or reducing the number of strings from what is stock or stripping away drums to their most *non*essential elements. Even changing keys chromatically, one half step, song to song can alter the attention of the listener. Anything to break and shake up the existing pattern.

Brazenly seeking out things which run counter to our beliefs and preconceptions, such as watching a puff-piece rom-com or engaging an opposing political party member in courteous conversation can also aid our cerebral flexibility.

Our entire nervous system is wired to find novelty, to notice anything new and ignore whatever is present and constant. The reality is we can adapt to almost anything that doesn't actually kill us, and no species is more adaptable than man: that is how we've come to proliferate and dominate almost every corner of the earth, no matter how frozen or sweltering.

Humility ceases whenever curiosity ends. One of the greatest wonders of our brains are their plasticity. We best live to, rather than fear, have our mind changed. A most fluid approach is to strive to be an eternal novice, ever eager to be wrong, and learn or relearn lessons.

Life is improvisation. Survival is adaptation. When imbalances occur, the world cries for correction. And when not listened to, it screams!

It can be powerful to refrain from speaking entirely for at least a day—a verbal fast—and (re-)discover how much is foreign, within arm's reach.

51

It's All in the Details

It is imperative to know who we are singing to. A truism is that immature singers scream what in real life would be murmured or whimpered (e.g., in nonstaged life, "I love you" is usually more of a plea than a demand).

Yes, performers often act out other people's id symbolically, but a better guide is to sing as we would speak words conversationally and not assume a different vocal affectation once the music starts. And, above all, to always put communication first, ahead of technique or concepts. Understatement is the Trojan Horse that people will almost unfailingly allow in, whereas being railed at is something that, for most, is repulsive. Great singers, rather than gushing, usually hold back some reserve. They "give all they can," but don't overreach for *more* than they can.

A trick of many great live performers is to pick one face in the room, even if it is an audience of tens of thousands, and sing just to them all night long.

Once artists begin to write for abstract "fans" rather than speaking directly to some*one*, their sales may increase, but their communicational abilities suffer.

They are aiming for a "mass audience." Literally, an undifferentiated mass.

Details are what seduce people—the clincher in their decision to buy a house is often something irrational and minor, but memorable to that buyer, such as having aqua, art-deco light switch covers in every room, or a person becoming fond of a town due to its one tree-lined block or a fountain or corner café near the city center. Similarly, what catches a listener might be the snag in someone's vibrato or the way two players dovetail around each other, both teetering on the age of fracas, but then pulling together just at the exact moment where they would have crossed a line into clear off-ness.

Joe Henderson related that he imagined having a conversation when he played, and a telling ritual of saxophone jazz great Dexter Gordon was to recite beforehand the entire lyrics of each ballad he was performing. Even though he was playing only instrumentally, he still absorbed the meaning of the accompanying text before attempting to transduce it.

And, sometimes refusing to reply at all can communicate quite fervently, as anyone who has ever suffered the "silent treatment" from a partner (. . . or an audience) knows all too well.

Often, the challenge is to tune out the loudest, in favor of seeking the meeker and more hidden offerings. As psychologists often advise—if you see someone from across the room and it's love at first sight: RUN!!!

52

Connectivity Through Sonics

Trying to help provide a soundtrack (versus mere background ornaments) for a person's life is a massive responsibility. Historically, in preliterate cultures, songs often were a primary means of preserving and passing down vital information in lieu of writing. And, music has throughout time been used to synchronize people's movements, labor, and feelings.

A brain's power is not measured by its size, but by its level of connectivity (e.g., someone with a big skull is not necessarily the brightest, and women routinely have more balance between the brain's two halves via more developed corpus callosums). Part of music's specialness is that it stimulates the mind on multiple levels and simultaneously in diverse regions.

One of the most robust aspects of memory is our ability to concoct meta-memories, memories *about* memories. (Further, many people's childhood recollections emanate *from* photos of their childhood, not the actual moment that the photos were taken.) Classic songs often serve the function of organizing time and emotion, with each listen creating and stimulating multiple layers of experience.

People will rarely reread even a favorite novel once or watch most films more than a time or two, but there are many songs that most of us have heard literally thousands of times in a lifetime—often *against* our will.

Hooks for some songs act as centers—instant orienting devices—that then generate an almost immediate nostalgia by way of their repetition ("Hey, I remember that . . . I just heard it thirty seconds ago."), and then take root in their host. We tend to be attracted to consistent, recurring patterns since they indicate life in much the same way that a baby bird's chirp does or wind and waves. And these things with easily definable structure are easier to process. Silence, contrastingly, indicates danger or lifelessness.

Though any single piece of recorded material itself remains consistent, the changing contexts it shares accumulate as it runs like a thread through people's lives, acting as a guardian to their existence—sometimes being summoned on command, and at others, popping up unexpectedly. And, what that song then triggers is a multisensory experience (smells, locations, etc.) that can span decades, or even back to infancy. When an auditorium full of fans pump their fists in the air to a band's signature song, a transparent circuit of connectivity is lit up invisibly, more elaborate than any laser light show.

Some songs have accompanied people their entire life, outlasting almost every other relationship, and often being the last remaining thread to a portion of their past, with even the senile sometimes still remembering snippets of songs (with music now having been scientifically proven to help counteract the ravages of Alzheimers far better than any chemical combo yet in existence).

53

Say It Loud, Say It Proud

To listen is to exist in anticipation, at the edge of discovery—our pulse modified by the action—with renewed hope, awakened from emotional hibernation. Preternatural songs are the peculiar ones that remind us that we exist, spurring us to remember this confusing miracle that we live daily.

Sound does not preexist, stagnant and waiting. Instead, it occurs and then departs, a sanctified event that returns us to eternity.

Timbre itself—the fingerprint of a sound—enfolds diversity, creating unity amid disparate elements, and from them shaping something new. And it is from voices which have been vacated, ignored, or discarded that the cornerstone of a true counterculture can be laid. Creativity not born out of reactivity to something already in existence, but instead from its own cloistered paradigm.

54

Castaway

True dialogue is not making love *to* someone, but *with* them.

Today, instead of the call-and-response vocal tradition, we are left with all call and no response. What is missing is the relationship. What is forgotten is that the entire vocal medium is designed as a way of spreading information (as whales and many birds do across vast distances), of relating something particularly meaningful. *So* meaningful, that it is worth raising our voice and reaching out for.

At worst, solo multitrack recording can be akin to a psychotic talking to themselves. The person is playing with and to themselves. It can end up being a sonic manipulation disconnected from the heart (. . . and admittedly, that is not always bad, *either*. Certainly, there is a place and time for cerebral music, too. Contrastingly, at its best, music made in strict isolation can be a form of meditation and introspection, of silent reading.).

But most live performances now are simulations of a document of something that in fact *never* happened: which means a group of people playing the exact same parts together in real time. (And, again, this way of recording is not "wrong." It just should not be the *only* way. Right and wrong are not the issue here. What matters in the end are the results.)

This is not to be misconstrued as saying that one of the beauties of recorded music is its ability to expose the interested to a much wider range of sounds than previously possible, as well as enabling artists to create works of a level of complexity that would otherwise not be possible.

Everything need not be a sketch. Certainly landmarks such as "Sympathy for the Devil" and "Like a Rolling Stone" testify to the benefits that can come from multiple drafts and "writing is rewriting" transubstantiation.

Neurologically, music making is decentralized. It cannot be tracked in the brain to any single spot. It literally comes from some other place. What matters is the connectivity, the mongrel pathways that are forged within, as the music flows into, out of, and between each one of us.

Plug-in a microphone or a DJ mixer and you are not coupling machines, but people together (…while often simultaneously repelling select others, as well).

At its best, music is an empathy-building action. It helps develop our heart as the major organ of receptivity, displacing the tyranny of our eyes and flesh. For what good is sight if our minds are already closed? To feel the music beneath our feet is an almost moral action, to use our entire body like an ear. It helps fine-tune our emotions.

But, increasingly, music is hijacked to promote superficiality, ego, and unreflective "thinking."

Music at its best helps people to be more objective, *not more subjective*, and assists them in coping with reality—through *temporary* escape—with a net result that grounds them, instead of inducing ever-escalating delusion. Otherwise, we are left with the self-exoticizing, fictionalized versions of our own daily lives, a trap that we all risk slipping into, if we aren't mindful.

55

If You're Not Having Fun, You're Not Fooling Anyone

We are not really ever playing music. It is playing us. What is often left out is just that: to be *playful*. Many jazz musicians have a wicked sense of humor that they demonstrate with moments of musical comedy—through juxtaposition, off-kilter homages, and by simply doing the unexpected. These moments are lost, though, on many of their pretentious adherents, who are there only for "serious" music.

Actors are often instructed to touch things continuously as a lifeline to believability and to eat during scenes for groundedness (i.e., since if you are really eating, then—everything else aside—you *are* doing something verifiably real). Similarly, the surest way to release tension is not by denying it, but vigorously acknowledging its presence. Not the reflexive "I'm fine" and "_____ doesn't bother me," but instead, "I am scared *shitless* right now."

Many buy into the conceit that force and agony are *necessary* to create. But instead, relaxation is the key. To find a flow and take the ride.

The Zomba Prison posse strikes some poses.

56

Home Base

Similarly, it is usually best to record around people that one is comfortable with and in spaces that speak to you in some way. Music comes from a place. If the inside of a studio in London is indistinguishable from one in Louisiana (as most studios usually are), then who really gives a fuck about their 20K pre-WWII German microphone.

Even if we examine these issues on a strictly technical level, the fact is that no decent studio anywhere builds recording rooms with parallel surfaces. You can't box in sound, it must at least be oblong, by design. (Even if one does ever have the good fortune of gaining access to world-class equipment, it is amazing how frequently people then unintentionally degrade it by processing it through some inferior, minor piece of equipment—a vintage mic run through a cheap and shitty compressor or cable. Better to just let the monster gear do its thing, unabated. To leave it alone.)

When you live in a hut you can't have a "garage band," only front yard yoddlers. It is cultures in decline that incarcerate noise. My own teenage band was shut down by a deaf-in-one-ear, former WWII artilleryman, who'd long before been a jazz drummer, but had literally forgotten how to "play."

Set up outdoors or somewhere with wood, stone, and/or an exterior view. Then let the life in.

Allow the music to be of this world.

An aerial view of the camp where Tinariwen's Grammy-winning "Tassili" album was recorded, in southeast Algeria near the Libyan border, just months before the Arab Spring.

SECTION VIII:

How Not to Memorialize Music

57

A Few "Don't" Champions
from My Past

To hear a Parisian engineer repeatedly screaming "Silence!" (which came out as "see-*lance!*"), without any hint of irony as to the contradiction between his own behavior and the word he was using, is something that will ring in my ears, seemingly forever.

And isn't commanding a group of musicians to be quiet such an odd objective to begin with?

Similarly, I remember recording my first album and the engineer interrupting constantly with a "No, no, no. No!" mantra. That sort of stop-shame-start-stop cycle did little to foster my getting into "the zone" that he'd claimed existed.

That I had made the mistake of working with him because he had a sixteen-track versus the smaller eight-track machine of a much more sympathetic producer acted as a punishing comeuppance to grasping the importance of not confusing technological priorities with aesthetic ones, and to try to always keep an eye on what the larger intentions are.

I returned one morning and neither I nor the artist could figure out why something now seemed to be missing from the cornerstone piece of the album. We were so convinced that we'd previously been experiencing a mutual delusion and had deceived ourselves as to the song's potency, that we began to discuss scrapping it entirely or starting from scratch, even though we had only days to deliver the finished album.

We came to realize soon enough that the methed-out, top-tier mix engineer had "fixed" the end section of an epic song. He had moved and aligned every single note of a raucous gospel rave-up onto a grid, and drained that passage of all of its life.

He'd completely disregarded that people almost always speed up when they are excited and their voices almost always rise in pitch also. The tone becomes more tremulous (i.e., vibrato) then, too, usually as a side effect of the adrenaline.

It is syncopation that keeps us guessing and listening and *feeling* the beat, rather than "knowing" where it is. Without that, our attention easily wanders, which is exactly what so much commercial music does—helps people to "zone out" rather than "zero in."

Asymmetry is intriguing. That is one of the reasons that few things captivate as much as the human face, since all of our faces are lopsided, with the right or left being the shrunken or swollen versions of its twin.

Tales of bands equalizing differently every note of a song or punching in each vocal word by word (or even syllable by syllable) smack of the obsessive-compulsiveness that is born of fear and neurosis, but tends to hide instead behind a charade of being a good "work ethic."

Internal complexity—an oblong stanza, a hesitation before a note—lends tension that suspends people into states of anticipation.

When a soccer-hooligan band member refused to sing live off the same microphone as his "favorite mate," it was clear to me that their division from each other would also set up barriers between the band and the audience, and that their efforts would wither on the sending side of the footlights. To watch them fall flat repeatedly, but never address the underlying issues and deal with their own intimacy, was telling.

The fact that engineers' main ability to communicate with musicians while recording is through a "talkback" microphone carries much of that term's baggage. And, that even in the most well-stocked studios, the mics used for this task are usually of lousy quality—so much so that they would not be thought of being used even at a public school assembly or for any other purpose in that same studio—clearly demonstrates the low priority that communication with the artist is given.

For me, whenever possible, I stay in the same room or area as the band, so that we can speak or gesture directly. An additional problem with any physical distance or barrier between people is that it forces one to be louder in order to communicate and this can easily lend itself to it unintentionally seeming angry or making it seem that irritability is present, when it is not. It is patently difficult to achieve rapport across obstacles, walls, and distance.

Too many are the stories of star producers whose shadow never darkened the door of sessions except to collect their paychecks—instead, having their henchmen execute their directions—or, at the other extreme, musicians scrambling to make changes every time a fascistic figure stepped out to the bathroom or for a smoke.

At one of the most famed studios in LA, I instructed the engineer to record *every-thing*—to not stop rolling the tape ever, unless explicitly told to do so.

It became clear that the scale the studio staff were used to working at was one in which many days were usually spent just tweaking a cymbal sound, so these "experts" moved at a snail's pace. The higher the hourly rate, often the slower people operate (and, relatedly, the more you're paid, the better people treat you usually. Which should be contradictory actually. And never is there a risk of being treated *worse* than when doing something for free.). To them, recording was always undertaken as an arduous and prolonged affair.

Later, when the artist was midway through a spot-on take of a seven-minute opus that was the pillar for the whole album, the engineer sheepishly turned to me to confess that he had failed to record any of it. I already knew more or less what the aftermath would resemble: seeing a man in his late fifties shatter his guitar against the meticulously prepared acoustic walls and storm out into the alleyway, refusing to return.

The methods of that Frankensteinian and wasteful world crystallized when that same engineer proudly recounted to me how the studio blocked out that same room for two years, with two engineers waiting there on standby nightly, every day of the week, only to have the artist *never once* step foot there. To be clear, this was at a cost of over $2,500 daily, totaling around two million dollars overall, to *not* ever record one second of music.

When the owner inquired later how things were progressing during another project, I was a bit tickled to inform him that with one of his former clients, we had recorded an entire double-album in one afternoon (a true story), writing the bulk of the songs on the spot, to boot. The greatest layer of the story, though, was his dismissiveness and utter unwillingness to believe that this was so.

At one of my first mastering sessions, the legendary figure at that establishment refused to acknowledge any of my input. The only seating for guests was on a low-rider couch behind him, as he helmed from an elevated throne housing his labyrinth of dials and faders. He sat with his back to me the whole time and kept muttering, "That's not right."

He monitored the music at ear-bleeding volume and when he was done at last, swiveled around in his deluxe rolling chair and smiled, "*Now* it sounds like a 'record.'"

What he had succeeded in doing was transmogrifying the deliberately pinched bongo sound into timpanis. And he'd turned a ukulele into something closer to a harpsichord.

He clearly took the "master" in mastering a little too literally. But for me—a bashful teenager—what I took away was an expensive and unintended lesson: to work with people who were open and kind, more than proficient, and also to always maintain a clear understanding about who is paying whom.

(Relatedly, as an aside, a good test of the balances of any mix is to play them as quietly as possible, on the shoddiest speakers that can be found—or even reduce to just mono—and see if it all holds up and communicates at even the lowest levels.)

An anal-retentive young artist once insisted on a record being entirely re-pressed in order to turn up the background vocal 1/4 db (!) on the second verse of just one song. To illustrate more luminously, he spent thousands of dollars to make a change that is scientifically imperceptible to the human ear—analogous to swapping out a 50-watt bulb for a 51-watt one (if such a thing even existed). But, self-fulfilling, it was all worth it to him.

He insisted, "Now it sounds *right*." (There's that troublesome word again.)

Though not a deception that I endorse, this sort of neurosis on the part of performers is why many engineers often pretend to make changes that they have not actually done, just to see if the musician even notices *and* in order to appease those who invariably contend something is resultantly "better," even when unchanged.

This is similar to why so many mix engineers insist on having no one from a band present while they work, since if the musicians were there what inevitably happens is that every last one of them advocates for more of themselves, and the entire thing just gets louder and mushier overall. (Consequently, some engineers *are* willing to have musicians present while they work, but charge substantially more for "attended" sessions, due to the extra work and stress that they unerringly bring.)

It was in the ancient cemetery where Edith Piaf, Chopin, Proust, Oscar Wilde (. . . and, yes, Jim Morrison, too) are buried that we were almost arrested for recording among the tombstones and trees. We chose the location for symbolic reasons, but also due to its being one of the only relatively quiet spots in the middle of chaotic Paris. The armed park-officers detained and questioned us for many minutes, even temporarily confiscating the equipment to review footage.

That upon exiting afterward, we witnessed a woman being maced and mugged on the sidewalk bordering the graveyard while the attacker managed to escape uncaught after knocking the woman to the ground—the back of her head slamming into the pavement—just minutes after we were being kicked out for "disturbing the peace" *of the dead*, only reinforced the often sad irony of police priorities.

In the Sahara, the permeation of the entertainment-merchandising complexes' influence was clear not only by the way that a person sang or played, but even by the way musicians held their instruments, their facial expressions, and their poses versus ease. It was almost instantly apparent who had spent time in Europe and/or the United States, and who had never left home. Many of the expats—minus a turban or if you listened with eyes closed—uncannily resembled the endless stream of lukewarm participants that afflict every open-mic that's been hosted anywhere in the states or United Kingdom since 1963.

Also, the recordings of the more polished came drenched in echo—the bigger, the better syndrome—instead of simply letting their voices speak for themselves. Like plastic-surgery-addicted trophy wives, too many musicians now "fix" every broken note and squeak, elements that were in fact maybe the *only* thing that made them interesting to begin with.

We watched aghast from the next room as the bandleader stood over the drummer, his crotch literally inches from the drummer's face, shouting, "Again. *Purr*-fect! Now try it again." This went on for hours, this game of interruptus. The same three seconds being drilled. The distinction of one take to another apparent only to him.

The words he spoke when he finally relented still resonate with me: He confided conspiratorially, "It just didn't have enough life before. It sounded too forced." The drummer threw himself on the couch, spent after that marathon of minutiae. It was no shock when he quit the band before the record had even been released.

The leader had bought into the slogan "no pain, no gain" as an inevitability. He'd not learned the art of letting go of that which we can never even hold to begin with, and the truism that if performing doesn't feel right, it usually won't sound right either.

Too often "the best" studios resemble nothing more than fallout shelters or crypts.

This is why I prefer recording outdoors. Or to choose a studio proper that at least has one window, if not *many*. And to open doors whenever possible and let a little light—and the world—in. Rather than working from what appears to be a bunker, the ideal is to seek out a place that has meaning personally for the artist (e.g., the house they grew up in) and whose specialness shakes and reawakens their outlook.

You want some "headroom" sonically? Go outside. You'll have the whole *sky*. (*Headroom* is a term engineers often banter about, to indicate a sense of air in a recording by allowing—as cushion—a mostly unused sonic space in the highest frequencies.)

When recording in the open air, a little grit always finds its way into the music somehow, one way or another. And, *usually*, that is a good thing.

58

Some Notes From the "Do" Files

A veteran star of over fifty albums, the artist confided in me that what he "hated" about recording was all of the twiddling and setup, and what bothered him most was singing with people on the other side of the glass.

The solution seemed easy enough to me. I taped over the control room with a blanket, so that no one was staring back at him, invited a bunch of his friends to sit in the room with him, and handed him a guitar the minute he walked in and then hit record. The entire album was done in a matter of hours this way, with him and me sitting knee to knee. Amid this relaxed environment, he played many songs he had long ago forgotten.

(This is not unlike a grizzled R&B producer who said he often bribed hobos to sit in the isolation booth. That some of the most sensuous, sex-you-up vamps of all time were sung to drooling, passed-out winos is not an image that's all that easy to shake.

By the way, "Isolation booth"? There's another nakedly contradictory concept.)

A young band was being funded by their millionaire leader who'd made his fortune at the dawn of the snowboard industry. The hiccup was that though they had spent nearly $100,000 overdubbing to a click-track in the "hottest" studio in town, they were unhappy with the results.

I asked them how they normally played, and they said, "Well, we all sit around in the kitchen and drink Budweisers."

So, no punchline here, I recorded them essentially doing just that. Over the course of two evenings, their entire debut album was finished, and later released to quite a heap of critical acclaim.

A questionably talented songwriter once, in a moment of frustration after hitting a creative wall, turned and began to serenade her cat. It was the most wide-ranging and adorned melody I'd ever heard her sing. Despite intense incredulousness and protest, she agreed to record it "with prejudice." It later went on to become the most beloved tune of her devoted fanbase.

An artist from a successful band reluctantly agreed to do a solo record. Very thoughtfully, he was concerned that by making more output, he was just going to be unnecessarily "adding to the human debris."

The first night in the studio, I witnessed him noodle on a banjo for five hours, warming himself to the new room. I had to literally obstruct the doorway to keep the overcaffeinated, in-house engineer from intruding so we could "stop wasting time and get started." That the artist is not a banjo player, doesn't play it all that well, and that banjo was not going to be on the record even, is of particular mention here.

What was important was the artist's process. In the long run, this proved hours well-spent, though, as once he'd reached the headspace where he was at ease, he became like a tidal wave, with ideas and music pouring out of him for twelve hours at a time, with not so much as a pee break. He had that razor-like focus that many overachievers seem to share.

To each his own, as they say. The most egregious gaffe is when a "one-size-fits-all" model is applied, especially with someone who is quite singular and quirky—and it was those very traits that attracted them attention to begin with.

Sainkho Namtchylak, the world's leading female throat-singer from Tuva, engages in her own masked artistic process.

SECTION IX:

Enlisting Limitations as Expressive Partners

59

Trained by Fire, On the Chopping Block

Arguably, no single musical instrument ever made has changed music as much as the invention of multitrack recording.

A paradox of all options is that as they multiply, it can be a case of diminishing returns. The more plentiful they become, the more overwhelming they can be, which consequently can lead many to then make no choice at all.

Those of us who were taught the ropes back in the dark ages with predigital equipment can take some comfort regarding the countless lost time executing tasks mechanically with tape, film, or paper, that can now instead be done in mere seconds (and with unending possibilities for reversibility and do-overs). We can at least try to believe that, experientially, we gained some deeper understanding of an overall process through these flagellations.

It best be borne in mind that before the 1950s all commercial recordings were mono. Singers and symphonies played together simultaneously.

This demanded focus and meticulous planning. There was no safety net. Forethought was headmost. The dark side of multitrack recording is that it can create a wishy-washy approach. Yes, freedom is a good thing, but at some point so is commitment. Even *more so* really, since ultimately that is what a recording is about: fixing something into a single, chosen finalized state.

It is hard to make a strong case for surmounting the pristine quality of recordings like Miles Davis's *Sketches of Spain*, that was recorded in a single, giant room (Columbia Studios in Manhattan), or at the other, grimier end of the sonic spectrum, the Chess singles which were done on only two-tracks, or the seminal Elvis Sun Studio sessions that were done on just one-track (in a room that Sam Phillips intentionally designed to be *more* reflective, so that there would be greater bleed between instruments, and not deadened as is the modern studio standard. And isn't it sufficiently blatant how misguided it is as an objective to construct a "dead" room in the first place?).

In the early to mid-1960s, three-track (!) recording was all the rage. But even then, Phil Spector still mixed those three measly tracks *back down* to mono, so that he could act as control freak for the listeners' experience (i.e., by his doing this, the mix would remain the same regardless of how many speakers it was listened through. He was actually withholding technological progress from the audience, preventing his singles from being panned and altered.) And, almost all of the Beatles groundbreaking work was done on only four-tracks.

John Golden, who has been mastering records for longer than almost anyone ever—fifty years and counting—worked for decades cutting vinyl lacquer-discs that had to be done unerringly in one pass or else thrown away at more than one hundred dollars a pop. That sort of painful exercise forges a very particular laser-like level of concentration, in almost direct counterweight to the fragmentation of consciousness encouraged by the Internet.

A mentor of Grammy-winning mix-engineer David Odlum (who himself comes from a family line of Irish producers, with a brother whose first word from the crib was reportedly "amp"), apprenticed for decades in a Midwest studio that was a bit of a sound factory, booking *two* back-to-back, eight-hour shifts daily, during which time an entire *finished* record—from setup to tracking and overdubbing, plus mixing and breakdown—was expected to be totally completed before the allotted time expired or else you would be terminated. That kind of trial by fire provides a level of training that is hard to mimic.

Planning, thinking on the fly, and just plain "knowing your shit" were mandatory. All the attitude, dumb luck, and connections in the world could not cloak deficiencies that would disclose themselves glaringly in less than a half-day's time.

One of the accidental side effects of physical records is that they literally limit what one can store (approximately twenty minutes a side), and this imbues a serious investment toward releasing only the best material, rather than the exhaustive lack of restraint that CDs and the Internet indulge. Does the world really need another covers record by an underground band leader's offshoot of a side project?

Examples of converting obstacles inside out are guitar legends like Django Reinhardt, who due to being badly burned had only two fused and *partially* functional fingers on his left hand, or Sonny Sharock who switched to the instrument not by choice, but only after asthma prevented him from pursuing saxophone. A personal example is an amazing harmony singer I know, whom I discovered years later had achieved a certain froggy character of tone—that he later was unable to reproduce—due to having had a cold during the days that we recorded. This illness had caused him to sing "better," since he had little choice but to submit.

60

What Do You Know?

A truism is to "write about what you know." The greater the detail and specificity, paradoxically—due to that very precision—the more galactic the impact spiritually. To extend this line of thought, potency is usually greatest when someone "sings about who they are" (instead of pretending to be someone else). This is much in the same way that you are more likely to get help in a crowd by pleading directly to any one individual rather appealing to the group at large, whereby the responsibility is diffuse and detachment normalized.

Not even the most blissed out and daft fan believes that Springsteen worked in a factory. But, having grown up with an often-unemployed father in a working-class district, Springsteen's words were formed from being a firsthand witness, not hearsay. And through the heightened observation of others, music can build empathy not just for the listener, but also the artist. By forcing them to lean in, look more closely, and learn.

61

Imperfect Pitch: There Are No Mistakes

A common refrain from musicians when recording or performing is, "I can't hear myself!"

Yet, more than hearing the sound they are making, what really is most needed is to *feel* it, on all levels. More than trying to control the outcome, the goal can be one of freeing the sound that already exists within.

The answer usually is not being able to hear ourselves perfectly, but developing the ability to converse *responsively*, which is not possible without closely listening to the other parties.

When someone is stirred emotionally you will usually hear it in the voice—"downstairs," beneath consciousness—before it is, if ever, revealed in words.

For instance, a change in volume or vocal force will almost always precede verbal abuse.

Punched-in, piecemeal recording has led to the elevation of the a cappella, car-singers. When it comes to a stylist like Mariah Carey, her performances can be so out of synch with her surroundings that it is as if her part has been grafted from an entirely different tune, as disjointed as if arising from unrelated tempos and keys. Even more telling is whether an individual's performance is integrated within their own bodies: does their musical phrasing and bodily movements/gestures synch?

Most modern duets seem more like duels, where the singers are singing not with, but *at* each other. When art begins to be pitted as competition and capitalism fuels an arms race for attention, then a compulsion is born to distinguish, not through nuance, but by sheer, unmotivated amplitude and *over*emphasis.

We are left with only the decorative aspects of singing—all glissando and grace notes (which are in actuality usually more like grace-*less* or disgrace notes), filigree without a core.

The plague of Janis Joplin-itis still haunts us, all pulmonary punch and hollow heart (. . . an affliction that has been known to be near fatal, by the way, both to the performer and listener).

Sonically, modern records are compressed, almost literally, to death—raising higher both the floor *and* ceiling, as well as bringing them closer together overall—which flattens the dynamics and contrast, so that the music screams for attention with a sense of "on"-ness, *even* in the quietest moments. There is no journey, festering, development, or crescendo. There is only one continuous peak. It's as if audiences are no longer trusted, but dictated to, with the greatest care given to some imagined lowest common denominator. The end result has all of the sledge-hammer subtlety of a TV sitcom laugh-track.

Yet, faith should be placed in "audiences." They rise to the occasion for the rare instances when something of quality like Nirvana or a low-budget film like *Once* somehow squeaks through and reaches more people, more easily. Almost all individuals hunger to learn more about their world. They are driven by a desire to improve their life, when and if ever more easily offered the chance.

62

Gauging the Atmosphere

Is a sound wet or dry? Ironically, warm climates may actually drain energy from residents, much opposed to the stereotype of hot-bloodedness. And isolated communities may seek connection, whereas those from a densely populated area may come to use music as demarcation devices.

Those from heavily forested spaces tend to be more ear-oriented due to the lack of sight to navigate the terrain. While those from open plains often use music to bridge distances. And nomadic tribes usually favor small instruments that they can easily carry, thus, their music usually eschews bass drums and other low-end instruments that require larger surfaces.

Cultures that are not straight (i.e., circular) usually have music that reflects that as opposed to being boxed-in and -up. Conversations there tend to not cut to the chase, but amble. And, thereby, variations are not made up of violent shifts, but gradual, almost imperceptible alterations. Rather than straight-line thinking, information tends to be processed and revealed in layers.

In environments without electrical lighting, among populations that have lower rates of literacy and therefore more dependence on oral culture, and anywhere that noise itself is less prevalent (e.g., an empty plain versus an eight-lane boulevard at rush hour), sound remains more tantamount.

Quieter instruments like guitar (versus the unifying power of drums) tend to get used as group cohesion declines, but then, ironically, these later end up being *over*amplified, shot like rockets from someone's basement to the world, in attempts to compensate, and reach out again.

Melody and harmony developed mostly indoors, whereas outdoor gatherings are conducive to rhythmic music that carries and translates easily. And, the warmer the air, the faster sound travels through it, which is sometimes mirrored by faster tempos in equatorial regions, and dirges arising from darker, damper environments.

Melodic phrasing tends to mirror the respective(s) language of a region, with consonant-heavy tongues tending to be more percussive musically as well, using the voice more like a blunt instrument. It's not quite happenstance that opera emerged from vowel-savoring Tuscans.

Musical forms that use little or no harmonic elements tend toward more elaborate scales, since more dissonant notes can occur in isolation and do not have to be consonant with any other note. One of the wonders of the ear's ability is that it can identify unique sounds from simultaneously played multiple notes by hearing them as chords, an integration that the eye is completely unable to do with separate, adjacent colors. We don't see things holistically, but with partitions (e.g., we can hear four different notes as a D-minor-7th chord, but not see ocean, cloud, and sky blended into some other single, separate thing).

Largely, instrumental harmony arose as a supplement to compensate for the absence of group voices, and it has left its mark wherever communities began to congregate less frequently.

SECTION X:

Racing Racism

63

Free for All?

In the twentieth and twentieth-first centuries, Caucasians have acted as claimstakers, appropriating and settling the territories pioneered mostly by African Americans.

That jazz, blues, reggae, rap, and electronic music have all been eventually overrun by whites, displacing and overshadowing the original architects is a crass trend and legacy.

The partial subtext predominantly being that:

1. The ruling class is entitled to annex anything they deem as theirs.
2. The ruling class can improve upon whatever other races do.
3. A white person excelling is less threatening than a non-Caucasian person doing so.
4. This commercial "success" brings fame and acclaim closer within grasp of the dominant audience, whereby, they are potentially capable of also learning the prescribed moves by rote and recapitulating them in the next increasingly diluted wave of trained-seal phoniness.

Indeed, it is a hazy border between imitation being "the sincerest form of flattery" and downright thievery. The dominant parties' ultimate privilege is stealing the sound of those who have struggled, without having to endure any of the oppression. A rapper may be able to sound "street" and strike the correct poses and facial expressions, but the fact remains that through a mere change of clothing (from sweats to pin-striped power-suit), makeup, and/or attitude, he or she has the luxury of being able to walk into a rest-stop restroom as a voluntary rebel/outcast and within minutes exit, transformed like a reverse superhero, having become a respected and unsuspect member of the dominant society, with the antisocial stance shed like the convenient costume it is.

When a blonde and buff frat-bro purrs "Redemption Song" at a beachside coffeehouse, that attempt at homage and/or solidarity has the stingingly opposite effect—hammering home that not only does this individual suffer a dire lack of awareness as to the degree of misery by birthright that he is foreign to, but worse yet, is so oblivious that he is unable to make even the slightest admission of his own *lack* of understanding, and the corresponding inaccessibility to the depth of those experiences.

64

Same Old, Same Old: Colonialism's Leftovers

Another vital consideration in the quest for authenticity is that often only a few select opinions—of questionable authority to boot—are granted and/ or assume an autocratic and usually mostly arbitrary role dictating what is historically relevant culturally. For instance, Leadbelly became a celebrity in his post-prison years, playing renditions that were force-fed to him by a self-taught, upper-class "expert" in American folklore—himself the silver-spoon son of a former slaveowner—whose versions of those songs were usually ones that expert himself had heavily edited, rewritten, and/or were composites from multiple and varied original sources that themselves were often of questionable validity to begin with!

Since all forms of racism, sexism, and bigotry are ultimately problems of vision—if not cases of complete blindness, they are at least certainly cases of near-sightedness—those in the position of privilege can never fully understand the experience of those who are without their advantages, and any attempt to claim such comprehensive awareness only adds to the ruling class' persistence of privilege. The condescension that they are all knowing.

Instead of "I totally understand," the more accurate admission is "I cannot even begin to really appreciate what that feels like, except to know that it must be truly awful."

More accurate than "I am not racist" is "I *try* not to be, and am hopefully *less* than some people (as if that comparison is even helpful, at all, particularly given the despicable conduct and beliefs of some)."

But, in fact, the term racist itself *is racist.* For we are but one species, despite our many manifestations.

The dirty, dark secret of "liberalism" is as open-minded as any one person may think they are: we are almost all more prejudiced than we believe ourselves to be.

One of the positive by-products of recording was that since it occurred behind closed doors, racial integration was possible in studios much more easily than in everyday society, and even long before it happened very often onstage. Those revolutionary sessions foreshadowed and helped direct the changes in society's makeup and direction.

Later, live, audiences would crash the dividers that separated races at early rockabilly concerts and intermingle. This was probably a little something like what we later witnessed in Algeria, when the Muslim men overran the women's section and the entire concert was halted three songs in by the police due to this "sex riot."

Certainly, the potentially clandestine act of decrypting recorded material makes it possible for people to juxtapose cultures with just the click of a button, cultures that in the real world might be separated by oceans and/or violently divided by ideation.

The reality is that culture "doesn't travel well." It is liquid and dynamic, and the minute you move it, it changes, for better or worse. Like Italian, Chinese, and Mexican food in America—whose cuisines are almost unrecognizable to people who have remained in the supposed places of origin of these dishes—the titles' essentially become misnomers. The food does not remain the same after it migrates (while, *concurrently*, the diets of those back home have evolved and drifted, as well).

Caesar Salad is a prime case: in America, it is associated with Italy, but was actually invented in Baja, Mexico, and then given a Roman name. It is *never* served in any authentic restaurant in Italy, though it is a must in most any Italian-American restaurant. My Italian wife and her friends actually use this dish as the acid-test for choosing Italian restaurants: if it serves Caesar salad, they refuse to go in. (The same fate awaits those offering Chicken Parmigiana.)

Similarly, a friend who had just immigrated from Italy was fired from her precious first job in Los Angeles—at an "Italian" restaurant—after a customer ordered a pepperoni pizza and she instead brought him a pie smothered with bell peppers, since that is the translation in Italian. Her confusion was understandable. There is no such meat at all in Italy, despite it being so copious abroad.

From my own family—one that almost pathologically celebrated our supposed Irish-ness—my aunts, upon visiting Ireland for the first time, were shattered to learn that not a single soul there recognized the Irish jig dances that they had spent years faithfully studying and mastering. It even extends to my own name, one that my "Irish" parents mispronounced as "*eye*-un" and burdened me with having to explain and/or defend daily, like some unintentional version of Johnny Cash's "A Boy Named Sue." (And through osmosis this error has now been transfused to another continent, due to a band member naming his son after me—a very dear tribute, but one that will probably prove burdensome down the line for his offspring, and could even lead to an epidemically mispronounced "foreign" name in that region.)

In Berlin, the raccoons that now infest the city, are offsprings of those few that escaped from a fur factory following an air-strike at the end of WWII. A North American species, they emerged with no natural enemies, and came to proliferate throughout a place where they "didn't belong."

Culture also doesn't age well either. For example, when my mother-in-law returned to Rwanda for the first time in decades, many residents there were unable to understand her words. They claimed she "spoke like someone from thirty years ago" (which was precisely when she had left and last spoke Kinyarwanda regularly). The language had not stood still, it had shed its skin, even in that relatively short span.

Another instance is how difficult it is to imagine the outrage in the 1800s United States that met the now touristically sanctioned, family-safe Hawaiian Hulu dance, which was labeled "smutty" and offensive back then. As was the waltz, the Charleston, and virtually every dance that has been passed through the amnesiac gauntlet that leads to acceptability.

Due to their portability, modern sounds face a bit of an identity crisis with any given song: is it a wedding reception dedication, a strip-club soundtrack, a sex-you-up rave, breakup counselor, lullaby sedative, or blaring wake-up alarm? Gym motivator or suicide note? Some tracks get used quite promiscuously. And stored music, almost always works overtime.

Another additional misstep of trying to limit music as a strictly regional phenomena is that it disregards the great diversity that can miraculously arise from a single environment. As much as disparate artists such as Frank Sinatra, the Ramones, Maria Callas, the Velvet Underground, Simon & Garfunkel, the Shangri-Las, Duke Ellington, and Run-D.M.C. can all emerge from the same city, should not similar unlimited variety be possible in "third world" communities? Especially ones that often have an even much larger population base than the world's largest cities?

65

You Call *That* Equality? Distracted by the Decoys

When you see one of the world's power couples performing together side by side, and she is bent over in only undies and bra, and, yet, he is donning multiple layers and a hat—literally exposing only his face, throat, and hands, the same as the most austere nuns are required to—then all of those screamed "female-empowerment" lyrical rallying cries are zapped of their power, and male dominance wins again. New packaging, same tired content.

The day we see the aforementioned duo perform with her in a burka and him sporting nothing but a G-string, back arched and ass-cheeks up and jiggling, only then will we all truly be free.

Relatedly, after a joke was made about this couple's toddler's hair, a writer was given the boot from the show that aired it. But the spokesperson who actually *said it* was "apologized" to by the network, for his being given the script. It seems that one is not held accountable for what they have said, if it is read. This is a scary precedent, considering that nearly every presidential statement is authored by someone else. This reeks of the childish "but he/she made me do it" rationale.

Beyond all of that, not a cry was raised as to the questionable parenting choice of any couple parading their child on worldwide television without the child being of age to give informed consent as to the forfeiting of privacy, in the first place.

Witnessing a mega-selling teen grace the cover of every major magazine in the country and be held up as a sex symbol, even though she's so painfully thin and frail that it appears that she has just been released from a prisoner-of-war camp, does countless harm to the psyche of young women (and men) across the land. That no one seemed bothered to even bat an eye or comment is even more dispiriting. One would be hard-pressed to think of a male equivalent, any case where a "hunk" is valued for his emaciation. Instead, the meatier and brawnier are usually the more fawned upon.

Then there exists the fact that in the first decade of this century *every* single Best Actress Oscar winner had appeared nude on film in her career—at least once and in many cases multiple times—but not one of their male counterparts had *ever*. It is a sick hazing and paying of dues. Please, don't get me wrong. I celebrate any individual's freedom to express themselves however they see fit, but certainly the statistics here are far from random and carry some significance.

Even more unnerving, male actors must agree to brandish firearms to become box-office megastars. Will Smith's fame skyrocketed after his film's poster stretched across city buses, featuring him in full-crucifixion pose, a well-hung gun pointing from each hand.

Ever recall seeing a gangsta' rapper having a slow-motion, pajama pillow-fight with friends in his video? Yet, this is a staple of most female pop stars. And the standard in advertisements that feature women remains that they are either prone and/or near-orgasmic in ads.

Gandhi's passive-resistance gets bastardized into what more resembles active-submission, rather than actual "empowerment" or reclaimation. When a pop star—whose primary audience is preteen girls—claims that she is portraying a "strong" twenty-first-century female figure, but ends up televised on her knees before an aging rocker who is old enough to be her father as he points his phallic-substitute guitar in her face, then it is clear just how things continue to (*not*) stand.

66

Stangered: Disproportionate Estimations (On the Outside, Looking *Out*)

Despite the many miles clocked, traveling musicians often have a very skewed vision of where they've been.

First, they generally have contact mostly with the more liberal elements of a region. And even in the midst of the most ass-backward regimes, there are alternative thinkers and doers. An avant-garde rock show at a club in Appalachia can make the society seem a whole heap more progressive than it actually is.

Second, if the band is successful, their contact is almost exclusively with the people that like *them*. Thus, these artists live in a cocoon of disproportion, insulated by yes-men and yes-women. For performers, often their experience can become quite rose-colored, as misanthropic as their aesthetics may be.

It must be challenging to put in perspective years or decades of experiencing audiences night after night that scream and/or rise to their feet at your slightest hand flick or dip of an eyebrow. (As a child, I witnessed Elvis, just months before his death, toil—due to his bloated belly and oversize belt-buckle—to pick up a scarf that an audience member had tossed at his feet. Yet, the casino crowd went apeshit with dysfunctional adoration at this failed and sickly display.)

To reposition "stardom" to scope: Even when a performer has sold out Madison Square Garden (which is certainly no mean feat, by any measure), that still translates to them having only played before 1 out of 1,179 of the residents in the metropolitan area. In other words, a small fraction of less than 1 percent of the population.

Generally, our greatest opportunities for growth are offered by the harshest spoilsports. Their evaluations may be over the top, but there usually is some grain of truth in their feedback. Those that hate what you do are at least *partially* right (for no one is perfect), whereas people that love you can be totally wrong, due to politeness and fear of hurting your feelings (e.g., someone who is "being nice" will almost never tell you that your zipper is undone or that you have spinach in your teeth, but an "asshole" will hardly hesitate. And their communicating these truths ultimately does us a favor, once we bypass any shock or offense.).

In every community, the true artists and musicians act as outlanders, the netherworlders, the boundary-sniffing and -busting explorers. Just because there is a language barrier and the person resides amid a traditional culture does not mean that he or she is not just a little bit off and/or that region's equivalent of a "weirdo." Every society has their versions.

Largely, the confusion is one of scale. Once while yonder in Baja, it took me nearly an hour to go less than a mile due to potholes the size of hot tubs. There was more hole than road. The map truly lied in this instance, as all miles are not created equally. Similarly, a driver cautioned me once that to try to go to the edge of Central African Republic—which appeared relatively small—it had taken him more than a week since the roads and checkpoints would only allow an advance of less than a hundred miles a day, maximum.

What looks like a dot on a page, can contain incredibly distinct and thorny microcosms.

When it comes to language, historically, water unites and mountains divide. Thus, in the Pyrenees mountains between Spain and France, there is the Basque language that bears no relationship to either neighbor, nor any *other* language on the planet. It is as if it just plopped down from outer space (. . . and maybe it did!).

Instead, due to sitting across from each other and being allied by a sea that is protected, relatively calm, and somewhat easy to traverse, Spanish and Italian share more linguistic similarities than the countries that they are actually adjoined to, like France and Germany.

Anywhere people meet—at points of crossing—is where language is shared, and the word from either respective tongue that sounds and feels the best advances and evolves, displacing its competitor (usually with the last syllable then later being dropped over time, for ease and expediency). This is how root words infiltrate other systems. And usually the longer that any language is spoken, the more that vowels have won out and consonants been discarded through this attrition.

67

Single Origin Fairy Tales

The essentialization of any group—defining individuals narrowly as one—is always rife with danger. All music comes from nowhere *and* everywhere at the same time.

That said, African Americans in the southern states of the United States have acted as the wellspring for almost all popular music. And this is nothing if not an understatement. There can be widely divergent theories as to why this was the case, but certainly there is no denying there are a complexity of reasons.

Captives were made to dance in chains to stay exercised aboard slave ships. Their accompaniment—African instruments that were crudely played by their captors and then summarily destroyed upon arrival to the states. Since instruments were forbidden for slaves—*especially* drums due to fear that they would be used for sending messages—music had to be internalized. And by self-report, many sought freedom of expression in music that they could not find in life. It was only in churches that they were allowed to make "joyous noise to the lord," since by accidental fortune, Protestant doctrine often encouraged nonverbal praise as the most supreme worship.

At many social gatherings, slaves were allowed to attend, but were prohibited from dancing, and instead only allowed the sadistic "privilege" of watching from the sidelines. Even more sickening is the reality that most bands were composed of African Americans, and that in the Deep South, audiences were especially partial to these "black" bands. Clearly, there was a deficit of self-reflection among the ruling class.

It is a fine line from patrimony to hatred. A population must be found threatening to be hated, and as any group's numbers swell, the segue from novelty to resentment is a precipitous one, from curiosity and "Aren't they a handsome people" to "Why don't you go back where you came from?" and claims of stolen jobs. Tolerance tends to come easiest from a distance.

What is often overlooked is that up until the turn of the twentieth century, the primary source of dance music was the violin. And in the 1890s, mandolin clubs—a most hillbilly of instruments—were quite the thing among African Americans (after the instrument's having migrated from Naples).

During this same era, "slave" songs (or as they were often referred to: "Ethiopian songs" . . . even though no known American slaves ever hailed from that country) were already the rage, being sung on college campuses. Sound eerily familiar? It is important to bear in mind that in the prerecording era, songs often remained hits for *decades* and sometimes even generations, dispersed via sheet music and wandering minstrels. They were not only viral, but resilient.

As romantic as single-origin theories can be, the reality is that most things arise from a collective hunch, slowly simmering to meet their zeitgeist. Then, once birthed, it is as if they were always there. Like mountaintops and rocks.

It has been theorized that the entire Mississippi Delta region was cross-pollinated musically by the African American boatmen who would travel up and down the river, singing as they worked. More than we can ever entirely grasp, music making is a case of reciprocal borrowing. Many "black" songs were actually imported from the military, following slaves being *forced* to enlist. And, in the early post-Antebellum period, black artists often stole back and reshaped minstrel songs from the racial drag queens of blackface that had popularized songs that were of extremely questionable African origin to begin with.

Despite Hollywood propaganda to the contrary, true-life cowboy trail crews were usually interracial and comprised of groups where, on average, one-third were African American.

An aside related to the lyrical content of gangsta rap is its part in a long tradition dating back not only to the nineteenth century and its ultrapopular "outlaw" hits about mythical figures like Billy the Kidd and Jesse James, but *much* further back to the first preserved Gaelic folk songs in the Middle Ages which were almost exclusively tales of rape, abduction, robbery, and murder. (None of this is to mention rapping's seventeenth-century origins in Quadrille dance-callers in New Orleans.)

Jimmie Rodgers, "the Father of Country Music," actually quoted blues couplets for a 1930 single on which he was accompanied by none other than jazz monument Louis Armstrong.

Norm Hamlet, longtime leader of Merle Haggard's backing band, explained to me how in the early 1960s, he had to build his own pedal–steel guitar from mail-order parts since the instrument did not yet exist as a mass-produced item. Each player had to graft together their own hot-rodded version, into what has now become the staple signature of country music. (He also confided how in the pre-Merle days, their band had been fronted by an African American singer who was quite a figure on the local scene of their redneck town at the time.)

For any that try to dismiss the African American influence as only being for "rudimentary" folk forms, it should not be let pass that no less than such classical greats as Stravinsky, Satie, Debussy, Puccini, and most explicitly and proudly, Dvorak, openly borrowed from the "blues."

On a global level, African American bands like the Fisk Jubilee Singers extensively toured Europe, Australia, Asia, and sometimes Africa, spreading influence *before* the turn of the twentieth century.

In fact, Orpheus McAdoo, Jr. (sometimes referred to as "the grandfather of World Music") is almost singlehandedly credited for sparking South African chorale music due to his 1890, smash-success, globe-trekking tour. In a bitterly ironic twist, that same vocal tradition's lineage was the one that Paul Simon infamously stole from nearly a hundred years later for his *Graceland* album's controversial appropriations.

When well-meaning types state someone is of "African origins," should they not more accurately explicate that they are of *recent* African origins? As is that not where we all hail from, ultimately?

68

Disgraceful by Association

Referencing cultural stereotypes to lend a sense of classicism? (E.g., an inconsequential Mariachi, anyone?)

Check.

A genocide museum's centerpiece art-installation being lifted without credit by a supergroup for their lovesick video?

Yup. (And, *yes,* that really happened.)

Then there's having a platinum-band prance down the street while wearing bygone, one-man band, busker contraptions, but strictly as costumes and never playing a single note on any of the instruments during the entire clip. And always at the ready is the catchall ruse of grifting "blues" or mojo to a name of a soul band made up of frat boys (or the word "bass," if you're a dance DJ).

Or Anglo bands flaunting Spanish words for no apparent reason at all.

And let us not forget one of the ultimate cultural transgressions: a white musician backing themselves with a Southern Baptist choir—usually featuring a heavy-set soloist—in a bid to lend themselves some sort of earthiness.

Shouldn't somebody be calling these illusionists on their shit? Where's the tribunal for *this* sort of feloniousness?

Somewhat facetiously, I'd gladly throw my support behind a petition for a "cooling off" moratorium on *any* music coming out of London, Nashville, or LA until, say, *at least* 2050. Maybe their headstarts could be curbed and the slate cleaned. It's high time instead for distant and distinct voices to be heard from.

That the cradles of democracy like the United States, United Kingdom, and Spain behave so undemocratically with music and film is disconcerting.

As to the therapeutic need for this, a primary marital-therapy technique is that of the Speaker-Listener. This process requires that each party have equal chance to speak, and as they do, the other partner can say nothing. Then, ultimately the only reply that is allowed is not one of rebuttal, but instead a word-for-word repetition of what has just been said, to ensure that those words have actually been heard.

It is worth considering that a key religious action is to take vows of silence, where one is forced to listen.

Recently, a vice president from a commercial radio giant had the moxie to claim to me that "we have no foreign-language restrictions on what we broadcast." This smacks of, if the NBA were to brag that they have no height-requirement (e.g., "We are totally open to any and all people. Even a talented midget, potentially!").

In practice, language really should not be much of a barrier for pop music since most people have very little idea, or downright incorrect interpretations, of what their favorite songs are about, sometimes even going so far as to love songs whose content they would abhor and censor if it were spoken (e.g., the sight of seeing "Sweet Home Alabama" being sung with gusto by a bunch of drunk left-coast liberals). As an example, with staged opera, *even most Italians* need to read the subtitles provided to understand the words, since the singers' pronunciations are so elongated and mangled.

Mon Hai, from the mountainous far north near the border of
Thailand, is reportedly one of two people left in the world
who play the Kann (a bamboo horn).

69

Outlaw Camouflage: Slumming in the "Underground"

When a member of ancient nobility accepts a Grammy award, and does so wearing shit-kicker boots, denim, and a street-skater key chain, isn't that as much—if not more—of a make-believe cartoon than KISS's makeup or Daft Punk's robots? It is as incongruous as a jailhouse face-tattoo on a WASP'y sorority girl or as inappropriate as suburban surfers' habit of appropriating African American slang as if it were their own. By all appearances, colonialism is alive and well, it has just shifted into the realm of culture.

That many roots-artists' sound features the banjo, a hillbilly instrument whose prototype was imported to the Deep South from Africa by slaves, only adds insult to injury. Is this not the twenty-first-century equivalent of playing in blackface . . . or maybe more apropos in this instance, "red-neckin'"? The musical counterpart of linoleum, hardwood floors, or a fake raccoon-fur, Daniel Boone hat?

Folk music has been appropriated from the actual "folks."

With singers like Lana Del Rey, Taylor Swift, and Lady Gaga having had their ventures into music careers underwritten by their East Coast millionaire businessmen daddies, and "underground" bands like Vampire Weekend being comprised of Ivy Leaguers that shoplifted the musical styles of Afro-pop, it is hard to make a stand for the relevance of rock music in the current landscape and instead not admit that it has fallen into the wrong hands. In this case, wealth has not been passed down, but been greedily and unashamedly siphoned upward. That one of the top "indie" bands in the land was founded by a duo who met at the same New England prep school as Facebook uber-nerd Mark Zuckerberg attended (as well as a Rockefeller or two), should rightly turn at least a few conspiracy-theorist heads.

To steal another's voice, particularly when personal expression may be the only power left in the possession of the unheard and/or underrepresented, is a staggering arrogance and assault. Much like when actors stoop to play disabled or gay people, as if there is no one among those populations qualified enough.

None of this is to disregard that these "tributes" might not sometimes benefit the pioneers, due to their consequently receiving the scraps and leftovers of the fraction of the audience that is willing to dig deeper following the inroads made by the commercial copping artists (e.g., those that later discovered T-Bone Walker by way of the Rolling Stones).

As Elvis was to Howlin' Wolf and Fabian to Elvis, Vanilla Ice was to MC Melle Mel and David Guetta is to Aphex Twin, ad infinitum, and the current crop of "modern" bands are again merely understudy, white-bread substitutes for the real thing. What is worse though than the thievery is the disingenuousness of their adopting stances as to being authentic or cutting edge in even the most remote way. It's a bit too much like watching diminutive, preppy posers like Tom Cruise handily take on droves of herculean villains and walk away with hardly a scratch or seeing pretty boys such as Brad Pitt that are seemingly driven by a compulsive, over-compensatory need to slum it and *act* tough, deifying hoodlum and serial-killer roles.

And isn't that why music always trumped Hollywood in pop culture? That it was real people, oozing sweat, spit, and flubbed notes onstage, instead of make believe.

In the final analysis, "keeping it real" is mostly a concern of those who are counterfeit and faking it. When you're being real, you don't have to work at it, much the same as with lying, which measurably drains more mental energy than telling the truth.

Now we are carried awash in a system where mediocrity is celebrated so as to not prove too threatening to the audience and thereby helping make them feel closer to the action. One of the most disturbing elements about Coachella and the like is the creeping sensation that out of the eighty thousand+ people in attendance, almost all of them have been, will be, want to and/or know someone who is performing or has performed at that same festival as a DJ or in their own fly-by-night, between undergrad and postponed-med/law school adventure, "alternative" band.

The underground has given way to the self-congratulatory dilettante sound. Yet, the actual relevance of the majority of the slot-filling musicians in the machine at these massive events is much like extras on a summer-blockbuster action film. The event itself has become the draw, and the content secondary (as is proven by many established festivals now selling out of tickets *before* any of the performers are announced).

Surface over substance is the order of the day, like the tattoo craze, which provides a purchasable salve to those starved for experiences that actually leave a mark—a proxy for anyone who has never really had to fight for anything and, as a consequence, suffers an absence of unwelcome adventure, war wounds, and survival stories, to demarcate their lives.

It becomes a competition of unintended conformity. One trip to the piercing parlor does not a revolutionary make. (Nor a jaunt to Africa, India, or South America, for that matter. People are changed by process, not events. There is no shortcut to interpersonal depth, no nip-and-tuck for the soul.)

Their's is an empty rebellion, a superficial subversion. Defiance without basis is not a virtue. It is simply going through the motions. Hedonism is no longer an act of defiance in a culture that is already liberated. It is then merely a self-indulgence.

And the charade of the practiced ambivalence toward success of the "underground" is the ultimate insult. With the indie-rock genre, audiences now customarily behave more like the stars, and the stars are disingenuously reluctant.

You are not a progressive because you drink hemp-milk and go to protest rallies. You're a progressive if you're willing to have your mind changed and admit rather then defend your existing beliefs.

A willingness to proceed through life with minimal expectation, maximum curiosity.

Though a performer would be ridiculed for staking claim to many visual aspects of a culture—wearing a turban or sombrero onstage, even if only attempted ironically or haphazardly—the musical elements are left unpoliced and free for the pillaging. Whether this is due to ignorance on the part of audiences or a lack of caring to investigate more astutely, the end result is comparable.

If someone appropriated a Holocaust photo for a clothing ad campaign, there would be (befitting) fury. But when a singer hitchhikes a ride from sounds born from another's experience—aping them sans the suffering—should there not be some similar backlash? Should this not somehow fall under the truth in labelling and fair packaging laws?

Social-tourism that travels upwards is derided as pretentious, "putting on airs." Someone adopting a French or English accent, or even so much as daring to demonstrate the audacity to correctly pronounce a foreign word, will be brought down a notch. But dumpster-diving and picking through the (white-)trash so to speak, is somehow apparently fair game.

I am far from being a Luddite—the slur that people so gratuitously hurl counter-defensively these days. The opposite is being advocated for here: *greater* diversity. This runs counter to conservationalism. (Nor is this simply a case of old-fogeyism. I was *far* more opinionated and less open when I was a teenager, as I fear too many people that I unintentionally offended or put off along the way could account to.)

It would be a very positive development if everyone deliberately created music. But *only* privately and without aims beyond the process itself.

Untold languages and customs have been lost throughout history and this is *not* necessarily always a tragedy. Not everything needs to—or even *can be*—preserved. Furthermore, art is mercurial and embodied. It alters with each inaction. Cross-pollination is an indispensable element in this. But to violently sever ties to and/or seize traditions wholesale that have been thousands of ceaseless years in the making is something that should, at least, stimulate the slightest modicum of pause and not be undertaken too rashly.

Before we deforest cultures, it is best to reflect and more fully appreciate the ecological implications of such massacres.

Any artist—no matter where they are from—will always be changed by exposure and success, and it is for them to then decide whether they want to maintain their original vision by will and choice, versus their previous relative naïveté that gave rise to it. If a "primitive" artist is sullied by the industrialized world, so be it. That is their right.

To someone who faces hunger each day or lives without electricity, discarding such luxuries as red meat and access to technology is unfathomable. It is almost impossible to explain why I am a vegetarian or don't own a television to someone who lives off the grid or without consistent nutrition, and not end up coming across as completely insane in the process.

But, in a world of social networking, where momentary infamy can be snatched via a single, wobbly, HD-camera YouTube video or a laptop-engineered Facebook single, how are bands who live without running water, electricity, or indoor toilets supposed to Twitter their way to the top, let alone keep up?

And, in the end, it might just be audiences, as much as anyone, who end up robbed when the cream of the crop is obscured and unheard, drowned out by the vacuum of frauds.

The glamour of "show business" where boundaries between
guards and prisoners can sometimes get blurry.

70

Are You Seriously "Serious"!?

From back in the day, I can recall the floggings in the press that Tom Petty ("vacuous pretty boys that mine the same three chords") and AC/DC ("juvenile cavemen who never change key") often went through. Time's passage has proven those pundits lacking some savvy as to these musicians' finer nuances and charisma. They may have made many meathead moves (e.g., Tom Petty modeling a confederate flag cap; AC/DC vaunting a skyscraper-sized, blow-up doll onstage), but each penned more than a few downright irresistible tunes. Often art must be unhinged from its era for purer objectivity to be found.

Regardless of the manifestation, superficial is as superficial does, though. Whether gift-wrapped in faddish identity-games, complex musical gestures, or "important" lyrical content, crap is still crap. This is the error in judgment that countless music and film critics, as well as tastemakers from the avant-garde often make: that if something takes itself seriously, then others should, too.

As a defense, many shroud themselves pretentiously by tackling weighty themes (e.g., *de rigeur* stances) or ambitious concepts. But I remain convinced that inside nearly every Death Metal devotee, there actually is a closet Sade fan, living in terror of being outed.

This is the same trap that adolescents fall into reflexively: not realizing that to rebel against something and define ourselves contrarily is to still remain in its shadow and under its influence. A more formal approach to life really cannot be found. Until we allow ourselves permission to make *any* choice—even the wrong ones and/or deviations from what is prescribed or acceptable—we can't be truly independent. (It's worth noting that Jack Kerouac was a full-fledged mama's boy, never "fully born," dying while still living at home, despite all his calls to the open road.)

Additionally, proving able to break a rule is far easier than replacing it with something as or more valuable.

How numerous are the promo pics that grasp for *gravitas* by featuring bands with a wall of exotic instruments behind them, but that they have no idea how to play?

A case in point is the West Coast band of caustically political "radicals" that claim that they "invented 'World Music'," but never even once wrote a ditty (or even a :28-second bridge) that anyone could remember afterward, sing along, or dance to?

It resembles when someone hides behind religion. Middling artists have always shrouded themselves and duped others by using "experimental"-ism or quirkiness for its own sake. Or "correct" politics as a dull crutch and shield—acting as self-designated "superegos" for the scene.

(Similarly, ethnic bands often trade on their otherness like used-car salesmen, tethering their tepid talents to a niche, and building marginal careers that would otherwise have never stood a chance. There are plenty of buffoons in every race, playing tourist to some usually *devised* cultural heritage, hawking copies of copies of perjured truths. Fronting and hiding behind their ethnicity and/or pimping out their ancestry, while willfully ignoring that very few traditions are passed down unbroken. And none, unaltered with time. Being the first in any medium grants privileges. But soon, as competition intensifies, that orientation and "being in the right place, at the right time" becomes no longer enough, anymore.)

Or, the trend of classical artists trying to begrime and toughen up their personas via S & M regalia, choppy hair, and custom, ellipsis-shaped orchestral instruments—usually made of some sort of transparent or incandescently colored material.

With so many modern musical practitioners, it is almost as if you can see the wheels turning in their head mind—"*this* (idea) will sure be good." They are preoccupied with results rather than process. The art doesn't arise from an innate place, but from intellect. So many today are detached from their own experience and emotional life due to playing judgmental spectator to almost every moment of their own existence. It is done with all the self-seriousness of a New Age didgeridoo player.

The result instead is often music that is all head (and Cliff's Notes) and no body. "Mind over matter," in the worst possible way.

For few things are harder to do than simple. Few tasks more challenging than restraint. It is literally harder to play slowly than to keep a beat at a medium or fast tempo. (This is since as the distance between each note becomes further apart, each note's place becomes harder to keep track of and gauge.)

Material having an air of "importance" does nothing to guarantee that it is, in the end, even marginally good. Someone may provide the soundtrack to a political movement—and that's all well and fine—but if the songs don't pass "the hum test" no one will be listening to them after the movement loses steam. Rare is the artist in any style that will ever give birth to a melody that will still be sung around the postapocalyptic campfires.

On the other end of the spectrum, since they make people laugh, comedians often are not taken seriously. Yet, the incisive critiques and concepts that they sometimes traffic in—iron fist in velvet glove, medicine hidden in sugar—are, most of the time, by far more penetrating and reach further than nine out of ten formal and overtly stodgy professors.

Since pop culture most often trades in aspiration and putting on masks, the alternative world has increasingly attempted to demand that artists don't "sell out." But the plot thickens when a real-life cartoon group like KISS pens one of the ultimate paeans of all-time to the carnal joys of simply rockin' out.

Is the irony lost that the "post-punk" breakthrough of Nirvana was made by their riding classic rock stalwarts Boston's riff? Or that a Lower Eastside poet's larger fame (Patti Smith) happened due to a cover of *another* writer's work (Springsteen), not to mention one from the theoretically unrefined backwater of New Jersey to boot? Sorry not to toe the party line here, but denying or ignoring facts only worsens the ills of a fractious culture. (And an unsettling historical truth is that the breakout songs of Joan Jett, Janis Joplin, Sinead O'Connor, Madonna, and Cyndi Lauper, were also written by men. Yes, that battle cry, "Girls Just Wanna Have Fun," was penned by a *he*.)

Skepticism is vital, as well as concentrated efforts to not be bamboozled into sloughing the tried-and-true for every new and flashy thing that turns heads.

71

Music Cannot Be Possessed, But It Can Possess

"**W**orld Music" sucks.

To clarify: I despise it as a genre.

"Exotic"-ness for its own sake just isn't enough.

Like all idioms, once artistic expression becomes codified, it risks growing calcified and commodified. And all of this stifles the original inspiration(s) for its formation.

What idioms kill is an *absence* of self-consciousness. It is rare today to hear singers who have *not* listened to far too many other nonlive voices. Yet, it is voices that have not listened to a lot of other recorded voices that communicate most easily without any seeming self-awareness, and instead deliver pure sound. Sound that originates from inside them, rather than external sources, since they have started with a more or less clean slate. "Soul music" that actually comes from the soul. Blues that emanates from actual suffering, not reverse-engineered affectations and gutted gestures.

All vocalizations develop first from that most primitive state, a baby's cry. That first scream, announcing, "I am (here)!" All sound that follows carries in it that mark.

Due to the physical limitations of most vocalists, melodies overwhelmingly walk up and down among neighboring notes—in stair-step melodies—they rarely leap. And they almost always frequently return home to the established tonal center. In essence, the more rudimentary the music, the more it is a homebody or "mama's boy" (or "girl"), risking only mere baby steps away from where they've started.

Pretelevision peer entertainment has largely been pulverized and artists have consequently been converted instead to craftsmen and consumers—filtering influences rather than creating naively. Rather than invention, we are given duplication. Impersonators rather than inspirers, stringing together hyphenated categories as if shopping were an act of creation and not simply one of appropriation. Not that collaging and recontextualizing can't be art. It's just that they are inarguably secondary due to their dependence on another seminal act of creation happening first. They therefore are, in and of themselves, finite dead ends.

It is not unlike the vampiric aspects of the pharmaceutical industry that sell people on the idea that solutions lay outside themselves and can only be purchased. When people begin to buy into the idea that they are lacking or imbalanced and that those needs can only be filled with a pill, then some autonomy is lost and dependance constructed.

Displaying good taste hardly determines the ability to produce anything *tasteful*. It is similar to the ratio differential between each person's receptive vocabulary being much higher than their expressive (i.e., productive) vocabulary. Or the way that aptitude in diagnosing (i.e., recognizing that there is a problem) comes so much more easily than the ability to prescribe (i.e., having any clue what to do *about* said problem).

Many are now imprisoned by influence, lost in an echo chamber of references. Left with lives that require footnotes to be lived.

72

False Friends: Raw Does Not Always Equal Real

The desire to find the needle in the haystack of an undiscovered, back-roads talent can often lead to trails gone cold. My initial rush and keen-ness have been exhausted, on more than one occasion, with what results in little more than chasing mirages.

For anyone who might misconstrue field-recording as merely pointing a hand-held doohickey at someone, be cautioned. We already suffer from an oversatura-tion of taped content. The current plight is about the inequity of how much of what is released is regional-centric, with most areas being blacked out, ignored, and silenced internationally. The larger ideal will be to improve the *quality, not quan-tity* of what is preserved *every*where, so that fewer gems are lost amid this static. The last thing that is needed is more shit out there, especially, if it misrepresents the potential of an entire country, and wastes their "one big shot," so to speak.

I in no way wish to unleash armies of microphone and camera wielding "white" people upon emerging nations. There are far too many already. We will know that the tide has turned for the better, the day we see legions of people from Africa scouring the globe in search of better and more "authentic" music *from* Europe and America. I personally, welcome that day.

This is not merely an imposition of Western values. There will always be a sliding-scale of subjectivity as to what any one person thinks is good, and these evaluations are highly fluid, as in leading to us "getting" something years later that we'd previously denigrated. For me the litmus test is honesty on the part of the performer. Someone who communicates clearly and uniquely. Psychologists have identified six core emotional states (fear, sadness, anger, happiness, disgust, surprise) that we come hardwired for. These are expressed and recognized universally, and are almost impossible to convincingly fake without "being fake." And they provide as good of a reference point as any.

Any act of recording—whether it be a child holding up a phone to his siblings, or an elaborately bussed, multi-input ordeal—is subject to subjectivity.

A recording and/or an artist can almost never be 100 percent "honest," since the act of performance itself is rife with unrealness.

A key tell is to listen for discrepancies between someone's speaking and "singing voice." If the tone that they use to sing with is something they take on and off like a shawl, then without a doubt they are "putting you on." Rather than dropping their guard and allowing others to see behind the curtain, they are in fact erecting an additional rampart between themselves and others.

Though I gravitate toward transparent and "warts-and-all" methods, that is not to be confused with intentionally low-fi results. My admittedly limited, technical skill-set may impose an unintended ceiling, but my aspiration is to present artists in the best possible light. My goal is truthful representation—what someone sounds like, not what they *think* they sound like or would like to be. The goal is a fly-on-the-wall sensation—but *with* as high a quality as circumstances and budgets allow.

This basic confusion was brought home to me when a world music label once sent back a record to be remixed three times because they thought it "sounded *too* good." The patrimonial message was clear: the higher powers had deemed that someone from a poor country must also, therefore, be represented with degraded sound. And that this was far more important than what the artist desired and/or what in fact existed on tape. (Adding insult to injury, was someone later deciding to *not* hire me because these recordings didn't sound professional enough, and they assumed this was my fault.)

Similarly, I have more than once had to switch engineers midproject, since many people approach unorthodox recordings as lesser and not truly worthy of their time, and therefore make almost no effort to maximize whatever the potential of the material is.

Kibera is reportedly the largest slum in the world. From the hillside above, it stretches as far as the eye can see, left to right. It is home to over two million people.

As I carried cases of equipment on my head through the pedestrian-only avenues, the streets became narrower. It was slick from the previous night's rain and difficult to stay upright as the road began to slope downward. The surface we were walking on was literally shit: meaning, human feces. There is no plumbing in the area and some people use what is dubbed as a "flying toilet," whereby, they put their excrement in a plastic bag and hurl it as far as possible into the dead of night. Lest anyone be struck, the distance and darkness make it more difficult to identify the sender. I had to actively thwart the temptation to keep eyeing skyward, for fear of what might be incoming.

I was being led to the home of a local, traditional musician and the deeper we went in the district, a growing crowd began to trail and jeer us. My companion, who outside the boundaries of the neighborhood had ridiculed my questions as to the prudence of entering, was reduced to a panic as the mob began to stalk our every turn.

Once there, in a single eight-by-ten room where more than seven people lived, we met the musician. Various capillaries in his eyes were burst, tearing with blood, and his breath smelled of death. A murky cloud of mosquitoes hovered, at chest height, as potentially deadly carriers of disease.

His instrument was homemade and in place of gut strings, there was a hodgepodge of multihued, day-glo knitting yarn. It was true that the musician was "authentic," but, despairingly, he just flat-out sucked. We had been duped. As politely as possible, thanks and tribute were given, and we made a quick exit toward the perilous and circuitous journey back through the claustrophobic maze of his stomping grounds.

In Kenya, a solo artist launched into a boisterous tune, using his right heel like a hammer to pound a four-on-the-floor pattern against a box. This promising start was followed, though, by his repeating essentially the same song regardless of multiple requests for different material.

"How about your slowest song?"

"Yes."

Then he would launch into the same key and tempo.

"Let's hear your saddest one."

"Okay. No problem."

Again, he would proceed to play nearly the identical tune (which it should be mentioned was quite a good song in and of itself. So, in that way, I guess he wasn't so dissimilar from most commercial artists who milk and/or rewrite their one or two good songs for decades!).

This went on for almost two hours. Each time it would seem as if he had understood and was amenable to the request, but instead what followed would be variations on the same theme. How much was lost in translation and how much was a result of limited ability seems destined to remain an unresolved mystery.

One Moroccan man sure looked the part of a wizened sage. His toothless grin, earthen bare feet, and spottily patterned and graying beard made him out as a sort of Berber Willie Nelson. His friends had hyped him in ways that might make even a SoHo major-label publicist blush.

With a broken acoustic guitar laced cockily over one shoulder using a bungey-cord for a strap, and a tale of the many miles he had walked since dawn to find me, a sense of optimism was in the air. But, this was quickly dispelled the moment he opened his mouth to sing. It was immediately clear that he was merely a swindler, trying to pawn off his amateurism for truth. Someone can be authentic and yet *authentically* incompetent.

He seemed almost relieved when his attempt did not have the desired effect, as if it was comforting to learn that not all Westerners could be tricked quite so easily—that it was not as simple as using a borrowed and battered prop. His compatriots seemed to take it all with good humor as well, that the bluff had been turned right back around on them.

Such was the locals' disdain for an artist that I believed in that they forcefully subjected me to one of their cronies who was "*much* better."

The man certainly was more polished—younger, cleaner, smoother in his social skills. Well-met, as the saying goes.

But as he sang, there was no sense that he knew what he wanted to say, nor that he meant a single world of it. When he dropped down to one knee, in a conclusive, dramatic Broadway pizzazz, every ounce of respect for his dignity had to be mustered to not burst into laughter.

The rub is that the "real" musicians are almost always fake. Someone who wants too eagerly be heard should be suspect, and instead room be made for the more timid and demure to be drawn out from the margins.

Tinariwen's renown is so strong in the Sahara that an ad hoc flock follow wherever they go, despite the best efforts to keep the band's goings-on top secret. Throughout our recording, secondary camps of those wanting to pay tribute were set up at a respectable distance down the canyon. Many of these were made up of aspiring copycats.

One so aggressively peddled his self-pressed CDRs that it felt as if he had been through one of those high-octane, weekend-marathon salesperson bootcamps.

And, on three separate occasions, different individuals claimed that *they* were the local musician Bombino. Most comically, it turned out in the end that, the truth was, *not one* of them had actually been him! They were all merely pretenders.

It seems that there's a little bit of LA everywhere these days.

Muhammed on a moto: He was riding a cherry-red chopper, with an acoustic guitar slung over his back, affixed by a piece of twine. He exuded a kinetic aura of vibrancy, so we cranked an illegal turn and gave chase through the streets. Sans helmet, he zigzagged through traffic, and we never would've been able to reach him had his mud-covered bike not stalled by the side of the road. He was one of the scores of "boda boda" boys, who taxi folks around and often act as distributors for covert outlaw activities, while they themselves are customarily high from chewing Mira weed. They are known to string rope across intersections, fishing other riders from their bikes and then robbing and—in many cases—executing them for sport.

As he frantically tried to restart his ride, over the sound of his sputtering engine, we attempted to explain to him that we were interested in meeting with him and hearing his music. After much urging, he distractedly gave us his number and then sped off. Sadly, we were never able to reach him again. Whether he would have been able to deliver or simply looked the part, unfortunately, remains anyone's guess.

We had been greeted at the Bosnian airport by a bomb scare, a lone carry-on trolley abandoned in a bar seat. The locals rolled their eyes and said it was a routine occurrence, as the special police unit pulled up and with little deliberation tossed the bag into their lead-lined container.

Few experiences were more sobering than being refused passage at a marginal kiosk checkpoint on the border of Bosnia and Croatia. It was up a long, narrow mountain road without guardrails, and being forced to turn around meant backtracking almost two hours versus merely driving the last few miles over the ridgeline to the five-mile strip of coast that stretches out from the body of the country like a pair of puckered lips, siphoning off the Adriatic sea, and just barely forestalling complete landlock.

When the two guards commanded that we turn off the ignition and exit the vehicle, and began flinchingly eyeing the perimeter of that lonesome pocket and then addressing my wife directly instead of me and repeating her name, there were a few moments of terrifying fantasy as to what might be their intentions. Especially considering that we hadn't encountered another car for dozens of miles.

We had come in search of folk music from veterans of the war in the area. In every town, we were told the same thing: "*No one* sings anymore." What we did find, though, were faded fliers stapled on the poles of each tiny, riverside hamlet. They were Photoshopped faces of the local casualties. However unintentional, these were formatted exactly like the all-too-familiar, "missing" child posters that haunt every US post office bulletin board nationwide.

Admittedly, there actually was one recording that *was* ruined by ambient noise.

We had set up in an open field just across the border in Uganda. The one-eyed, glue-huffing rapper had failed to deliver on his boasts of being a "superstar." But more beleaguering, we were positioned right beneath a flight-path. Every five minutes or so, a low-flying biplane would buzz the ground.

We had already moved once, after being verbally accosted by a spear-wielding Masai warrior who was cross that we had apparently ventured too near to his cattle (which were still more than a football field's distance).

For the first time, the recorded tracks proved unsalvageable later. But, from this experience I at least did learn to always also look up, and not just around, when scouting locations—and to literally broaden my horizons.

Deep in the heart of the Appian Mountains in Tuscany, we sat in a mostly abandoned village that had literally been sliced in half by the Nazi's Gothic Line of defense during World War II. This village of less than one hundred people sported its own language. *Not* just a dialect, but a separate, government-accredited *language*—one that was completely unintelligible even to my mother-tongue Italian spouse.

With most of the population elderly and nary a person under forty years old to be found, sitting in the plaza and listening to the men converse conspiratorially as the sun set was like bearing witness to the rattling death gasps that have befallen countless cultural elements throughout time.

I cringed when screening an award-winning documentary about a local female empowerment group in Rwanda. The work featured Caucasian, Western activists onscreen to such a degree it was squirm-inducing. Worse yet the filmmakers utilized generically "African" music for its soundtrack. That awards could be given to a film with the insensitivity of plastering onto central Africa an artist from such a distant and different region as the Ivory Coast was the geographic equal of using Peruvian panpipes in a film about rednecks from Alabama, as if they were in even the slightest way a match.

A personal reminder of to just what extent the scale of Africa can be mutilated is how often well-meaning people have asked me if I am alright following incidents in Mali. These inquiries are due to their having confused Mali with Mal*awi*, which is almost six-thousand miles away—the distance of driving across the USA... twice!

Equal opportunity dumb-down: In the name of scrupulousness, I have deliberately left the band unnamed here, but there is really nothing quite like riding in an overstuffed van with a group of drunken, middle-age, Middle Eastern, traditional "religious" singers. More than one of them wet themselves along the way, and seeing this group of men in ceremonial garments, post-show, stagger and blabber, angrily rebutting the driver's insistence that they wear seat belts, and then insisting that we pull over so that they could puke by the side of the road, is not an experience I will forget anytime soon.

More than a spiritual encounter, they brought back a distinct "*boys*-gone-wild" flavor from my hard-rock adolescence in the California suburbs. More *Animal House* than mystic.

The "World Music" folks certainly outdid the "heshers" on this occasion.

An African television producer recently berated me before his staff, questioning whether I "cared" about music. His claim was that there were "proper musicians" from his country of origin that I should have championed instead of the group that I believed in and that had had unexpected, but resounding success.

I pointed out to him that many of the most outstanding artists of all time were often unappreciated at home in their own lifetimes (e.g., Emily Dickinson,

Kafka, et al) or had to travel overseas to first find appreciation (e.g., Hendrix to the UK), and the most creative were rarely also the most virtuosic. He barked at me this was beside the point.

I then asked him to name some of his favorite musical artists of all time. When he stammered and cast his gaze heavenward, grasping for even one name, it became quite evident who might really not "care" so much about music.

Our hazing into the Sahara was to be taken captive on a 4 x 4 joyride by the band's leader. We had arrived in the middle of the night and just predawn he, a reticent man, invited us into his vehicle. He tore off, chuckling as he relished spinning us up, down, and all around on this roller coaster of sand, and we bumped and bounced, sliding into each other across the plastic seats. At speeds in excess of one hundred mph, we often took air. In the end, the trail he'd carved out led to one of the longest and most uncleft, 360-degree vistas I've ever witnessed, one with not a single manmade construction visible in any direction.

I learned later that as part of a promotional crusade, an automaker had loaned him one of their upscale SUV vehicles that they had named after his tribe. That he had managed to return the vehicle, utterly destroyed after only a single weekend of true "off-road" use spoke volumes as to image over substance.

The person that I have worked with who was by far the most resistant to trying things was a self-identified "experimental" artist. For her, every detail had to be decided in advance, down to the most elaborate scripture. She even suggested that maybe we should tape our discussions, if needed for reference purposes later. She was unwilling to leave anything to chance and had been almost brainwashed into stock, industry recording methodology, insisting that the drummer had to play in a separate booth, etc. That there was "*a* way" that things must be done.

Witnessing a group of Ugandan schoolgirls rushing down a stairwell so as not to miss the latest *Hannah Montana* rerun of Disney Channel can be a chilling experience.

But worse was when a group of gregarious men on the Congo border pompously declared to me that the local group Konono No. 1 (one of my favorites of the past two decades, in any genre) were "horrible" and "nobodies," despite it being clear that none of them had ever even listened to them. Minutes later, the suspect acuity of their evaluative abilities was brought home to me as I witnessed them excitedly gathering around the television to watch a central African "Pop Idol" show. The program featured off-key and generically overwrought vocalists from all over the region, who forced out notes that could make Christina Aguilera seem as raw, tapered, and truthful as Nina Simone, in comparison.

Nonetheless, the Congolese critics literally leaped out of their seats with glee and high-fives, as a heated feud followed as to which lousy contestant was "the best."

One married member of an esteemed nomadic, high mountain group cyber-stalked a female friend of mine for months online, declaring to her that "she was the most beautiful woman in the world." The group carries a cryptic and sage mystique among their international fans, with many holding the musicians in awe and above reproach due to their armor of exoticness. In contrast, their homeland peers openly declared to me that they are "just impostors" and not the *real* thing (i.e., the "Big in Japan" phenomenon, transplanted).

There is no culture without narcissists, and those traits and its effects are universal. Through a further process of selection, the arts inordinately attract self-serving individuals, and from their inception, always have.

What I ascertained while living among this group is that what many misperceive as a transcendental vibe is actually more a case of their being permanently wasted. That if one scratches past the exterior image and differences, hanging out with them reeked more of stoner Todd from Ventura than anything even remotely associated with the divine.

One group from Kinshasa encompassed three members from that ghetto, but the fourth had been raised in relative affluence due to having been taken in by nuns when he was young. That member, when asked to add to the polyrhythm of a song, kept straightening out the time. His immersion in European sensibilities manifested in the music, with him playing on rather than *with* the beat. He valiantly tried, but an improvised musical dialogue escaped him, and he instead defaulted to a prescribed and predictable pulse.

He was "churchy," in the worst sense of the word. I relented with my attempts, when I found myself having unintentionally blundered into the unflattering, double-bind of being a cracker trying to coax an African to be funkier.

73

Thinly Veiled Bigotry (The Patrimony Dies Hard)

Amid a band's big finale, a middle-aged fan once interrupted me persistently while I was clearly working in front of the stage. As such, I inferred it was something important. Turns out that she'd stopped me only to admonish that the group should "lose the drums," which she emphasized by making a cutting motion across her own throat. Her presumptuousness was shocking. First, she had assumed that playing Western instruments was *my* idea, when in fact I had discouraged the band from doing so. Second, would she ever even dream of attempting the same stunt in the middle a Radiohead concert? Or to try to give an artist she respected arrangement instructions—ever at all, even under much more casual circumstances than in the middle of a show!?

This same group often experiences audience members insisting on the band providing the name of their remote village (where only a few dozen people live total), as if it is the fan's right to know. Yet, would these random people ever brave to request a Western performer's address without risking being marked as a stalker and given the old heave-ho? In a world where one pop starlet reportedly just bought a *matching* Manhattan penthouse across the hall from her own—for additional tens of millions of dollars—simply to house her round-the-clock security team, this sort of gumption hardly seems likely or even possible.

In some sort of backhanded compensatory bid, I have more than once been denied the standard backstage hospitality meals (and even tap water!) by white promoters who meanwhile dote a bit too effortfully on the "foreign" bands I'm with, going so far as to making menu choices for them as to "what I think *they* would like." Similarly, once in Australia, a patronizing fan wanted to buy the band "an ice cream," as if they were children.

Somehow it strikes me as doubtful that the members of Slayer or the Geto Boys have ever once been made such an offer.

A successful band I know that is shrouded in exotic mystique often tours without their charismatic frontman and leader, an individual who tends to prefer staying home in the countryside to go for days hunting by himself. Yet, the majority of the audience doesn't ever even notice his absence, when he is not there! If Axl Rose were ever to pull a no-show, there would be a riot (as there once *was* when he cut a concert short in St. Louis). Would Bono not appear, every person there would demand their money back.

In Kenya, we attended a showcase of various regional folkloric forms. What seemed to have been put over on the audience was that the "different" tribes were actually a rotating cast of the same people who had simply changed costumes repeatedly backstage. When I was able to spot a stellar musician in the bunch, simply by the way he played a simple metal percussion ring, the locals were astonished that I had been able to ascertain this guess from so little. Their esteem toward me ascended when it turned out this man was actually the leader of the entire troupe, an instrument builder, and skilled on various instruments. To this day those same folks tell me that they have no idea how I deduced that insight, and have dubbed me a "witch."

In Paris, it was a squirm-fest, trying to sit through a Caucasian woman in her early twenties, who had crashed an "Afro" activist meeting to long-windedly lecture them about their "history," as per her largely erroneous master's thesis. (A scholarly paper that would no doubt be cited later as indubitable fact.)

A member of a scenester Brooklyn band once contacted me, repeatedly refusing to take no for an answer regarding her pining to "jam and hang out" with a band I knew in Mozambique. What she seemed to have little sensitivity about regarding her little arty-safari was the dire conditions that these folks lived in day in, day out. Conditions that did not allow for such frivolities as "grabbing a cappucino," not to mention the barely restrained and veiled disdain that many musicians view most "mzungu"—their slur (though, sometimes it is also a precarious term of endearment) toward Caucasians. It is a name by the way whose origins refer to "someone who wanders *without purpose.*"

Once, a man literally ran after me at a festival to inquire if the band I was working with was "intimidated by the superior musicianship of the other artists?" My reply was to ask him to hum *one* tune by any other band there, a feat which he, nor almost anyone else could do since the majority were light in the songwriting department.

Without sturdy songs or the possession of a singular voice, all the jamming in the world is hardly worth the pipeline of hot air it is built on.

As a person of mixed race, my wife has never entirely gotten over her disappointment when after a lifetime of battling bigotry in northern Italy (her father's country and her own homeland), she anticipated finally fitting in somewhere upon traveling for the first time to her mother's country of Rwanda.

But after arriving, we were met with the sorrowful truth that most people there regarded her as "white" and completely equivalent to and interchangeable with me racially.

At a tribute show for an underground alt-country figure whose lore has grown outsized—largely due to his having overdosed at a tender age—his now middle-aged daughter bounded on stage and blurted out, "My daddy had a nanny. *I* had a nanny. Now here they are, the . . ." as way of introduction for an all black gospel choir. It was hard to appraise which was worse—her having made such a mortifying bungle or her lack of awareness at just how lacerating it was. Sometimes, all the twang and peyote in the world can't mitigate the taint of being the Harvard educated, third generation namesake of a southern agricultural magnate.

In a hotel lobby one night, a gang of drunken locals collared a group I was working with as they entered. The young, male revelers literally stood a head taller than the musicians. They held them in the pseudo-friendly, menacing headlock of the intoxicated and refused to let go, insisting, "Play us some music, *man.*" It was issued more as a challenge than a request.

I'm sure in their own clouded way, this was some attempt at cross-cultural outreach. The band, who do not speak a word of English and originate from an introverted culture, were left trembling from the experience. As the accosters attempted to follow us down the hall to our rooms, I was only able to free the band by the hairiest of escapes from a five-against-one fisticuffs (i.e., that one being *me*). The staff of the supposedly high-end and full-service hotel demonstrated convenient inattention to this prolonged incident, which couldn't have been more different from how aggressively they'd scolded us earlier that we could not eat food from outside sources in their lounge, even though we were multi-night guests.

The next evening, a group of teenagers fled the sandwich place across the street where we were eating. They covered their noses with their sweatshirts, waving their hands in front of their faces to displace the air, and complained of the "stink." And, then almost on cue, they tore off in their truck blasting a hip-hop track, without the slightest hint of irony or contradiction.

The truth is that when people speak of something smelling or tasting badly, what they really mean is that it smells *differently* than what they are accustomed to. Their filter has been opened sensorially and that stimulus has become conscious and noticeable, as opposed to the other elements which they have acclimated to, as we humans are so adept at doing, for ill or for not.

As the family member of two disabled individuals, I can certainly attest to the negative attention that being in the minority can attract. A childhood of misguided and clumsy fisticuffs stands proof of this.

Prejudice can cut both ways, though. This can lead to the overreactive, counter-imbalance of inverted bias that drives the adopting of mascots. Uniqueness rarely escapes notice, and there are invariably some folks, with meager boundaries, who are overeager to solicit and champion any odd-person-out. This in part accounts for the "gay best friend" sensation currently sweeping the nation (as well as the individuals who seem to handpick, collect, and curate friends based on their exotic quotient and/or accomplishments).

For instance, being the only redhead in school carries disadvantages. But it can bring unexpected advantages, too. Guaranteed, whoever is unique will not escape notice of *some* kind.

My unintentionally prejudiced view of my aged Italian landlord was that his life's score was made of wafting mandolins and Gregorian church-choirs. It was much to my surprise when he said, "You've probably never heard of something old like this," and then whipped out a waffled Emerson, Lake, & Palmer (ELP) album, singed with old bong resin stains. Little did he know that, as kids, I and my stoner friends had listened to that exact same record, tucked away in a carport hideaway after school.

The dominant culture tends to digest the tides of youth, so that through the aging process itself, most slowly succumb to their upbringing like some sort of preset homebase. And all that's then left are the tattoos, and some washed-out Polaroids on the fridge, as mementos.

A holier-than-thou German nonprofit agency once agreed to pay for a group of band member flights from Africa, but refused to bring the founding member— who was a recent African emigre—for the trip, since she now lived in Europe. Their willingness to distinguish who was "African" enough was particularly chilling, especially given the eugenic history of their own country.

Repeatedly, when on tour for the first time ever with bands that have never before left their remote regions, many know-it-alls will nonetheless claim, "Oh yeah, I've seen them before. They're great," continuing to insist that this true, even after I've informed them that it is literally impossible. Such are the dangers of essentialization (seen one banjo player, I guess you've seen them all, is the "logic").

Walking through the streets of Havana during the post-Buena Vista Social Club breakthrough, it often felt like every street corner and café was holding a contest to see who could most out "spice" the next for the tourists. That the more mournful sound I heard while there was from an elderly Asian man, singing beside an open window deep in the heart of Chinatown, was a master class in migratory studies.

The next night when an overly gregarious young trumpet player, who was visibly of an almost psychedelic mix of ethnicities, whispered unsolicited that I should "watch out for the blacks," the equal-opportunity imbecility and complexity of racism was again brought home. All the blockades, reclusiveness, and embargoes in existence can't keep the best and worst of human nature out. Ignorance has a way of sprouting up anywhere, like a weed. Even from the more unlikely of sources.

A redneck is a redneck, whether they wear a KKK Wizard's hood, a turban, or a priest-collar. A fundamental truth is: almost everybody in the world—no matter what their color or belief system—is probably a bit more prejudicial than what they think they are.

This was reminiscent of the shock I felt when an acclaimed Senegalese music master informed me that he would collaborate "with white people *only*. No Asians! No Indians or Muslims!" He had even unabashedly put this in writing. Then he had allowed me to reread it many times to make sure that my eyes weren't deceiving me. I informed him that this sort of ideology was completely untenable and thus aborted the project, at a significant economic loss since I'd already paid for his nonrefundable flight and hotel, etc.

SECTION XI:

The Battle for Democracy in the Arts

74

How Music Dies

A primary subtext of pop music is that being yourself is not enough. That you must pretend to be someone else to compensate for your deficits. This trend helps perpetuate the system it hosts from, since those who feel they are lacking and must fill a void make the best consumers.

Adolescent musical forms (rap, punk, et al) often provide reverse sanitized histories, dirtying up someone's background to make them appear "street," when in fact they aren't. Rather than exposing truth and helping to emotionally enlighten, this peddles moldy fables.

Worse yet is the concept of "front people." It is born out of misplaced and knee-jerk competitiveness—a jock mentality intruding on the arts. Shouldn't any truly unified band stand in one, unbroken line, with no one ahead of, behind, or above another? Yet, so many play against rather than with one another. They leave no space for dialogue, in the favor of monologues.

Crowd barricades themselves are antithetical to forming a connection. Big rock production often positions performers so far from the audience that the closest are *farther* than *any*one would be in a normal-sized club. Rather than unity, separation is created. As a youngster, my band once played a grand amphitheater that literally had a moat in front of the stage. And the effect was exactly like that: drowning.

Instead, a performance space should at best provide a temporary asylum, bridging superficial divides between individuals like race, age, sexual orientation, and gender—creating a shared space, where short-term safety seems almost promised by the unity.

Often big-name bands—usually made up of former best buddies—each ride on their own separate tour bus (and yet also often have the gall or the lack of insight to hypocritically speak out publicly about the "environment" and protecting the rain forest, despite their energy-inefficient ways). They talk to one another through respective personal assistants and managers, and see each other only onstage, if they dare make eye contact, at all. The franchise carries on, long after the camaraderie has gone.

As a cautionary note for anyone trying to first start a band: rather than searching for the "best" musicians, more fruitful results will almost always come from recruiting your truest friends to join. *Even* if that means having to teach them to play an instrument, you will almost always have saved time in the end.

Otherwise, trying to back-engineer the magic will almost always fail. Chemistry cannot be dictated. Usually, it just is or it isn't. And all the conviction and well-wishes in the world cannot will it into being.

Art is a soft science, at best. What should work on paper—having all of the requisite elements—can fall flat in reality. While other, unlikely pieces inexplicably work, being undeniably moving to most people that witness them.

75

Cheapshot

Easily mass-copiable and disseminated forms, over time, have an exponential increase in their content being copied. Each reproduction suffers a loss of data and quality, and that which we consume begins to consume our imaginations, like an intestinal tapeworm stealing nutrients from its host.

Any anthropologist worth his or her salt will tell you that the more widely spread an object, the more primitive it is. So what does that say about our "products"? This is why only one Van Gogh-like visionary is found anywhere on the planet, but scribbled hearts and initials are ubiquitous.

Mass-dispatched content itself is intentionally dumbed down, since less *and* simpler dialogue in film and television equals massive savings in redundant voice-over and subtitling costs overseas.

There could hardly be a more apt metaphor for the objectification of musicians than recently when one of the nation's biggest "first adopter" insider conventions featured bands on a giant stage made out to look like a vending-machine.

76

A World of "Superstars," Minus an Audience

It started with Madonna and Arnold Schwarzenegger (the latter who became most famous for portraying a robot, the actorly equivalent of a musician basing their career on not making sound). For the first time, business acumen became more important for an artist than any discernible aesthetic ability. No longer was it the best artists being sold by the best salespeople. The middleman was promoted and in this triumph of capitalism, artists were reduced to mostly public-relations personnel, selling *themselves* rather than their talent, so that the primary talent became "me"-ratification as an end in and of itself. Rather than musical instruments, public figures now *played* themselves and the hype-machine like masters (e.g., "Did you like my version of the resurrection myth? How's about that rendition I did of, 'The way parenthood has changed me for the better'? Or what did you think of the mock excitement generated by my third consecutive fake-retirement/farewell/reunion tour?").

Rather than musicians, we now have media-ticians.

In an age where reality shows are scripted, scandals orchestrated, and marriage/romantic partners for the famous, cast, performers become their own product-placement. Instead of a commercial break, there is now *no* break. It is continuous, hounding, 24-7 via your blinking phone.

The point of the punk-rock revolution had not been that anyone could be a star. It was that there should be *no* stars, at all. It was about anyone being able to play music, not for an audience, but noncommercially for self-entertainment and community-building and bonding.

But this lowering of the bar artistically was seized by the egos of the masses, and amateurism was fetishized and elevated to art. For the delusional systems of the majority to be courted and sustained, the new decree called for movie stars and singers whose most extraordinary quality was their own *ordinariness*, lest they be too threatening. This degradation of quality perpetuates the sense that one's own potential for acclaim remains within reach, and as a result we suffer the wounds of the resulting sonic shrapnel.

There has inevitably always been self-absorption. It just hasn't before been so glorified. Arguably, cynicism and irony have been the major cultural movements since the moment musical forms stalled in the late 1970s. Cynicism and irony's rise coincided with pop innovations sputtering out. It is not that irony didn't exist before—as evidenced by Moliere or Oscar Wilde—but never in such massive doses.

Today, trendy subcultures often resemble fickle pep-squads, before which a steady stream of finger-paint da Vinci's offer limp compositions as if they were the Second Coming. Yet, these works are ones which bear only the faintest distinction to their predecessors. Many now seem to have confused being able to finger a G-suspended-4 chord with the same momentousness as finding the G-spot. And it becomes near impossible to hear anything above the sound of everyone patting themselves so strongly on their own back.

To rehash Freud: we can easily go astray amid the narcissism of marginal differences.

In broad strokes, popular music has been an anorexic, reductive trajectory: from complex symphonic density to an almost bare-bones pulse. Jazz reduced instrumentation, rock dismantled most harmonic elements, rap gutted melody in favor of the beat, and techno expelled the human voice almost entirely, coronating metronome as king for the balletically impaired.

77

The Myth of Purity

S cientists call it "genetic fitness." The larger the pool of DNA to draw on, the stronger the outcome for the offspring. Intertribal breeding produces more exceptional children than incest, at the other pole, which commonly leads to defects. The wider the net cast, the more resources there are to select from.

Artistically, the more diverse the voices, the greater the benefit to the culture overall. Otherwise, stagnation is inevitable.

But as access to being heard narrows to the inner circle of the famous and their associates, we are left with impersonations *of* impersonations—elite individuals whose greatest influence usually derives from make-believe elements via media rather than anything resulting from their lived life. A dead end is reached when people begin to regularly reference fantasy as more compelling than actual experiences (e.g, how often it is that we hear someone describe an event as, "Just like something out of a movie.").

As the collective storytelling is overtaken by one class—and increasingly dynasties are formed by the uppers—it is inevitable that the messages will lose touch with the experiences of the majority, who are struggling just for a paltry existence on this earth.

When art is transformed into product, and products become generalized due to losing their individual voice, differentiation must then be manufactured by promotion and advertising. Since no real distinction really exists at that stage between one "artist" and another, celebrity becomes the distinguishing and decisive element. Once this marketing trickery becomes a necessity, then power is stolen from the creators, artistic effort is demoted, and the "para-artistic" capitalists become the arbiters and dictators of aesthetics, where he who has the most powerful soap-box wins. And, as it's been since time immemorial, convincing would-be buyers that the same-old is "new" is the most vital selling point.

Any medium based on replication lends itself to repetition and homogenization. Differentiation then can only be made through "paramusical" elements like fashion, haircuts, etc. But even these ingredients get co-opted and drained of meaning, and all things become harnessed for one purpose: to *sell.* Thus, former street-level symbols of rebellion and angst become mere window-dressing and fodder for the consumeristic monolith (e.g., five-year-olds replete with blue-colored mohawks and spiked leather jackets).

The cutting edge is more likely "future quaint," due to its being almost instantly postdated.

Performers by default end up hand-puppets to a market's demographic dictates (e.g., the perennial favorite of a misunderstood, youthful "rebel"). Meanwhile, recordings perform the sorcerer's trick of making, at will, sound disappear and then reappear otherwise later, becoming so estranged from its source that the person's voice can even be heard long after they are dead. Often, by far more people—and sometimes even for the *first time*—after their death.

This experiential shift—an extension of the written word already having divorced information from its original source—has caused a before/after chasm in human behavior. People are now often split in their experience, potentially giving greater attention to that which isn't actually occurring in their immediate environment. This severs us in two places at the same time and contributes to not being fully present, anywhere.

In this state, one is usually, literally, reliving the past. And what is a recording ultimately but a mummy, a revisiting of that which has all transpired?

78

In Their *Owned* Words

Even New York taxi cabs now come equipped with television monitors, as if the cinema of the city were not far more rich with its one-of-a-kind, homegrown live(-d) entertainment.

Corporations increasingly steal more and more of our expressive space by going so far as to patent and brand preexisting words right out of our mouths (think Yahoo, Apple, or Kindle, just to name a few formerly idiosyncratic choices that have been sapped of their potency. This skullduggery usually involves converting words from verbs into nouns). Henceforth, they can no longer be used without containing invisible quotations marks around them and/or lending an unintended endorsement for *said* companies.

Rather than helping people be more revealing, this acts to restrict language and brings baggage to formerly purer forms of meaning.

A company like Amazon even claims the world's largest jungle for themselves. Through this same sort of linguistic "squatting," an Indian tribe's name (Winnebago)—one which was viciously persecuted to near-extinction—is metabolized into being synonymous for gas-guzzling recreational vehicles.

Bands like Oasis, the Talking Heads, Journey, and the Rolling Stones have hijacked words and terms as their own. And Madonna, Genesis, and Nirvana have even appropriated religion. While words and phrases like "Imagine" and "We Are Family," if uttered, almost demand being sung back as an echoed response.

Meanwhile, Microsoft co-opts the word "Word" itself, as staggering a metaphor as can be conjured.

The ultimate accomplishment of corporate language is when a brand name subsumes the noun it is based on—bandage becoming Band-Aid, tissue transforming to Kleenex, Coke converting cola, etc. And that substitute usually is some nonsense, phonic-amalgam, lacking any explicit meaning—a term such as Kotex—hatched from a boardroom focus group.

These thefts that impose reductions on people's ability to better express themselves are far from victimless. Content has literally been seized.

And with recording, sound can now be owned and controlled, with one person's larynx being memorialized and extended around the globe and bounced out into space, rather than their words and breath simply expiring in the air before them.

79

Wire-Monkey Music

The absence of tactile and vocal contact with mothers has been scientifically proven to result in depression, violent tendencies, and psychotic qualities in our fellow primates. A question then is what is to come from those reared with mostly nonanalogous and compressed sound? Formative years spent repetitively staring at the same staged scenes must have *some* detrimental effects. It seems that the flat-screen kid generation is upon us.

When parents entrust their children's imaginations repeatedly to corporations like Disney, it is as if that caution has been thrown to the wind. Despite most people being terrified today of their child talking to strangers or even saying as much as hello, they turn right around and allow their children to be nannied by commercialism and co-fathered by technology.

Can it really be that a billion-dollar enterprise with worldwide retail outlets doesn't have at least *some* ulterior motives in the messages they impart? Often the same parties that panic if their child ingests one bite of candy bar allow the same child to gorge themselves on music and images that lack positive emotional nutritional value or even contain destructive content.

"Organic" food is the craze, so how is it that culture has been left behind?

At least on occasion, most of us consider scientific measurements to monitor our caloric intake. Not dissimilarly, it could be referenced that when tested, the "guess" is supported that neurologically someone is working harder listening to the complexities of John Coltrane than, say, deliberately dumbed-down fare like Whitney Houston (R.I.P.). And when an artist of Elliot Smith's nature sings, emotions are to varying degrees more engaged than with aggro music that—by design—stimulates the reptilian stem, not introspection.

Only the suicidal knowingly swallow poison, but almost all of us are enveloped by cancerous interpersonal elements from the media that often go almost unnoticed or are discounted as not mattering much.

In the past, when the same bedtime stories were told and retold by parents, these encore performances were slightly different with each recurrence and the sound was born from the acoustics of the environment. Now, the repetitiveness is rigid, without variation, and originates from an artificial source. Rather than a connection to the parent—through the exposure to their voice, which in most cases was the first sound heard consistently in a child's infancy and sonically equals home base—media acts to sever families, drawing children's attention somewhere else, to places that, in fact, don't exist at all.

A young father recently boasted to me how good it was that there were all of these advances in mobile equipment since now, "I can watch one movie and my son another, and his sister whatever she wants, too. That way we don't have fights. We can all be sitting there together eating at McDonald's and enjoy ourselves as a family."

I am not making this up. It is word for word. And, I am not trying to mock this man, either. I have no doubt that he loves his children very much, probably more than anything in the world.

But, what seems to have been missed is that the reason that they are not "fighting" is because they are not *interacting* at all, and that sharing, compromise, and developing problem-solving skills suffer as a result.

Imagination has been put up for sale.

We now engage middlemen to dreaming, and are faced with the all-too-common scene of distracted throngs raising cell phones like decoders between them and reality. Rather than directly viewing the events before them, they take photos and videos: ones that they are unlikely to ever look at again more than once, if at all. Only adding to the impersonal absurdity of stadium events, often what the audience is documenting is not what is actually happening before them, but rather a magnified video-screen projection of the action.

80

Organically Grown: Truth in Advertising

If one's diet is made up strictly of processed food, we know that this will eventually result in negative physical consequences. It is not that far of a reach that overexposure to artificiality in the media—the newscaster with an ambiguous grin on her face reporting a shooting, a nine-year-old overemoting about romantic love or even sex—might also have injurious upshots emotionally. It is not so different from the epidemic for those who work in customer service all day long—where repression of emotions is rewarded—and then go home and struggle to make meaningful personal connections. Truth cannot be turned on and off at will like a faucet, but must be practiced.

I'm not advocating for legislation or interference with free will and choice. The hope is instead that there would be greater caring, respect, and education devoted toward the cultural selection process itself. Just as with other forms of pollution, sound and manufactured imagery matter, too. And the culprits are not just the obvious concerns about excessive volume—as usually is the focus with sound—but of nuance also.

The more holistic worry is that any attention given to something less coherent can displace the opportunity for all to share an objectively more profound experience. So many people are so careful about every last nutritional ingredient that they take in. What about their ears and minds?

And much like with food, live face-to-face music making that is born out of the moment and from existing relationships is made without artificial preservatives. It is fresh and "bio," Zero Kilometer music. What is missing from most mass-produced music and food is that most important of ingredients: that it is made with love.

81

Every Man for Himself?

Ours is not the mythological, market-driven, "survival of the fittest" capitalism, for the majority are never even given a fighting chance to be heard from the get-go. They are disguised by the sheer noise of clichéd niches being played out disingenuously as renegades.

The rare absorption of an underdog is made all the more deadly on two fronts: first, it is an exceptional individual who can resist the temptation to selfishly indulge in their good fortune and not feel that they are destined and deserving, rather than simply chosen. Second, the occasional bone of inclusion that is thrown to the masses perpetuates the illusion that we *are* actually living in a meritocracy, where the "best" is what is made available to us, instead of having whatever the system distributes most aggressively being pushed forth as the best.

That leaves not the most talented on top, but the more connected. A case of politics conquering art.

Nepotism generally kills creativity. With the heirs of the famous, what we end up with are usually prettier, but less talented versions of the parent. Due to their own success, such is the net equation of "geniuses" customarily marrying up in the looks department.

The by-product is "Artist-*lite*"—new, improved packaging, with little of the nutritional value. These privileged-borns are gifted in an entirely different way than their parent. Not through ability, but inherited social station.

Pop culture is becoming more and more of an aristocracy, with worth prized on pedigree, who you know, and fame-worshipping. Objectively, it's hard to respect the statistical absurdity of any single family's talents being superior to the broader net of resources from seven billion people globally! Our allegedly level system increasingly is becoming an *access*-tocracy. Paradoxically, the more the population swells, the more the number of those who have direct links to those few in power shrinks, since though the competition against sheer numbers becomes greater, the number of slots remains virtually unchanged. That in the supposedly enlightened twenty-first century we are being revisited by this sort of privileged classism is a threat to a healthier future.

Good-bye, Communism. Hello, Connected-ism!

In other words—except for that brief interval in the mid-twentieth century, and even then only among some *very* lucky western countries—society has returned to how it more or less *has always been*, lords and serfs. To play devil's advocate for a minute: maybe this mode is all well and good, but regardless, we should at least drop all of the pretense about fairness and "open" markets.

These all indicate movements away from know-how, and toward know-*who*.

When did this all take a turn for the worse?

Before 1996, cross-ownership of any major daily newspaper and a radio or TV station in America was not possible within the same city. This was to ensure that a broader range of voices could communicate. Today, media giants not only own multiple platforms in every major population center, they often own *every* major television, radio, newspaper, publishing house, retail outlet, venue, *and* billboard. They literally have us flanked no matter what direction we turn.

What greater metaphor could there be for the shrinkage of informational channels than the trend of media conglomerates often broadcasting one station across the country *and* also issuing it from multiple signals in the same local market? That means, where once there were three different stations to be found, there is now instead just one being broadcast from three different places on the dial.

82

Too Much "Like," Not Enough Love

Certainly, the child of an artist may be gifted in their own right and almost without fail has a deep history of nurturing within a bohemian support system (i.e., a head start). The issue is not one of talent, but access. Yes, the individual can have ability, but how often is it superior to hundreds of thousands of other struggling artists? And without their surname, would a soul really care?

Often, superstar-semen children whine about not being taken seriously enough or respected in their own right. They speak about how their heritage is a "burden." What they so conveniently fail to recognize amid the spoils is what a luxury it is in the first place to even be *considered* and then disregarded, at all. This experience itself is a privilege most will never have. The lucky-born are bestowed a level of attention that they feel entitled to and take for granted as if it is beneath them. Yet, countless other more talented souls would kill for a smidgen of their opportunities, but will never receive them. It is so easy to believe in a system of fair-chance and that the cream rises to the top, when you are already aloft.

For most of us, anger stems from not having certain things at all. But, for the entitled, their rage is driven due to not having *more* (e.g., "Yes, I am a doctor. But not at a prestigious hospital." or "Sure, I've been nominated. But I didn't *win*.")

Really what could come more prefabricated than the descendants of the infamous? And this tilt toward coattail riders just makes the lazy and daft hoopla system's job that much easier by piggybacking on the leftover fumes of a parent's waning legacy and cashing in on the low-hanging fruit.

Given enough opportunity and atypical support to gestate, a certain aptitude *will* develop over time with almost anyone in most anything. That is the danger: popular artistic forms are basic enough that a passable aptitude is not all that burdensome to achieve (i.e., it is far from the high bar of neurosurgery or the World Cup finals, that clearly only a rare few can reach). What results is the celebration of adequacy and watered-down facsimiles being pawned off as top-notch. Far from the survival of the fittest, these endeavors come ready-built with a cushioned fall.

Stand-up comedy is the one undertaking that cannot be faked in this way, for the failure to succeed is audible (i.e., people are either laughing or they're not). Try to name one offspring of a famous comic who has even dared to try to step onstage. Even the most known comedians state that previous success and notoriety only buys you a few minutes. If you have not made people laugh decisively by that time, then you're dead in the water. Unfortunately, popular music and serious "acting" can more easily camouflage themselves, by way of ballyhoo and bombast, by adhering to the prescribed steps, toeing the party line, and fronting. Especially if there is a wall of sound backing you up.

As marketing personnel infringe more on the creative process, the media increasingly resembles a school play for the elite, one that the rest of us are expected to dutifully attend and play cheerleader to the clique.

Now that even famous stars regularly lip-synch during live concerts to their own pretaped and pitch-corrected voice, the shower-singer onslaught has been unleashed. The fact has become that propped up by the required technology, literally, anyone given the chance can potentially also do what the "pros" *don't do* either. And, so rather than reality tests, where experience provides objective feedback, vain delusions are enhanced and extended.

Don't get me wrong, being able to fix one or two notes in order to potentially resuscitate an otherwise one-of-a-kind performance can be a magnificent thing. But when the repairs *become* the performance, then things have gone horridly awry, indeed.

If a celebrity musician progeny truly want to be self-made and treated equally "like everyone else," then they should live like fugitives on the run—flee the country, dye their hair color, and surgically alter their face to a point of unrecognizability, assume a new name, and then try starting a band and see if *any* other local players will even agree to audition with them, let alone, that the group will after years of paying for a cramped and smelly rehearsal space, via a demo-tape, be able to secure even a last-minute, opening-slot gig at the local dive bar on even the slowest Monday night of the year.

83

The Talking Dead: Rest in *Pieces*

T he act of giving permanency through recording to something that is by nature transient presents many cultural and philosophical hazards. If one even dare enter into such an endeavor, hopefully it is at least not undertaken lightly. For with this alteration of an experience into an object, there is responsibility entwined.

It is a power not afforded most to disembody and multiply one's range of communication. Almost none of us will have representations of our faces and voices beaming off satellites for generations after our death, as Marilyn Monroe or John Lennon have (and quite possibly would not have wanted to be exposed to this voyeuristic shade of necrofilia). Nor will our words be regurgitated for centuries more in classrooms, or pressed into paper and imprinted on gray matter, like Shakespeare or Dante.

The greatest lie of commercialized music is that it exhaustively represents *all* musical possibility. There has always been and always will be music that exists outside any monetary system or marketplace. Superstars are not needed for people to sing. In fact, the disproportionate emphasis on them actually works to silence the masses. And what we are left with is an illusion of options that ignores the vast majority of music that exists on the planet.

Generally, those in the minority are forced to use intensity in compensation for their infrequent access or exposure. Performance becomes a question of quality versus quantity, and this sort of imbalance can breed extremism in all stripes (e.g., people can only be excluded for so long before they splinter off to their own fringes). Minorities and women are required to outperform to even be considered equal.

Contrastingly, the media's machinations now inundate us with imagery that actually shows very little—the barren content hides important information awash an avalanche of minutiae: reports about rumors, "news" stories on old news stories, or previews of upcoming broadcasts. Previously one stunningly crafted photograph or line had the power to change public opinion, but now we are left with sometimes weeks' coverage of fake news.

84

Oversharing

The creative statements of artists now have often been reduced to a new haircut or makeover, relying on external reinventions to signal the significance of their latest recording. Instead of being cloaked in mystery—as were many pre-MTV artists whose photographs were not included in even the most elaborate album artwork and whose images were often instead defined serially by a single artist's illustrations—today many celebrities work is almost entirely paramusical (e.g., a dust-up with a rival or a wardrobe malfunction have become almost obligatory) and their endeavors bear more than a passing resemblance to prostitution.

Seeing major female singers appear at an annual televised lingerie runway show, during which they are often *even more* scantily clad than the official underwear models, serves as an apt metaphor unto itself.

These attention-desperate panderers are gratuitously explicit about every last detail of their personal lives, *except* the one area where specificity is needed: for the act of lyric writing. Instead, pop lyrics exhibit a poverty of content, bathed in "it's," "forevers," and unspecified "fights," that contain no literal meaning and resemble the scribblings that junior high students make on their forearms and BFF's spiral-bound notebooks. Words then are drained of all content, and subsequently performances become blank canvas upon which free-floating significance can then later be projected. These odes to nothingness act as advertising in that they, whether by design or through ineptness, are sooooooo vague that they leave room for the consumer to place themselves in the middle, and flesh out underfed, skeletal works.

Music was the original "self-help," a way for people to independently make themselves feel better (or at least to feel *something* other—to alter their own state). But market forces have conspired to instead have people dependent on outside supplements—that usually come at a price—for this same process to occur. For all of the faux-empowerment messages of pop lyrics (i.e., mix-and-match Hallmark slogans with an attitude), the subtext is clearly one of learned helplessness, if not full-on addiction.

Referring to celebrities on a first-name basis in the media imposes faux kinship. An odd, collective mental shift has occurred that finds us with more people looking to the "stars" for inspiration and direction than raising their eyes and searching the actual night sky for guidance.

And those celebrities who subject themselves to the feeding frenzy of the media have now become *their own paparazzi* via oversharing of bathroom selfies and "leaked" home sex tapes. It's an arms race for attention and the casting couch is the entire nation. No longer occurring behind closed doors, but instead in the most public of forums possible.

Yet, the hunger for spiritual connection persists, as we see with so many teenagers turning webcams into confessionals.

That songs have become placards for careers in spectacle—more than private manifestos or offerings of rapport—is made all the more harrowing with the realization that most parents no longer sing to their youngsters the tunes that their mothers sang to them (and their grandmothers before them), but instead they hum jingles, television themes, and/or bygone "hits" from their own youth.

This point has been brought home to me in many countries where instead of blasting the radio, carpenters and bricklayers today still sing ancient ditties to help pass the time. Often, these vocalizations are spontaneous and/or profane encouragements to one another that the workday will be over, soon enough. Rather than irritating, I found it almost comforting to be awakened predawn by laborers serenading one another in Bergamasque dialect.

Most often, musical expressions in the western world now—be it dancing or crooning—are not taken on full-throttle with sincerity, but doused in look-at-me, "ha, ha, ha" irony. A one-foot-in-the-door, one-foot-out that allows them to remain supplements observer, commenting on themselves all the while, and not allowing that they ever be completely overtaken by the expressive urge.

Instead of carols, we get mix-tapes (and forwarded links)—passive replays, rather than active creation.

And sadly, frequently, those dancing are dances of derision, not celebration.

SECTION XII:

How Music Dies: $$ and Its Wake

85

If You Can't Beat 'em, Get *Them* to Join You

Almost anytime an unnecessary intermediary is introduced into a process, it is a regression. To witness that so many people's first impulse when encountering extraordinary events is to pull out a phone to record it with—thus distancing themselves from the proceedings rather than simply being—is heartbreaking. With the online diaspora, this middling makes spying on our actions easier *and* enforces an involuntary toll on otherwise gratis or cheaper behaviors.

The ever-escalating corporate mergers, bolstered by smoke-and-mirrors speech about "free markets," actually decrease competition and have built up an infrastructure where most of us reside within a de facto, open-air company store (e.g., malls having gutted downtown centers, with identical shops then installed in every said mall). Most everything we buy is now owned by the same few. That sucking sound is the profits from transactions being siphoned out of our local communities and into the hands of a dizzyingly privileged, parasitic minority, a form of nongovernmental taxation by the rich to the poor, for merely existing.

In the postcolonial age, the high-and-mighty had two revelations:

1. Rather than forcing people to do something, if you can sham them into wanting it themselves, then there is no resistance whatsoever.

   The idea that individuals would not only advertise for corporations, but actually *pay* to do so—for the "privilege" of wearing a Nike emblem or brand-name purse—is so absurd that even the most ardent capitalists could not have initially believed it was possible. Without a doubt, the first person to propose this at a company board meeting was laughed out of the room (e.g., "You mean you're suggesting that people would not only advertise for us for free—on their person even!—but actually pay for the privilege? That is totally ridiculous! Stupidest idea I've ever heard! You're an idiot.").

Ashamedly, it was musicians who were the pioneers of this type of bodies-as-billboards merchandising—T-shirts, baseball caps, stickers. When people care about something, then their support is voluntary. And when people do things voluntarily, they are statistically proven to actually work *harder* for them than for money. This is because their effort is not measured and meted by external means. The difference is that instead of doing what they have to do, they are doing what they *want* to.

The surreptitious revolution that corporations have succeeded in is getting people to care about abstractions—to be inspired not by material goods, but by the things that they (allegedly) represent, through association.

In an overly cutthroat, capitalistic ideological milieu, the supreme currency is attention and a sense of superiority. Far more valuable than mere money, these are sensations that people will not only pay to have, but in some extreme cases even kill for.

2. Instead of fighting the opponents head-on, it can work much better to simply co-opt their "cooler" image while retaining your same lackluster formulas. With political conservatives we now have ruthless ideology neatly packaged using female and/or minority candidates as fronts. And in the pop world, we find half-naked, tattooed, and drug-addicted "personalities" with artistic content so vapid it would make Pat Boone or Barry Manilow green with envy. (Yesterday's hair-raising metal guitar-wanking finds reuse today as a brain-dead, reality-show "conflict sequence" soundtrack.)

The turning point was during the Reagan/Thatcher neo-con overthrow, when blind greed was perplexingly recast as butch and "courageous." This recoding stands as a particularly diabolical setback for the likelihood of mankind being able to progress as a more enlightened and empathic species.

And, just as missionaries in the nineteenth century would enwrap existing regional holidays and rituals into the web of the new religion they were hawking, McDonald's now offers salt-and-sugar, token versions of local fare to lure in patrons from each region.

86

Now You Don't See It (and Now You *Still* Don't)

T he marketplace is driven by two primary sleights of hand:

1. Bait and switch: You incite a desire for someone to *have* something. Then once the buyer is properly aroused, their target is switched to something of lesser quality and/or higher price. Ideally both!

    a) Specifically, with market-driven music, often artists are browbeat into offering up a fawning and unrepresentative single (usually written and/or played by someone else) as a sacrificial lamb to lure in audiences. Rarely is this strategy tenable, though, since buyers quickly tire of albums and concerts that do not resemble that which drew them in the first place.

2. Illusion of options: Through packaging, differentiation is feigned, so that one nearly identical item becomes more desirable than another by way of the emotional response its aura creates. How a laundry soap can be perceived as sexy or an automobile smart can only be a symptom of diseased appetites, where the preservation instinct has become unhealthily linked to things that actually kill us—cigarettes, alcohol, junk food, cars, etc. This is what pop culture has now done by way of niches and aperture

being filled by cartoon versions of rebellion, that actually only help perpetuate the system that they supposedly are revolting against. Could there be any more pro-establishment figures today than a Jay Z or Kid Rock or (you fill in the blank here)? They are beneficiaries of privileges for the elite staying *exactly* as they are . . . or even *increasing*. For they are among them!

And isn't that the most skilled and ancient tactic for conquest of one's opposition? To simply enlist and assimilate them, silencing and taming them by satiating and lulling them to sleep with rewards, all without throwing a single blow. The old "keep your friends close and your enemies closer" routine.

Through the mass-facsimile of Che Guevera's image or James Brown's howl, they are gradually emptied of almost all their former sting, and revolutions become gentrified. (And recently seeing Gandhi's likeness on a bottle of malt liquor led me to believe that the microbrew was proposing a whole new method for staging "passive resistance.")

87

Image Cannibalism: The Media as a Gigantic Mirror of Infatuation

Technology now allows people to consume themselves as entertainment, photographing every movement and moment, Tweeting out trivial thoughts, and monitoring people's reaction to them. It is now possible for people to cast in a recurring, starring role their favorite person: themself! Clearly, there has always been youthful vanity. But with adolescence increasingly prolonged, vanity is no longer a development stage, but a permanent, narcotized station. And the longer that stage is prolonged, consequently, the less frequently generational shifts in perspective occur.

The personal-technology industry's colossal win has been enabling and indulging an individual's addiction to their own image and professed potential, *without* requiring any corresponding achievement. Since juveniles have been targeted as the most lucrative sales demographic, prolonging this mind-set promotes consumption. And it is the capitalists that end up the primary beneficiaries of this otherwise undesirable emotional immaturity and infantilism.

Additionally, for the cycles of overbuying to perpetuate themselves, a materialistic society must be conditioned to equate what is newest with what is "best." Consequently, it is necessary that youthfulness is pushed to the forefront and celebrated.

The healthy role of role models, though, is not so much to be domineering evidence that you aren't good enough. But, instead, to serve as an indication that we could be *more*. Rather than acting as a force to validate lack of emotional growth as normal or desirable, imagery at its best can instead potentially give us something higher to aspire to.

88

Manufactured Competition: Don't Believe the Hype

O ur media culture is driven by superlatives. This extremism leads to disappointment and distrust, since the vast majority of communications people receive are exaggerations and false. (A significant consideration is that most advertising's imperative nature would be considered rude if it occurred in face-to-face contexts.)

Advertising is bathed in radical, all-or-nothing language to ensure maximum provocation and authority. Throughout the ages, this sort of propaganda was largely nonexistent and rarified. Today, it is almost inescapable and consequently has influenced the way people think. This element has altered and harshened our cultural climate. Largely, this is due to marketing's goal being to provoke anxiety while simultaneously offering a solution to resolve it. Rather than finding a need and filling it, propaganda strives to *manufacture* needs that then must be filled (to then again be perpetually displaced).

The desire for the "best" can only lead to disappointment. For there rarely exists such a distinction. With a planet of billions and counting, the concept that chosen individuals are so superior that they should be listened to or looked at exclusively, and the majority silenced, is a profit-steered construct.

Managers, agents, promoters, and music companies protect their interests, in the same manner that petroleum giants hire mercenary armies in oil rich, undeveloped outposts. Profits foil the greater good, and artists past their prime are propped up like straw effigies, kept going by artificial life support, so that we can be subjected to the decades of dribble from them. Many a one-shot writer's, idiot savant's, or prodigy's gifts were ephemeral and, in some cases, even killed off *by* the trappings and/or ramifications of success.

Worse yet, usually very few of those that are trend-riders outlive the novelty phase. They fall into the quick fix of bell-bottom sounds that come forth with a pre-issued, ready-made expiration date, a cultural shelf life.

Instead, classic works free us from time. And these almost always emanate in the absence of ego. Often, *so* much so, that the contribution was made anonymously.

Not that any of those lottery-lucky performers deserve being begrudged, but in a more holistic and aesthetically minded culture, ailing artists would be issued *anti*-record contracts and paid to *stop* making albums. Or even more, paid to *un*release their paler efforts.

"In the name of 'eminent domain,' you'll need to step away and hand over that Les Paul *now*, sir."

But, instead, once-visionary groups are allowed to degenerate into tribute bands *to* their former selves, releasing ever fainter facsimiles of their apex, in an endless string of hollower "comebacks." This is done, rather than recognizing and admitting that the limits of their own imaginations have already peaked and been duly strip-mined. They, instead, loiter in the collective consciousness. The hero of today is almost predestined to become the despot of tomorrow, should they not self-terminate and bow out gracefully.

Far too often, once an artist has become a cash-cow, they are milked dry and paraded around like Stalin's corpse. (I had the misfortune of witnessing, by chance, the final performance of a blues giant, weeks before he passed on. He had to be led by the hand to a chair, did not once touch with his hands the instrument set in his lap the entire time, babbled incoherently and sporadically somewhere *around* the vicinity of his microphone, and it was clear that he had only the foggiest idea he was even on a stage. I expected at any moment for him to start singing, "Get out of my house! How did all these people get into my house? Somebody, call the police!" In such cases, it would seem that more than a paying audience, Elder Protective Services should've been on the scene.)

This is not about ageism. Clearly, some artists are delayed-bloomers and their greatest work comes late (Little Jimmy Scott; Norman Maclean's first novel *A River Runs Through It* being published when he was seventy-three).

Drugs and other indulgences aside, few things are more deadly than the pride (and the self-consciousness and grandiosity) that the star-system engenders. The instant an artist even dares to conceptualize a "legacy," the muse has left them for purer portals. This is night and day from an artist at their peak, overflowing with so many ideas, that they are indefatigably outpaced by them and driven to distraction. Inspiration is a restless thing. And, if that person is further insulated by yes-people and the bloated "G"-word gets bandied about too liberally, then the quality of their output will predictably fall in direct disproportion to that wicked word's use.

The fact is, if remembered at all, even a venerated author's entire work is often depleted down to a single misquoted or misattributed touristic blurb (Capote for Venezia, Mark Twain for something he *never even said* about San Francisco).

89

Sin-ergy

An eye-opener for me was recently guesting on the same radio program as an ultraslick, megahit producer who had become a billionaire by devising some of the sappiest and most reductionistic pop of the eighties. Though unassailably worlds less severe, hearing him relate that he had quit the business because music had become *too* commercial and calculated, *even for him,* was a bit like hearing Joseph Goebbels speak out against anti-Semitism, claiming outrage that it had all gone too far.

Even most diehard fans would often be hard-pressed to aurally identify their favorite pantie-packaged vamp in a blind-taste test. Part of the reason is because audiences have never really heard that person's true voice, but are instead familiar only with a synthetic process triggered by said person's vocalizing. The real stars now are often the engineers. They are the ones pulling the strings by costuming the singer's voice in this game of dress-up and acting as a musical stunt-double for the star's artistic limitations.

Historically, pop singers have cloned one another, chasing trends. This is nothing new. And sometimes they even *improved* on one another—sometimes entirely by accident—through this copycat process. The difference today is that it is often entire sound templates that are replicated whole and then onto which the singers are them simply slotted in—almost as an afterthought—merely one element of literally dozens or hundreds of separate, stacked ingredients coloring a three-minute recording.

In the girl-group and boy-band eras, singles were often phantom sung by far more talented, but older and less visually marketable vocalists (e.g., someone balding or hefty). Instead today, singers are shadowed *by machines* that literally "correct" their voices to some standard that a techie has preprogrammed.

This is day and night from hearing someone like Pavarotti singing the end of "O Soave Fanciulla," where it is evident that *even from offstage* his voice is more resonant than any other dutifully trained and top-notch singer is when front and center.

How can a truthful experience be shared with an audience when even "spontaneous" bits or mistakes are scripted into many live shows, during which the lead singer's mic temporarily becomes audible so that they can make known how normal and down-to-earth they are? (Nothing humanizes an icon more than a staged fall or a celebrity mugshot. Ironically, for some, bruised and/or mascara-streaked police photos become the *most* enduring image of their careers.)

Lighting-cue directors and video-feeds come to dictate what occurs on stage so that the performer is shackled into being just another moving part of a gigantic stadium spectacle machinery (and performers literally can get killed if they miss their mark and are standing in the wrong place at the wrong time). Audiences pay to have simulated "live" experiences, rather than weathering the risks that come from unrepeatable, discrete, but imperfect musical performances. Instead, they witness lip-synchers playing ventriloquist dummy to an idealized and manipulated version of *themselves*.

One of the eeriest cultural images I have seen in recent years was watching a band soundcheck at a stadium without the "star" being present at all except via his prerecorded voice, which played oracle stand-in for the spotlit but completely bare, altar-lit center stage.

90

Don't Believe Half of What You See

For all the images of "freedom" music videos wantonly project, the trauma that they inflict is their dictation of only one vision for a piece of music. And then that very restrictiveness gets *re*inforced repetitively. What is lost is the intimate and idiosyncratic relationship that can bloom naturally and randomly—mostly in the unconscious—for each listener to a piece of music.

In this post-aural, persona-driven era of "music," manufactured-by-committee, machine-hygienated songs often are nearly indistinguishable from one another and strikingly unmemorable. They tend toward a mush of sound.

Rather than ear worms, we are given eye candy.

Even ardent fans often cannot hum a hit song back to you as it is so lacking in melody, and they often have not the mushiest what the lyrics mean since they are such empty, word-salad fragments that have been deliberately left completely open to misinterpretation. *But* those same people can tell you *exactly* what the video looks like. Instead of musical hooks, we are left with visual adhesives. And that optical hook is often somebody's booty or six-pack abs—usually stand-ins for the star.

The eye usurps sound again, reiterating its supremacy.

91

Fabricated Identity: Bands as *Brands*

In this life-lived-as-replay era—where many photograph their food before they've eaten it—we end up in the wake of cultural backlog, with the gap between innovation and impact being ever lengthened, like an aesthetic equivalent of the Doppler Effect. Documentation should help memorialize, not trivialize. In the recent past, we only photographed major life events like weddings and newborns, now we photograph *every* thing. Many today can hardly take two steps without stopping to snap yet another picture, and then often immediately review, delete, and redo it.

By the time a form is acknowledged and reaps rewards commercially, it has long since been reduced to mere nostalgia for the more attentive. And, thus, in the marketplace, the status quo remains the same and revolutions-deferred get submerged, appearing only tardily when they are sold down the line as a concept and brand-name (frighteningly far more Ramones T-shirts have been printed since their demise than their records ever were in their entire career).

Though hundreds of thousands of "alternative" bands have tried, not one has yet outstripped the template set forth by the inauspiciously received bands, the Velvet Underground and Big Star. The rub is that the successors are working from a schematic, and that can hardly be construed as "independent."

It is embalmed. And all that is left is ritual, like a spiritual movement whose charismatic leader has died, and is then followed by competing charlatans quarreling to fill the void for their own nefarious reasons. The primary result of reliance on consumption and source materials for creative action is neutered vision.

It is but a faint memory now what an uproar was stirred when Lou Reed appeared in and allowed "Walk on the Wild Side" to be used for a scooter advertisement (circa 1984). Sadly, he acted as a pioneer regarding selling out, too. Since that first hallowed ground was ruptured, there has come a flood, where now musical bands not only endorse products but have even *become* their own brands—via clothing lines, cologne, etc.

In his most outlandish musings, it is almost guaranteed that obscure British balladeer Nick Drake never dreamed that decades after his suicide, one of his songs would go on to help sell automobiles and make millions, if not billions, for complete strangers. But this is the delayed assimilation that we are caught within.

Music doesn't have commercial breaks like traditional television, so corporations have found a way to use them *for* commercials. And with films, they insert themselves via the cameo intrusions of product placements (a trend which all too many supposedly "street" rappers have introduced a tad too lustily by name-dropping within their rhymes). Now entire films act as chamber of commerce tourist brochures for famous cities that are used as "characters"—which ironically have often been filmed mostly in *other* less famous but similar cities that offer far cheaper permits.

92

Sub-*merged* Substitutions

What remains of most corporate labels are now headed by alumni from the promo departments, rather than those with a grounding in and love of the arts. This only intensifies highly commercialized trends. Playing matchmaker to stars—so that can gain a symbiotic boost—passes for inspiration versus truer and less-calculated creativity. Instead, it is essentially opportunistic, symbiotic micromergers that are made. These are prearranged, marriages of convenience, like any "good" aristocracy.

Similarly, many studios build and bill themselves almost entirely based on very loose associations. For me, the knowledge that "Pink Floyd used this board to mix _____," or "Kurt Cobain sang into that mic," or the claim that a certain engineer has become the go-to person for an ailing veteran star is the least of my considerations.

Patterns are of interest. Isolated incidents might only be lucky accidents or anomalies.

Even more pathetically, there is the food-chain, pecking-order whereby people feed off associations that are even secondary and tertiary—and often anemic ones, at that—overzealously name-dropping what amounts to *no*-names (e.g., "When I was mixing with my friend Dave, who sometimes plays keyboards with _____'s solo band . . .").

Similarly, a classic artist endorsing someone often lends that named artist undeserved credibility by association, particularly if it is cross-racial. When attempting this sort of prestige mortgaging, it is almost comical the exaggerated reverence that many otherwise obnoxious celebrities grovel in, whereby they wear other races and/or another's fame like fashion accessories.

One empty corporate-creature has even has implemented a sure-fire songwriting system which involves lyrics that follow set steps:

1. start with a greeting
2. make a declaration of self (e.g., "I am hurting.")
3. ask a question of the listener such as "Will you come and help me?"
4. give a simple command (e.g., throw your hands in the air)
5. spell out a word and/or count (i.e., 1-2-3-4)
6. use immediate repetition—either by restating the same short line twice or by deliberately stuttering (e.g., "B-b-b-baby") a single word
7. and, most importantly, use catchphrases that roll off the tip of an audience's tongue because they already know them.

This entire method encourages formulaic sameness, helping nondeviation from the norm become even more the norm.

And, it goes without saying that almost every pop song ever written is done so in the second-person: Yes, it's all about "*you*," babe.

93

The Superscar System

If a person dies within days of not being able to eliminate their own feces, then what happens to a culture that has been constipated for decades? After the inarguably unparalleled explosion of musical creativity in the wake and throes of Industrial Era America, what entirely new musical form—not just variation on a form—has emerged since the 1970s? Try, zero.

Subgenres and splintering, yes. Radically new genres, no.

"Rap" officially emerged in 1979 and the groundwork for dance and/or electronic music was certainly set in the seventies by the likes of Giorgio Moroder, Brian Eno, Kraftwerk, and the cross-dressing, Bach synth enthusiast Walter/Wendy Carlos. Scientifically, stasis of any system is identified as when descendants stop being spawned and a family tree branches into a dead end (or maybe more aptly, a suburban circle).

The more "skilled" they become, the greater the likelihood that artists are to analyze and use logic and methodology rather than run on pure creativity. As a result, the more polished and "professional," usually the more limpid their output. Focusing on the surface manifestations of inspiration (chords, equipment, attitude) and venturing to try to trace magic backward is a confusion of values. They fall back from art, into the comfort of craft. Rather than "fake it till you make it," this becomes a case of fake it till you *break* it, since almost all of the most precious ideas arise from the unconscious—in unguarded, relaxed dream states. It is easy to end up in a purgatory of paralysis as the conscious and unconscious work in opposition rather than harmoniously. A state of repression rather than *expression*.

A common syndrome is to unconsciously sabotage progress due to a fear of the unknown. Past success can make people risk-allergic and lead to a favoring of the familiar—even when it is negative and destructive—due to the sense of relative safety (e.g., that thing, as bad as it may be, at least has not proven lethal . . . yet), as well as the nostalgia it evokes.

And, past-orientation—being unable to "let go" of something—is one of the chief giveaways of clinical depression.

Fear is the primary emotion at play, the only one necessary for survival. But it can *interfere with* our survival as well, by rendering us frozen due to being overly loss-aversive. It is imperative that we find a way through, to somehow metabolize and integrate our experiences and sensations.

When people speak of forever and "history," they do so in direct ignorance of commercially recorded music being just over one hundred years in the making, that the delivery formats have regularly metamorphasized during that time (and continue to do so at an ever-escalating rate), and that the majority of the biggest-selling singers and most celebrated actors of each era are *already* forgotten, buried beneath the avalanche of content, whose volume is ever proliferating.

If entire nations are less known than a single family's name or—even worse yet—a globally identifiable first name—then the bandwidths have clearly become clogged and constricted. The healthiest system would be one based on *how* (well) something is being done, not *who* is doing it.

On the upside of all this, do not singular voices like Chavela Vargas, Bill Monroe, Chet Baker, Bjork, Yma Sumac, Nusrat Fateh Ali Khan, and Biggie Smalls (to name just a few) deserve to become artifacts and heard for generations?

Yes, they do and *that* is recording at its most purposeful. Much like the cries of a dying person, they are sounds that leave an involuntary mark on a listener and can change history slightly. The concern are the armies of clones that follow in their wake, and in a noxious double-whammy, clog the channels of content *and* camouflage the sounds of new and true artists, by infesting listeners ears, along the way.

94

Standardized Forms, Fear of the Random: Living in Boxes, atop Grids

R ather than unique entities and diversity, we are increasingly encapsulated by standardized forms. Architecture is one example of this, as more and more buildings since the 1950s have come to resemble boxes, more than domiciles.

There is an understandable comfort for people amid the known. Chain stores and restaurants epitomize this. The trade-off is one of consistency for quality.

Living beside the freeway in a new tract of condos wedged amid an hour's-long stretch that was virtually indistinguishable to all but the most studied, a family member of mine recently explained how much she preferred, "The Target store at the next exit rather than the one here at ours, across the street."

Seeing tourists gobble down McDonald's in South America or stand in line for Starbucks in Europe are but sad examples of opportunities lost for discovery.

The ultimate benefactors of standardization are the manufacturers, since it is easier and cheaper to just clone or simulate the same recipes and designs in mass quantity. But this action is antithetical to progress; it runs counter to the process of adaptation that advances any species.

These standardizations now extend to indistinguishable talking-heads on television. A trend is that the hosts of most TV and radio talk programs now have an eerily, pod-like similarity regardless of their region.

Even in typing this book, the trend of standardizing encroaches on this very document due to the tendency of automatic spell-check to change words *wrongly* to their more common counterpart (e.g., Milli Vanilli becomes Milli Vanilla. Though it may arguably be a more accurate handle for the group, this is an error that was caused through the "correction" process and the dominance of one word over another).

In live music, around the mid-1990s, venues with circular or semicircle stages were badgered to conform and make costly remodels, when major artists began boycotting anywhere the dimensions did not meet the single standard that their tour's sets and lights were designed for. Instead of embracing the break in routine of a months-long tour and rising to the challenge to work with different rooms and environments—where people might be beside or even behind the artist—these behemoth, concrete-and-steel spaces themselves were forced to collapse into one unchanging format, with all artists confined to the same fifty-foot-wide box that fit the mandates of the basketball courts that they were actually playing atop.

And a most spooky tableau from almost anywhere I've visited in the world that has continuous, twenty-four-hour electrical service available is the nightlight glow of television sets throbbing beside almost every bedroom window.

Another self-crafted instrument from recycled parts—*DO* try
this at home!

Odds and Endings: They Couldn't Keep Doing It Without All of the "Little People"

95

Souls Sold for Convenience

In the future everyone will have their own television show . . . that only they will watch.

To borrow a philosophical quandary, if a blog goes unread on the web, does it make a sound?

Rather than disregarding the attention-starved—who rabidly curate *themselves*—it is worth noting that the preponderance of cult leaders (Charles Manson, David Koresh) were failed rock starsand many terrorist extremists are aspiring rappers. When one endeavor fails, any other available vehicle will do, because the art was never truly the goal in the first place, but glorification. As the Twin Towers came down, posters of Bin Laden went up on the walls of disgruntled adolescent misfits across the Middle East who suffered from free-floating angst. Osama had achieved a level of abomination that in seconds turned yesterday's gangsta instantly antiquarian. Tupac and Danzig suddenly paled in comparison.

It is not so much that there is some grand conspiracy scheme at play. Capitalists are by design opportunistic, not visionary. It is far less taxing to observe and replicate than create. Business is run by settlers that come after the revolution, not the pioneers, who often languish in poverty and obscurity. An "if you can't beat 'em, join 'em" blueprint. Which then becomes a "get *them* to rejoin that which has already been stolen from them" undertaking. During the "alternative" phase, corporations sorted out quickly that most people didn't actually care if they were being anticonformist, as long as they could invest in what made them believe that they were.

The history of most cultural movements is one of the rich invading and pillaging the territories of the innovators, and those displaced originators then being forced to abandon ground and move on to greener pastures to forge new movements and trends, keeping the torch of "now"-ness alive in some reborn form. With music, this usually is demarcated when that which formerly involved a dancing audience becomes listening music, and followers are subsequently relegated to become stationary, detached, and "polite" spectators. This couldn't be much further from no audience, only participants—that return to the "we" that reduces the "I." (In a related phenomenon: as a general rule of delineation, the more "proper" and accepted a musical form becomes, the more the diction of the performers improves.)

A delusional population is not healthy for democracy. But totalitarianism thrives on denial and distortion, not truth. The battles of the future will not be so much between people or states, but more about corporations' assault on culture.

In a culture that worships underdogs, candor becomes scarce since almost everyone then wants to portray themselves as having "struggled." After scuttling an official aristocracy to found the US of A, now even most "liberals" cuddle it unreflectingly in the arts.

The corporations' bottom lines revealed that not only did they not have to lose money fighting for censorship, they could actually *make* money by gaining greater control of distribution, peddling placebos, and then marginalizing dissent—drowning it out through sheer volume alone, instead.

96

Corruption and Arrested Growth

kin to how puppies are vulnerable to having *any* surrogate imprint as
their identified mother, corporate brigades like to hook them young, so
that their brand becomes a source of comfort, akin to a warm blanket or
breast milk. These acts of predation have become almost blasé.

I am fully aware that even though I'm not "supposed" to, I still get teary-eyed
at moments during the first two *Rocky* films, and that the bands Rush and the Bay
City Rollers (!) both hold a special place in my heart that it is doubtful they could
have gained in my more august years.

An argument can be made here for inoculation rather than isolation, that
being out in the world and embracing the sloppiness of it all can actually produce
its own hybrid power and resistance to metastasization.

In many ways, I feel bad for the kids that are raised involuntarily swaddled
in Dead Kennedys and Johnny Cash jumpers, before they even have any idea
who the sponsored musicians are! This coercion of coolness inflicted on children
leaves them meager opportunity to fearlessly explore and possibly *fail* at finding their own ears, eyes, and heart, and allows them limited freedoms in making
meaning from the sea of stimulus that they are faced with. All should retain the
God-given right to be an unintentional nerd, milquetoast, and mainstream in their
tastes, or to latch on to whatever transitional fascinations best suit their burgeon-
ing little selves along the way.

In fact, often boy-bands with their honeyed hits act as transitional
training-wheels to popular culture, a gateway drug for fans, who as they age, will
usually seek out and follow knottier offerings.

97

Who Are You Calling Crazy?: The Romanticization of Mental Illness

A minor tragedy is how often people buy into the myth that artists must be crazy in order to be substantial. Anyone with more than a passing exposure to true mental illness knows that not only does madness *not* abate productivity, it actually incapacitates and destroys it, since disorganization and depression are the rule.

Further, those who try to make relativistic arguments about the verifiability of even the existence of certain clinical diagnoses (e.g., "But aren't we all a bit 'crazy'?"), need only spend a few hours in a locked psychiatric facility to see that certain conditions like schizophrenia are prevalent and palpable.

The confusion here is trifold.

Firstly, almost all people that are above-average performers in any field spend much of their time in a *hypo*-manic state. They are more energetic than the average individual and have racehorse minds, but are usually not fully "bipolar." Therefore, they are able to do more, but without fully crossing the line into the fragmentation that comes with mania.

Secondly, those who open themselves up more empathically can also be more prone to depression due to this sensitivity. But the self-professed belief that one is exceptional in any way (such as artistic aspirers who often claim to be more "sensitive" than the common person) leads to delusion. Everyone is selectively vulnerable and their status is in flux. It is best to define people using adverbs rather than adjectives—what they are *doing*, not who they are—for no one is that one-dimensional as to be merely an "asshole." (Though, some sure do come close.) Further, attempts to describe ourselves are futile as they are always limited by our own ego and subjectivity. We are literally too close to the subject at hand.

Lastly, what game-changing artists do require is a lessening of social obligation. The line between dropping the veneer of nicety in favor of truth, *but* not crossing over to life-size sociopathic behavior is often a thin, almost overlapping one.

With many fledgling artists the affliction is monochromaticism—they always try to be nice, instead of honest. And the kind of credibility and transparency that are needed to create great art cannot be turned on and off at will, like a faucet, when needed.

It is true that there are a select few leading figures who were also genuinely afflicted with clinical mental illness. But those few created *in spite of* the illness, not because of it. These sorts of individuals are sometimes so exceptional that they can function high above most others, even when they are compromised. A physical example of this is a former private anger-management client of mine who suffered from massive addiction issues, yet still decisively dominated as world champion in his sport for years, even during the times when he competed so drunk he could barely stand up.

Due to my background working as a counselor in mental health facilities, I gained somewhat of a reputation as having a special facility with "challenging" artists.

The fact is though that the most raucous evening at a nightclub, almost without fail pales in comparison to the most ho-hum Saturday night in a locked psychiatric facility, and what most in show-biz label an "emergency," rarely is. Not to mention that your "craziest" and most salty, loose-cannon songwriters or singers usually can't hold a candle to a garden-variety manic or schizophrenic in a florid state of their illness.

98

Records Don't Kill People, *People* Kill People

R ecordings at their best give people the ability to be influenced by kaleidoscopic sounds, without ever leaving the confines of their home or car. At worst, they encourage conformity and reductionism, whereby creation becomes merely an act of tracing and copying.

Corporate confections and branding, through their insidious imposition of values, can be as willfully deluded and sinister as the nineteenth-century "Carry Me Back" genre, in which white songwriters sold fictional tales of free slaves who preposterously longed so woefully to return to the "security" of the plantation life that they had now come to miss. The difference today is that instead of just preaching to the choir, it is those who should most actively be rejecting these limitations (e.g., young adults who are having their choices increasingly censored by omnipotent and displacing presences like Subway and Starbucks) that usually snuggle and even *covet* this self-limiting propaganda the most.

Beholding a crowd of wealthy Arabs lurch drunkenly on the beach in front of a festival stage on the Persian Gulf, just spitting distance from Iran, and belt out "Redemption Song" in anticipation of one of Bob Marley's children appearing, stands out. That this anthem for the oppressed was being sung by some of the richest people in the world, their Rolex's and nail-extensions shining in the moonlight, was made even more ironic by the fact that it was the performer's *father's* song that they were celebrating, not the offspring's own (of which it can be assured that no one there would be able to even name a single song from, let alone sing), and the father himself had died more than four decades earlier. That Mr. Marley's own privileged, legacy-coasting son had cancelled at the last minute and was not going to appear after all, was just the *coup de grâce*.

It might be hard to create a more vivid metaphor for the aggressive viral nature of mass-media than to hear the founder of an orphanage for the victims of napalm (Agent Orange)-related birth defects—the chemical that the US military rained down to defoliate jungles near Laos and that still has genetic repercussions today for those living in contaminated regions—share how the children there will only rap and not sing at all. And that the rapping they do is in porous, phonetic English, not their mother tongue.

99

Open Season

There is the ever-popular, relativistic, "I watched tons of those movies when I was a kid and I am fine" argument.

But, really? *Are* we fine?

Much like the adage "you are what you eat," there must be some residue to what we ingest aurally and visually. Lifetimes spent watching dysfunctional and damaged porn stars, simulated murder, and insincere expressions of emotions cannot be without some effect.

Just because someone hasn't directly killed someone, it doesn't mean that they have not passively participated in and contributed to a murderous subtext that plays out in our everyday milieu of cynicism, compulsive competitiveness, and the paranoia that those lead to. For every murder or act of vengeance that actually gets played out, millions if not billions are imagined inside our skulls. We never act entirely alone. Extremists manifest and act out the unresolved, cultural undercurrents, cries for correction.

With subjectivity touted as truth, it now often suffices as enough to simply believe and feel, than to actually be or do something. What the self-help gurus neglected to factor into their geometry was that "positivity" boosting was meant as an antidote for those who were wounded and lacking in self-esteem, *not* as fuel for *further* egocentric indulgence.

The most dangerous personality structure is excessive ambition and arrogance, held without any corresponding ability. This is the quintessential mass-murderer/serial-killer cocktail.

The result in daily life are café baristas that serve up cappuccinos with all the self importance of brain surgery and yuppie grocery baggers that carry themselves with the swagger of NFL stars.

100

Conditional Love

Something that I've experienced in less money-oriented societies is that when entering a business establishment in those environs you are expected to greet *every*one there, and to fail to do so is regarded as rude. This is very different from in capitalistic milieus where generally the only person spoken to—if at all—is the person that any cash will be exchanged with. In fact, to speak to anyone else in these public spaces is usually reacted to as if it is strange and maybe even threatening.

Increasingly, it is common to have professional exchanges (e.g., airport security) where no mutual acknowledgment occurs whatsoever, since the cash-flow is indirect and the worker often is under the misimpression that they are solely beholden to their employer, not the individuals that make their employment possible in the first place.

On the interpersonal front, those who rummage around for friendship or romance based on shared consumeristic patterns (i.e., liking the same things) are bound to be disappointed by the lack of longevity down the line. It's not so much that opposites attract, as that what is missed in the like-type pursuit is a more fundamental connection. Seeking a partner with empathy—regardless of their questionable proclivities in movies or music—is likely to prove far more rewarding than someone who uses their own personal preferences as a way to ridicule others with less debonair tastes.

It's not that a Celine Dion or Hollywood franchise film fan necessarily has a bigger heart. But certainly he or she is less of a perfectionist and elitist. One not driven by the hunger to prove themselves special and different by every last, little thing that they buy or believe in. Instead, they are relating to whatever it is each thing makes them feel.

Often, casual listeners are much better judges of the longevity and universality of a classic than "serious" music fans. The more disinterested listener doesn't usually so much interpret, but instead just "knows" what they like, with little prejudice or interest in the baggage or context.

Somewhat paradoxically, the more hard-core music buyers tend to be the most materialistic, more so than commercial music fans who ironically often instead expect (and increasingly *get*) things for cheap or free. The true music-heads are the ones willing to shell out top dollar for some rarity, box-set or limited-edition color vinyl. The social-currency and symbolism of membership and one-up-ness is often of greater importance than the content itself (as so many unopened completists' items attest to).

But due precisely to its wide dissemination, music is so devalued that even the most cherished collector's items rarely go for more than one hundred dollars, even in bidding wars. Compare that with someone paying over three hundred million for a painting, and some of the ramifications of mass distribution can become better elucidated.

There is no single, easily playable "original" recording ever. Every copy *is* a copy. Even "master tapes" are often lost or disintegrate over time, and the only true original would be if you were actually present while a record was being recorded. And even then, in the era of multitracking and staggered performances that can be dragged out over months or years, even that experience would probably bear little resemblance to the finished (un-)real "thing" that results and becomes known.

A central investigation is: does the music unite indiscriminately or divide selectively, acting as a sort of new world country club, one with a new haircut and worse manners? A culture that substitutes things for relationships *and* self for others erodes our humanity since one of our defining characteristics is a human's potential ability to choose self-sacrifice on behalf of the greater good (e.g., a stranger drowning in an effort to rescue a child).

In the end, believing someone might be your "soul mate" simply because they like Tom Waits too is not really any more advanced than a pair of toddlers claiming that it is proof of their undying friendship that pistachio is both of their the favorite ice cream. Bonds of common consumption, as well as using intimates as a looking-glass to bask in one's own glory, are likely to leave one hungering, forever chasing that elusive buzz.

101

The Collective Jukebox Is Stuck: One World, One Store

Unregulated capitalism is not the self-monitoring organism its proponents claim. Consolidation and mergers lead to ever fewer checks and balances. When corporations that already produce the majority of material goods and consumables proceed to absorb most competitors into one glob—while also controlling most of the major media—we are faced with more than a theoretical conflict of interest.

A great imbecility of those that claim that it is a "dog eat dog world" is that the phrase is a factual inaccuracy: dogs almost never eat (nor kill) dogs. They are highly cooperative, pack-based, social animals. Even more dumbfounding is that many of those that most staunchly espouse this concept are actually proponents of Creationism, not evolution. But they conveniently borrow from nineteenth-century quasi-science ideology, whenever it proves convenient.

The difference in nature is that systems will collapse to restore balance—the world begs for correction. But with corporatization, as it grows, the masses only continue to feed it more (and often unintentionally, due to the illusion of choice that is fabricated when one conglomerate owns many "diverse" stores at a mall or online).

With centralization of media, "cut-and-paste journalism" results. Fact check-ing, consulting multiple expert or eyewitness sources, and secondary verification and review is thrown out the window. Instead, press releases are routinely quoted whole.

Thereby, promotional parties with vested perspectives and designs end-up *dictators* of the news, and whatever it is that they claim is then prone to getting copied ad infinitum on the Internet, thus dethroning fact. (More than once I have found myself having to weigh whether to adjust to an error that has proliferated on the worldwide web—such as a foreign word misspelled or a historical date misstated—or else risk being faulted as wrong, later, by the hive-mind mentality that *does* believe everything that they read.)

Next, advertising begins to shape the news (e.g., editors avoiding or softening certain content that might offend the sponsors or bigwigs), and ultimately news *becomes* advertising via fluffy coverage of upcoming blockbuster events and media works.

Ernest Hemingway style war-reporting, this ain't.

And as the objective ethics of journalism deteriorate, the news media is allowed to distribute content during daytime and primetime hours—borderline child-pornography, snuff films, slander—that would likely get an indie artist run out of town, free speech be damned.

102

"Forever" Is a Very, Very Long Time

What constitutes a true celebrity or "star," anyway?

On more than one occasion, when traveling overseas, this point has been brought home to me due to witnessing sightings of regional public figures that create near pandemonium, while to me that same individual is unknown, seems utterly nondescript, and in no way intrinsically remarkable.

For instance, Ethiopian singer Tilahun Gessesse's funeral parade was attended by over one million people, yet, very few people in the rest of the world have even heard of him. Similarly, in 1975, millions lined the streets of Egypt to pay respects after improvisatory giant Umm Kulthum's passing.

Johnny Hallyday has reigned in France as an Elvis-like figure (something that most countries have their own equivalent of, by the way) since 1960 and sold over one hundred million records. On his last tour in 2009, he sold out *five* nights at Paris' main soccer stadium with a capacity of over eighty thousand people. Similarly, the crooner Charles Aznavour sold upward of one hundred million albums in France, which equals almost two records for every citizen of the country.

Udo Juergens (Germany), A. R. Rahman (India), Nana Mouskouri (Greece), and Alla Pugacheva (Russia) have all, also, sold *over* one hundred million records, dwarfing the career sales of relatively minor stars like Bob Dylan, the Beach Boys, and Metallica. In Japan, Yumi Matsutoya and Ayumi Hamasaki both have sales of more than fifty million albums each while in Pakistan the late vocal great Nusrat Fateh Ali Khan produced no less than 125 separate albums!

Some of the biggest-selling artists of all time are completely unheard of outside of their own homelands. Their enormous sales figures are made even more startling by the fact that many of these same countries are prone to huge bootlegging syndicates, thus official sales figures account for only a fraction of the actual records in circulation.

Being a household name is almost entirely dependent on *which* neighborhood one is living in.

Art is nothing if not subjective, with beauty truly being in the *ear* of the beholder.

103

Guilty as Charged

It is not lost on me that I can easily be accused (and probably have unintentionally lapsed into) some of the types of exploitation that I rail against.

Due to avenues being very closed to non-English or Spanish music outside the borders of all other, smaller linguistic areas, there is virtually no money to be found in "international" music (i.e., even the sales of the largest "world music" stars like Youssou N'Dour are feeble compared to most other pop icons). This fact seems to have done little though to dissuade some from harboring great apprehension toward anyone involved in cross-cultural efforts.

Ruefully, I learned way back in my early days of charitable work and activism that "no good deed goes unpunished," and that some of the biggest "star" egos ever to be found populate the "helping" community—much more than are usually found among most mere musicians. Many despots started off by doing good works, but then somewhere along the line lost their rudder.

That most international recordings are labors of love that actually *lose* money for the producer *and* record companies involved seems to have small bearing on audience members paternalistically suggesting that "I hope that at least *some* of the profits find their way to the band somehow." That I don't even own a car, nor house, and that the few items of clothing I do ever possess almost always end up being "shared" with materially less-advantaged artists—literally giving the *shirts* off my back—would probably hold little sway with these blanket convictions.

Rather than risking territorialism and seeing any area of the planet or forms of music as my turf, I openly encourage more people to seek out and find new music and fresh(-er) voices. To help chaperone to the fore, "forgotten" faces and places . . . that is, *as long as* they are treated with the same tough-mindedness as any other contemporary artist from anywhere.

Ultimately, we can all only benefit from a smorgasbord of greater diversity and equity. As with love and compassion, it is hard to imagine that a crisis we are ever likely to face anytime soon is from having too much of these precious elements.

And, if it were ever so, what a great "problem" that would be to have.

Conclusion:
The Earth Is an Echo

P ut down that handheld device, click off the TV, close your laptop, and sing. Not for others, but for its own intrinsic value as an action. *Play* music with the instruments that perpetually surround you, just waiting to be reanimated—your hands, feet, chest, the ground.

Truly ethical living disregards the presence or absence of an audience as an influence, in favor of consistency and unfiltered truth. Unfortunately, the post-television era has encouraged and enables the opposite of this ethic, with pop stars literally directing people to "vogue" and strike a pose.

Rather than consume music, *live* musically. Not for the benefit of any performance, but simply for the sake of being. Co-compose your own existence.

Most importantly, hear.

Similarly, wear clothes, rather than let brands wear you. Eat food, not products. And in place of amassing possessions, be possessed by *experiences*—particularly the unplanned and cost-free ones.

Turn away from the prescribed sonic channels, and listen to and through the noise. The more we hear, the more we can potentially learn and, consequently, the deeper our connectivity to the world becomes. When we attempt to understand one another—to embrace, rather than silence difference—empathy can grow, and in empathy's presence, neither hate nor deliberate violence can coexist.

Empathy displaces them, in favor of the all-inclusive balance of its perceptive and nurturing grace.

If there is a God at all, that being is certainly nothing, if not a listener.

The women of Zomba Prison making the best of their
environs.

Epilogue:
Open Ears, Open Mind

To be clear, I potentially love *any* music, regardless of its source. My goal is not to trade one inflexible, supercilious paradigm for another, but to celebrate anarchy toward monetary value(-less) systems of distribution. Technology, when employed as one of many possible means to an end, can be breathtaking.

Loops are often amazing, and multitracking opened up unforetold possibilities sonically.

Inspiration can and should be found wherever it resides—from the most pre-fab, preteen crap to a thirty-second corporate television commercial to formally "composed" music. The proof is in the hearing (as well as the dancing, and, *most of all*, the feeling). That unmistakable tingle down the back of the spine, that careening rush is what most of us hunger for and, of which, this world can never get an overdose of.

Just as there can never really be and never has been too much love on this earth, genuinely realized artistic expression is far too scarce, but desperately needed. When it comes to quality and vision, the more the merrier, genres be damned.

Paraphrasing the great MLK: It is not the color of one's skin, the fortunes of one's ancestors, or what neck of the woods you hail from that should matter, but ultimately the depth of one's content and candor.

This book is not a call to arms for a counterprotectionism, but *inclusion*. Regional music is constantly in varying stages of growth, stagnation, and instability. Innovation is nomadic by nature . . . and always has been! It is nonsequential and often impetuous. Outside and varied influences are not only *not* a threat, but to be encouraged, in order to ensure the continued health and progress of any form.

Cross-culturalism is nothing new and is actually inevitable. If one could be transported back to ancient Rome, there is little doubt that the diversity there must have seemed planetary, akin to the bar scene in *Star Wars*, with the interaction of so many now-extinct tribes and languages colliding from across much of the globe.

We are all immigrants. Every last one of us a "traveler." None of us will remain in this world.

Even one person can sometimes be a catalyst (particularly, if they have charisma). Musicians have always been commissioners of cultural change. Not so much for what they even do artistically, but first and foremost due to the simple fact that they have usually been travelers. And, travelers are the ones that import new clothing, religions, ideas, instruments, clothing, spices, diseases, loaned words, and, above all else, stories of what they have seen and experienced beyond the horizon.

The western world's distribution system allows it to bully trends into being, with themselves in the role of the speaker and other countries, relegated to gagged listeners or by-the-book, rote imitators. What is needed is conversation and dialogue, with both sides having more equal say and sway, rather than one-way communications.

Left-field mash-ups are welcomed occurrences, but the jeopardy of literal sampling becoming a dominant means is that it restricts creators to consumeristic roles and regurgitation (as does strict traditionalism of all stripes, also), with creativity reliant on preexisting material versus spontaneous birth.

In other words, output does not have to correlate to input and be dependent on external elements. A goal is to find the aria(s) *already* within us, fueled by emotion and manifested by the way we move and speak. The wellspring for an idea can be solely visceral and some similarities can actually just be the result of parallel, happenstance inspiration versus derivation.

The irony is not lost on me that advances in digital equipment have made my remote forays in the field stupefyingly easier, both in fidelity and portability. Even at the start of the new millennium, I was still left lugging around ADAT VHS decks and a separate mixer, with a combined weight that was close to a hundred pounds.

Do I expect (or even *want*) this book to change even one person's mind about music or their favorite bands?

No.

Nor should it really.

There is the hope, though, that it may spur some individuals to commit more heartily to investigating their own beliefs, and thereby become less anesthetized when facing corrupting corporate influence's onslaught. All the better, if this book leads any individual to an increased reflection on the importance that music plays in their daily life, and even to our very survival as a species.

In the end, it doesn't matter how a song was made or by whom. The crux of the matter is if it has that special spark that can manifest itself in myriad ways—infectious groove, literary lyrics, ear-worm melody, et al. If the superior output turns out to be from oil rich, private school boys in Qatar, then so be it.

But the reality is that the system does not work so democratically after all, that our "free market" is far from liberated. What is needed is a revolution, a revolution of fairness.

Music *does* matter. It is one area of culture we potentially have much control over. But it is to the capitalists' advantage to trivialize it, making it easier to manipulate culture's unfair distribution.

What is a solution?

That we vote with our clicks. That we take a more active role in the music and films that we consume, and not just accept whatever slop is hurled our way as distraction. Violence is not necessary for this veering away, for if we simply step outside the company store that corporations have turned most global city-centers into, and turn our backs on the emperors, refusing to so readily feed them our dollars, they will wither and stall. Talk back to performers, get thrown out of clubs. Don't be courteous, when it comes to things that truly matter. Communication should be a two-way street. Let's reclaim our right-of-way.

Just as mandatory nutrition labeling on food has given rise to more people being aware of and selective about what they eat, a deeper investment in and caring for what music we choose to listen to is beneficial and helps demonstrate that far from being frivolous, music truly *does* matter. It is an invisible but audible connectivity that runs through time, between people, across the world, and within one's own life history. That its power is immeasurable and has so much fluidity, only makes its effects that much more magical.

Song is the embryo of speech. We all screamed, babbled, and buzzed before we spoke.

If you can no longer dance, you're already dead. If you refuse to sing, you've surrendered your voice.

And only those who don't listen are truly alone.

There is no "us and them." There is only us...*all* of us. And, like it or not, it is together that we will stand or fall.

Overview

I. How Music Dies

1. Due to the repetitive listening and wide distribution it enables, recorded music contributes to the homogenization of art.
2. Amid a plethora of releases, differentiation can only be created byway of a "star" system, where one person is extolled disproportionately, and usually quite arbitrarily. Through this process, the promoters become more powerful than the audience or performers themselves, in determining popularity.
    a) As musical styles merge, calcify, and become indistinguishable, paramusical elements become more important than the art itself.
3. Art forms have become empty shells whenever they meet some preset physical criteria, but are left devoid of the spiritual content that first brought those forms into being.
4. The splitting of audience from performer creates a milieu where exceptional beauty exists only outside oneself—it can only be purchased and consumed rather than created—and is thereby commodified, with corporations acting as middlemen in this unholy apartheid.

II. The Perils of Recorded Music

1. Recording transforms music from being an action to becoming an object.
2. The reinforcement of identical, single performances leads to some arrestation in growth for the listener and the performer(s).
3. By dislocating sound from its source, the range of any individual voice is magnified excessively—not just beyond the moment of its inception, but even long after the death of the person who was its author.

The silver lining of recorded music is its capability to potentially expose any one person to an exhilarating range of music that would otherwise be impossible to experience.

    a)   Therefore, the greatest challenge and danger ultimately faced is not due to the technology itself, but through the inequitable distribution of whatever content it captures.

III. How Art Can *Live*

A few possible actions:

1. Listen to at least one song a day in a language you are not fluent in.
2. Watch at least one film a year from another country, outside of the English-speaking world.
3. If given the choice between art created by the dominant class, gender, sexual orientation, language, or race, or a performer who doesn't exploit the sexuality of themselves or others to sell their music, choose the underdog.
4. Buy from owner-run businesses, whenever possible.
5. Be wary of descendants of the aristocracy and/or those that use their fame in other forums as a platform, in favor of those who have made due on their own merits alone.
6. Try to consciously make music for at least one minute daily.
       a)   Try to dance for the length of at least one song daily.
7. Volunteer for a cause you believe in at least one day annually (and on nonholidays, when the need for help is the greatest), so as to participate deliberately in some nonmonetary work relationship.
8. Refuse to buy shirts with massive advertising of a brand on them.
9. Regard with suspicion any solutions that are offered that require an external and commercialized source (e.g., the pharmaceutical and tech industries).
10. Write letters of complaint to or petition businesses that colonize spaces with excessive sound and/or images (e.g., airports that have not a single accessible silent-spot throughout their entire campus, even outdoors.).
11. In lieu of commercially manufactured instruments, try to customize, recycle, or *invent* new ones (e.g., I can guarantee that a well-mic'd and eq'd box or jug can sound as good as most sanctioned kick- or tom-drums).
12. Strive to monitor and select your intake of art, with at least the same level of care that you do personal nutrition.

About the Author

I an Brennan is a GRAMMY-winning record producer and has produced four GRAMMY-nominated records. At age six, while staying home sick from school, he by chance he saw an old Elvis Presley exploitation film on rerun television and was inspired to pick up the guitar. It immediately became his obsession and "life-jacket" for surviving childhood and adolescence. He recorded his first album in 1987, during the pre-Pro Tools, dark ages.

He has worked with artists as diverse as Merle Haggard, filmmaker John Waters, Flea (Red Hot Chili Peppers), Fugazi, Green Day, Tinariwen, Kyp Malone & Tunde Adebimpe (TV on the Radio), the Blind Boys of Alabama, Nels Cline (Wilco), and the Vienna Boys Choir, and has repeatedly traveled the world in search of music. Among others, he has discovered and produced groups who went onto be the first international releases in the indigenous languages of their respective countries, Rwanda, South Sudan, and Malawi.

During his leanest years, he supported himself by day working as a counselor in the locked emergency-psychiatric unit for Oakland, California. This led to his becoming a violence prevention "expert," lecturing on the topic over one hundred times annually since 1993, at such organizations as the Betty Ford Center, Bellevue Hospital (NYC), UC Berkeley, and the National Accademia of Science (Rome), as well as on various continents—Africa, Asia, the Middle East, Europe, and North America.

He was a published poet by age nineteen and has written about music regularly for *Zero Magazine* and *Guitar Player*. He is the author of three other published books. *The Boston Phoenix* called his lyrics,"a model of economical, unpretentious, narrative songwriting," and the *Readers+Writers* journal praised his novella, *Sister Maple Syrup Eyes* as, "A beautiful book. Achingly beautiful."

He was born in Oakland and raised in the far east Bay Area. In 2009, he relocated first to Paris and then later to Italy as a homebase.

Index

 # Books from Allworth Press

Booking Performance Tours: Marketing and Acquiring Live Arts and Entertainment
by Tony Micocci (paperback, 6 x 9, 304 pages, $24.95)

Guitar Encyclopedia
by Brian Tarquin (paperback, 8 ½ x 11, 256 pages, $29.95)

How to Grow as a Musician: What All Musicians Must Know to Succeed
by Sheila E. Anderson (paperback, 6 x 9, 256 pages, $25.50)

Making and Marketing Music: The Musician's Guide to Financing, Distributing, and Promoting Albums
by Jodi Summers (paperback, 6 x 9, 240 pages, $19.95)

Making it in the Music Business
by Lee Wilson (paperback, 6 x 9, 256 pages, $24.95)

Managing Artists in Pop Music: What Every Artist and Manager Must Know to Succeed
by Mitch Weiss and Perri Gaffney (paperback, 6 x 9, 288 pages, $23.95)

Profiting from Your Music and Sound Project Studio
by Jeffrey Fisher (paperback, 6 x 9, 224 pages, $24.95)

The Quotable Musician: From Bach to Tupac
by Sheila E. Anderson (paperback, 7.6 x 7.6, 224 pages, $19.95)

The Songwriter's and Musician's Guide to Nashville
by Sherry Bond (paperback, 6 x 9, 256 pages, $19.95)

Starting Your Career as a Musician
by Neil Tortorella (paperback, 6 x 9, 240 pages, $19.95)

Insider's Guide to Music Licensing
by Brian Tarquin (paperback, 6 x 9, 256 pages, $19.95)

Insider's Guide to Home Recording
by Brian Tarquin (paperback, 5 ½ x 8 ¼, 224 pages, $16.95)

To see our complete catalog or to order online, please visit www.allworth.com.